BUSINESS ISSUES, COMPETITION AND ENTREPRENEURSHIP

THE POWER OF ENTREPRENEURSHIP

BUSINESS ISSUES, COMPETITION AND ENTREPRENEURSHIP

Additional books and e-books in this series can be found
on Nova's website under the Series tab.

BUSINESS ISSUES, COMPETITION AND ENTREPRENEURSHIP

THE POWER OF ENTREPRENEURSHIP

DAAN DIRKSEN
EDITOR

Copyright © 2019 by Nova Science Publishers, Inc.

All rights reserved. No part of this book may be reproduced, stored in a retrieval system or transmitted in any form or by any means: electronic, electrostatic, magnetic, tape, mechanical photocopying, recording or otherwise without the written permission of the Publisher.

We have partnered with Copyright Clearance Center to make it easy for you to obtain permissions to reuse content from this publication. Simply navigate to this publication's page on Nova's website and locate the "Get Permission" button below the title description. This button is linked directly to the title's permission page on copyright.com. Alternatively, you can visit copyright.com and search by title, ISBN, or ISSN.

For further questions about using the service on copyright.com, please contact:
Copyright Clearance Center
Phone: +1-(978) 750-8400   Fax: +1-(978) 750-4470   E-mail: info@copyright.com.

NOTICE TO THE READER

The Publisher has taken reasonable care in the preparation of this book, but makes no expressed or implied warranty of any kind and assumes no responsibility for any errors or omissions. No liability is assumed for incidental or consequential damages in connection with or arising out of information contained in this book. The Publisher shall not be liable for any special, consequential, or exemplary damages resulting, in whole or in part, from the readers' use of, or reliance upon, this material. Any parts of this book based on government reports are so indicated and copyright is claimed for those parts to the extent applicable to compilations of such works.

Independent verification should be sought for any data, advice or recommendations contained in this book. In addition, no responsibility is assumed by the Publisher for any injury and/or damage to persons or property arising from any methods, products, instructions, ideas or otherwise contained in this publication.

This publication is designed to provide accurate and authoritative information with regard to the subject matter covered herein. It is sold with the clear understanding that the Publisher is not engaged in rendering legal or any other professional services. If legal or any other expert assistance is required, the services of a competent person should be sought. FROM A DECLARATION OF PARTICIPANTS JOINTLY ADOPTED BY A COMMITTEE OF THE AMERICAN BAR ASSOCIATION AND A COMMITTEE OF PUBLISHERS.

Additional color graphics may be available in the e-book version of this book.

Library of Congress Cataloging-in-Publication Data

ISBN: 978-1-53615-114-5

Published by Nova Science Publishers, Inc. † New York

CONTENTS

Preface		vii
Chapter 1	Heterogeneous Analyzer Typology Organization: The Role of Strategic Entrepreneurship *Mikhail Kozlov*	1
Chapter 2	Entrepreneurship and Research Skills in SMEs *Ileana Hamburg, Emma O'Brien and Fikret Öz*	45
Chapter 3	Applying the Global Entrepreneurship Development Index Methodology to Assess the Entrepreneurship Performance in Vietnam *Ha Thi Thu Nguyen*	77
Chapter 4	Local Economic Development Theory and Practice in South Africa: Forcing Square Pegs into Round Holes? *Danie Francois Toerien and Johannes Wessels*	121
Chapter 5	Who Is an Acadepreneur? Towards a Conceptual Framework of Acadepreneurship *Raouf Jaziri*	163

vi   *Contents*

Chapter 6	The Role of Venture-Sitters in Creating and Managing Knowledge Ecosystems for High-Expectations Start-Ups *Diego Matricano*	**201**
Chapter 7	An Epistemological Criticism of Social Entrepreneurship: Is Social Entrepreneurship a Sound and Scientific Field of Research? *Amir Forouharfar*	**225**
Index		**297**

PREFACE

The Power of Entrepreneurship begins by addressing the idea that the rejection of change is likely to occur when opportunity seizing by analyzer organization is accompanied by proactive strategic typologies. Strategic changes in digitization are also discussed in respect to the case of the Microsoft Corporation strategic transformation initiated with the goal of moving beyond the niche associated with Office products to outstrip the market of cloud technologies from its leader, Amazon Web Services.

The authors go on to explore how the discipline of entrepreneurship has evolved, the role of entrepreneurship education, and how research skills could facilitate the development of entrepreneurial culture and innovation.

This compilation also measures entrepreneurship performance in Vietnam at the national level through a new approach, the Global Entrepreneurship Development Index. Results indicate that nine bottlenecks of fourteen pillars are performing with very low scores, in which the highest policy priority is given for including risk acceptance, opportunity perception, internationalization and technology absorption.

Brief reviews of the evolution of local economic development policies and practices and of quantitative entrepreneurial research are followed by a case study to reflect the value of such analyses. It examines proportional relationships between demographics, entrepreneurial development and economics and provides evidence that entrepreneurship in South Africa is not limited.

The next article emphasizes the dilemma proposed by the new concept of "acadepreneurship" especially its two facets of intrapreneuring (intrapreneurship) and extrapreneuring (extrapreneurship). The authors stress the boundaries of "academic entrepreneurship" and draw a conceptual framework of the neologisms of "acadepreneurship" and "acadepreneur".

Aspiring entrepreneurs aiming to launch high-expectation start-ups can be at a critical juncture. Five research propositions are offered that intend to form the basis for scholars carrying out further studies on this matter. Practitioners may also leverage on the insights provided in order to facilitate the creation and development of knowledge ecosystems for high-expectation start-ups.

The closing paper examines (1) whether "social entrepreneurship" is an oxymoron, and (2) the characteristics and sources of social entrepreneurship knowledge.

Chapter 1 - The work is supposed to help resolve the problem, how the resistance to changes, determined by some studies as the main barrier for the implementation of digital transformation, could be mitigated. A hypothesis is advanced that (a) the rejection of changes is likely to occur when opportunity seizing by Analyzer organization is to be accompanied by its transition towards more proactive strategic typology, and (b) it is the presence of strategic entrepreneurship construct dimensions in such organization that is instrumental in carrying out its strategic innovation responsible for the organization difference in strategic transformational development to exploit business opportunity outside its current market. To overcome the limitations of Miles-Snow typology static character and of its inappropriateness to describe the process of transformation of one adaptation type to another, new conceptual model is proposed to analyze how a niche strategy organization moves away from the defensive Analyzer's typology to a proactive reaction to new opportunity. The new Heterogeneous Analyzer dynamic transitory typology is determined in the Miles-Snow space alongside the key strategic dimensions of entrepreneurial, engineering and administrative problems, who is trying to "align" itself with the opportunity in its environment by building alternative solutions to the three problems. The model regards implementation of the Heterogeneous Analyzer strategy in the form of organizational strategic innovation, for which strategic entrepreneurship acts as its driver. The role of strategic entrepreneurship construct dimensions in solving entrepreneurial, engineering and administrative problems of the organization is analyzed. For verification of the conceptual framework case study of the Lausanne Federal Polytechnic Institute strategic transformation is examined by structuring the materials of its entrepreneurial, engineering and administrative problem solution in terms of the strategic entrepreneurship construct dimensions. The Heterogeneous Analyzer case study findings are identification of entrepreneurial, engineering and administrative problems derived from the proposed model in conceptual part of the research. The study is supposed to be the first where Analyzer organization at the stage of its transition to more proactive development is examined using new framework based on strategic entrepreneurship construct dimensions. Provisions of the proposed model, applicable to the analysis of strategic changes in digitization, are also discussed in respect to the case of the Microsoft Corporation strategic transformation initiated with the goal of moving beyond the niche associated with Windows / Office products to outstrip the market of cloud technologies from its leader, Amazon Web Services.

Chapter 2 - An Entrepreneur is a person who identifies a need and starts a business; Entrepreneurship could be defined as a capacity and willingness to develop, organize and manage a business venture (https://searchcio. techtarget.com/definition/entrepreneur). Entrepreneurship and Entrepreneurship Education have an important role in social and economic developments. The EntreComp framework outlined by the EU commission in 2016 highlights that Entrepreneurship should not be limited to those people setting up businesses, but in all aspects of life. "**Entrepreneurship** is when you act upon opportunities and ideas and transform them into value for others. The value that is created can be financial, cultural, or social." (http://publications.jrc.ec.europa.eu/ repository/bitstream/JRC101581/lfna 27939enn.pdf).

There are more Small and Medium-sized Enterprises SMEs than any other organizations in Europe. Because SMEs are small, and their resources are constrained, their staff need to regularly adapt to changes and learn new competences and skills relatively quickly. To survive, they need to be proactive and look for new opportunities, in addition to the daily operations of the company. Due to limited capacity, owner managers together with employees need to develop an entrepreneurial culture. Slevin and Covin (1990, p. 43) highlight that "a successful firm not only engages in entrepreneurial managerial behavior, but also has the appropriate culture and organizational structure to support such behavior." Most entrepreneurship programs are targeted at new business owners or startups. There is, however, less research on the relationship between entrepreneurial skills of employees in existing SMEs and innovation capacities.

The ongoing Project Reinnovate focusses mainly on providing workplace research skills to encourage all employees in SMEs to develop an entrepreneurial mindset, increasing the chances of the small firm's survival. Reinnovate "Practice based research to enhance the innovation capacity of SMEs through learning and ICT supported collaboration" is an Erasmus + Project, with project partners from five European countries (www.iat.eu). Within the framework of the project, an intense cooperation with SMEs, research organizations, and representatives of higher education is crucial. The provision of a training program and model accreditation will assist employees in SMEs to find/create the knowledge required to become more competitive, to develop a culture of entrepreneurship, and become more innovative. This chapter will explore how the discipline of entrepreneurship has evolved, the role of entrepreneurship education, and how research skills could facilitate the development of entrepreneurial culture and innovation. Finally, it will detail a program being developed by the REINNOVATE project to develop entrepreneurial culture in SMEs through the provision of research skills.

Chapter 3 - This study mainly aims to measure entrepreneurship performance in Vietnam at the national level through a new approach - the Global Entrepreneurship Development Index (GEDI). The Global Entrepreneurship Development Index (GEDI) consists of three sub-indices, including Entrepreneurial Attitudes, Entrepreneurial Abilities and Entrepreneurial Aspiration, which are divided into fourteen pillars and can be further subdivided into 28 variables. By analyzing these pillars and variables in comparison to two Southeast Asian developing economies - Thailand and Indonesia - which have similar cultural, economic and social characteristics, the study identifies the best and worst performing variables of the Global Entrepreneurship Development Index (GEDI). The research results indicate that in Vietnam, nine bottlenecks of fourteen pillars are poorly performing with very low scores, in which the highest policy priority is given for four pillars, including risk acceptance, opportunity perception, internationalization and technology absorption. Finally, the Penalty for Bottleneck (PFB) methodology, which is considered as the policy application of the Global Entrepreneurship Development Index (GEDI) methodology and a simulation of "optimal" policy allocation are suggested to alleviate the weakest performing pillars, aiming to achieve the greatest improvement of entrepreneurship performance as well as reach the desired five-point increase in Vietnam's Global Entrepreneurship Development Index.

Chapter 4 - Two decades of disappointing South African local economic development (LED) outcomes are possibly due to inattention to quantitative research of entrepreneurial dynamics. Brief reviews of the evolution of LED policies and practices and of quantitative entrepreneurial research are followed by a case study to reflect the value of such analyses. It reflects on proportional relationships between demographics, entrepreneurial development and economics; provides evidence that entrepreneurship in South Africa is not limited; explains the concept of entrepreneurial space and the LED implications of its quantification; presents evidence that the churn rate of enterprises in South African towns should be considered in LED policies; provides evidence that the enterprise richness (i.e., the number of different enterprise types) of towns is linked to productive knowledge, the lack of which plays a role in poverty and unemployment; examines the link between poverty and entrepreneurial development and its implications for pro-poor LED policy; and explains why officials and academics involved with the development and consideration of LED policies and practice in

South Africa have ignored the quantification of the characteristics of human settlements in the United States and South Africa. The analysis concludes that the paradigms underlying South African LED policies and practices should be reconsidered and debated in-depth.

Chapter 5 - "Academic entrepreneurship" is a polyphonic concept. Therefore, there is no precise definition adopted unanimously by researchers within the field of entrepreneurship research. However, the emergence of the neologism of "acadepreneurship," seeks the transcription of an entrepreneurial logic within the university mainly in its extrapreneurial and intrapreneurial dimension. This article emphasises the dilemma proposed by the new concept of "acadepreneurship" especially its two facets of *intrapreneuring* (intrapreneurship) and *extrapreneuring* (extrapreneurship). In fact, the authors want to stress boundaries of the "academic entrepreneurship" and to draw a conceptual framework of the neologisms of both "acadepreneurship" and "acadepreneur."

Chapter 6 - Aspiring entrepreneurs aiming to launch high-expectation start-ups – which are knowledge intensive ventures anticipating high growth rates – can be at a critical juncture. On the one hand, they need to get external knowledge and mix it with previously hold one in order to develop new knowledge. On the other hand, however, they can be not able to catch external knowledge in order to create new one since they can miss necessary capabilities and skills or instruments and tools. In such a scenario, a major role is played by venture-sitters, i.e., a kind of knowledge promoters, transformers or gatekeepers who look after new high-expectation entrepreneurial ideas to ensure they are nurtured, developed and exploited through the launch of start-ups. Such experts can support the creation of voluntary and specific knowledge ecosystems and their management. This chapter offers five research propositions that are intended to form the basis for scholars carrying out further studies. Practitioners could also leverage on the insights provided in order to facilitate the creation and development of knowledge ecosystems for high-expectation start-ups.

Chapter 7 - The paper was shaped around the pivotal question: Is SE a sound and scientific field of research? The question has given a critical tone to the paper and has also helped to bring out some of the controversial debates in the realm of SE. The paper was organized under five main discussions to be able to provide a scientific answer to the research question: (1) is "social entrepreneurship" an oxymoron?, (2) the characteristics of SE knowledge, (3) sources of social entrepreneurship knowledge, (4) SE knowledge: structure and limitations and (5) contributing epistemology-making concepts for SE. Based on the sections, the study relied on the relevant philosophical schools of thought in *Epistemology* (e.g., *Empiricism, Rationalism, Skepticism, Internalism* vs. *Externalism, Essentialism, Social Constructivism, Social Epistemology, etc.*) to discuss these controversies around SE and proposes some solutions by reviewing SE literature. Also, to determine the governing linguistic discourse in the realm of SE, which was necessary for the authors' discussion, *Corpus of Contemporary American English (COCA)* for the first time in SE studies was used. Further, through the study, SE buzzwords which constitute SE terminology were derived and introduced to help us narrowing down and converging the thoughts in this field and demarking the epistemological boundaries of SE. The originality of the paper on one hand lies in its pioneering discussions on SE epistemology and on the other hand in paving the way for a construction of sound epistemology for SE; therefore in many cases after preparing the philosophical ground for the discussions, it went beyond the prevalent SE literature through meta-analysis to discuss the cases which were raised. The results of the study verified previously claimed embryonic pre-paradigmatic phase in SE which was far from a sound and scientific knowledge, although the scholarly endeavors are the harbingers of such a possibility in the future which calls for further mature academic discussion and development of SE knowledge by the SE academia.

In: The Power of Entrepreneurship
Editor: Daan Dirksen

ISBN: 978-1-53615-114-5
© 2019 Nova Science Publishers, Inc.

Chapter 1

HETEROGENEOUS ANALYZER TYPOLOGY ORGANIZATION: THE ROLE OF STRATEGIC ENTREPRENEURSHIP

Mikhail Kozlov[*]

Moscow Business School, Moscow Technological Institute,
Moscow, Russia

ABSTRACT

The work is supposed to help resolve the problem, how the resistance to changes, determined by some studies as the main barrier for the implementation of digital transformation, could be mitigated. A hypothesis is advanced that (a) the rejection of changes is likely to occur when opportunity seizing by Analyzer organization is to be accompanied by its transition towards more proactive strategic typology, and (b) it is the presence of strategic entrepreneurship construct dimensions in such organization that is instrumental in carrying out its strategic innovation responsible for the organization difference in strategic transformational development to exploit business opportunity outside its current market. To overcome the limitations of Miles-Snow typology static character and of

---

[*] Corresponding Author Email: mkozlov@mbschool.ru.

its inappropriateness to describe the process of transformation of one adaptation type to another, new conceptual model is proposed to analyze how a niche strategy organization moves away from the defensive Analyzer's typology to a proactive reaction to new opportunity. The new Heterogeneous Analyzer dynamic transitory typology is determined in the Miles-Snow space alongside the key strategic dimensions of entrepreneurial, engineering and administrative problems, who is trying to "align" itself with the opportunity in its environment by building alternative solutions to the three problems. The model regards implementation of the Heterogeneous Analyzer strategy in the form of organizational strategic innovation, for which strategic entrepreneurship acts as its driver. The role of strategic entrepreneurship construct dimensions in solving entrepreneurial, engineering and administrative problems of the organization is analyzed. For verification of the conceptual framework case study of the Lausanne Federal Polytechnic Institute strategic transformation is examined by structuring the materials of its entrepreneurial, engineering and administrative problem solution in terms of the strategic entrepreneurship construct dimensions. The Heterogeneous Analyzer case study findings are identification of entrepreneurial, engineering and administrative problems derived from the proposed model in conceptual part of the research. The study is supposed to be the first where Analyzer organization at the stage of its transition to more proactive development is examined using new framework based on strategic entrepreneurship construct dimensions. Provisions of the proposed model, applicable to the analysis of strategic changes in digitization, are also discussed in respect to the case of the Microsoft Corporation strategic transformation initiated with the goal of moving beyond the niche associated with Windows / Office products to outstrip the market of cloud technologies from its leader, Amazon Web Services.

INTRODUCTION

Digital transformation describes the deep changes in production and organizational activities, processes and competencies necessary to use the opportunities and respond to the challenges generated by the new digital paradigm. The impact of digital transformation can't be only reduced to the creation of smart and connected products (like appliances, thermostats, cars, watches and many other), but is also determined by the depth and comprehensive nature of its effects on competitive dynamics, business models, value chains and competences of firms in the field of production and services (Porter and Heppelmann 2014), (Porter and Heppelmann 2015).

In the transition to global digitization, the capability of a firm to adapt is becoming its core competence, since its level determines whether the firm is capable or not of employing an identified lucrative opportunity through the early introduction of a new business model. The software company IFS surveyed 750 decision-making managers about the significance of various barriers to digital transformation. The main barrier to firm transformation in that study was determined to not accept changes, marked by the largest share of 42% of the total number of respondents. According to top managers of some leading companies, overcoming barriers to digital transformations is about creating an organization that has the ability to constantly change as soon as the organization itself becomes the subject of the change.

In this connection, the task of developing conceptual models of organizational changes in the form of strategic innovations arises, making it feasible to determine the extent to which a firm is capable of a responding in proactive way to an emerging business opportunity, and what strategic transformation may be needed to impart such capability. One example of such a case is the strategic transformation of Microsoft, initiated in 2014 with the goal of becoming capable of successfully competing in the cloud digital market with Amazon Web Services, which occupies a there a leading position. This paper attempts to put forward an approach to analyzing this case through a constructed model of strategic organizational transformation based on the use of a combination of modern concepts of strategic entrepreneurship with the elaboration of a Miles-Snow typology of organization adaptation to changes in its competitive environment. This model is developed by further structuring the strategic transformation case of the Lausanne Polytechnic Federal University (Kozlov 2018).

To develop a model describing the organization's transition from the defensive typology of adaptation by Analyzer archetype organization to prospective typology, it is advisable to amend use some of the Miles-Snow approach provisions with some elements of strategic innovation and SE concepts. Although Miles and Snow strategic archetypes represent a useful perspective to analyze the organization's adaptive cycle in respect to making its decision whether to employ new business opportunities or not, the approach is sometimes criticized for being rather static. To some extent, the critics seems to be valid, as the theory doesn't imply any option for a description of how organization modifies its strategic archetype in favor of more proactive strategy, the event that occasionally happens. However, the availability of some recently elaborated tools of strategic entrepreneurship makes it sensible to examine if Miles and Snow strategic archetypes in terms of three typical problems of adaptive cycles may be extended to embrace the cases of organization transition to another strategic archetype. Such tools as SE construct dimensions have not received yet any noticeable attention in the studies of organization strategic typology. One of the newness elements of this work consists in the extension of Miles-Snow strategic typology to develop a conceptual framework of Analyzer's transition from defensive to prospective typology in its competitive development. Verification of the proposed conceptual framework is carried out by Analyzer development case analysis.

The second element of the newness of this work is manifested in the choice of Analyzer organization at the stage of its transition from defensive to prospective typology as its case study object. In this paper the conceptual framework of strategically entrepreneurial Analyzer transition to catch-up development is put forward and verified by case study of the well documented success story of the Lausanne Federal Polytechnic Institute, or Ecole Polytechnique Fédérale de Lausanne (EPFL) spelling in French.

Therefore, the lack of conceptual framework for dynamic conceptual framework applicable for the examination of defensively oriented organization's transition to more proactive development in terms of SE perspective consists a gap in strategic transformation research this study aims to address. To resolve the research problem the study focuses on the following key research questions:

Q1. Could Miles and Snow strategic archetypes be amended and developed to present a dynamic conceptual framework for the specification of defensively oriented organization's transition to more proactive typology?

Q2. Given the results of the employing of the conceptual framework of defensively oriented organization's competitive development, how engineering and administrative problems of the organization's strategic transformation can be formulated and solved?

Q3. Given the definitions of engineering and administrative problem, does SE play any significant role in the solution of engineering and administrative problems of the organization transformation, and what administrative problem organizational process can be used as an instrument to ensure the positive outcome of the transformation?

Based on the research questions above, the general structure of this study is to develop a conceptual framework of dynamic conceptual framework, applicable for the examination of defensively oriented organization's transition to more proactive development, based upon Miles and Snow strategic typology extension. The framework is applied to unfold the process of organization's transition to more proactive strategic typology and SE role in EPFL opportunity employing case study. The concept was verified using the case of EPFL managed to accomplish a transition to more proactive strategic typology to become a research intensive university and significantly increase its competitiveness in global research markets (Fumasoli 2011). It belongs to a rather thin group of the most dynamically developing universities and recipients of grants from the European Research Council (ERC). The critical significance of the university transition to more prospective strategic typology for exploiting newly discovered opportunities, enhancing the level of competitiveness and advancing in international rankings, is strongly articulated in the Plan of Strategic Development of EPFL.

"We need to ensure a global presence throughout the world, to excel and innovate faster than the competition and to acquire adequate critical mass in key sectors. In other words, if Switzerland is to retain its international reputation in the fields of education, research and innovation 10 or 20 years from now, the institutes of technology must go one step beyond on the path to growth so as to face worldwide competition and make the most of the new opportunities offered by globalization." (EPFL 2011)

Depending on the case study findings, the hypothesis would be confirmed or rejected. As the case study is expected to evidence complete correspondence between SE construct dimensions of conceptual framework and those identified at EPFL case study, the outcome of the empirical investigation would be a confirmation of the hypothesis.

The building of the EPFL transformation case was carried out by structuring the materials and numerous interviews with and publications by its charismatic President Emeritus Patrick Aebischer. The EPFL case is based on analysis and interpretation of mostly secondary data available from numerous publications on its success story rather than on collecting as much new data as possible.

In summary, this research contributes to the existing literature in the following ways:

First, this study demonstrates that Miles and Snow typology can be applied to describe the way an organization changes its adaptation capability to that is expected to enable it to serve new customers or to offer new services to extant customers.

Second, the study extends the original work by Miles and Snow (Miles and Snow 1978), as it introduces a new dynamic heterogeneous typology that ensures more comprehensive understanding of an organization's process of its transition from a former defensive strategic orientation into the new one.

Third, the dynamic heterogeneous archetype enables understanding of the strategic transformation decomposition in terms of definition and solution of the entrepreneurial, engineering and administrative problems as well as identification of the process stage being most critical to the success of organization's strategic transformation.

Finally, the findings of the EPFL case study deliver an evidence in favor of the views that SE presence contributes positively to the introduction of the process of managing human capital strategically which plays critical role in the solution of heterogeneous typology organization administrative, engineering and, eventually, entrepreneurial problem.

The chapter is divided into five sections. Following the introductory section, the second section discusses the concepts of the strategic innovation, strategic entrepreneurship construct dimensions and Miles and Snow strategic typology. The third section introduces the conceptual framework of Heterogeneous Analyzer typology. Next in the fourth section the Heterogeneous Analyzer typology revealed from the framework of the former section is verified through case study of EPFL. Finally, the last section outlines most significant conclusions and suggests directions for future research.

STRATEGIC INNOVATION AND STRATEGIC ENTREPRENEURSHIP CONSTRUCT DIMENSIONS

Strategic Innovation

Strategic innovation is a specific case of the business model innovation, and throughout the research strategic innovation is regarded in the context of discovering and exploiting new emerging strategic positions in the industry (Markides 1999), also known as 'unexploited pockets of profitability' (Larsen et al. 2002). Therefore, "strategic innovation focuses on changing firm level strategy over time to identify unexploited positions in the industry ahead of rival firms" (Larsen et al. 2002). Since such unexploited market gaps in the industry positioning usually occur due to changing market and industry conditions, an organization's proactive behavior, related to managerial intentionality (Bosch et al. 2003), is very instrumental for its managerial sensing, selection and exploitation capabilities in respect to the industry positioning gaps (Markides 1997), (Hamel and Prahalad 1994), (Hamel and Välikangas 2003).

Thus, "strategic innovation focuses on changing firm level strategy over time to identify unexploited positions in the industry ahead of rival firms"

(Larsen et al. 2002). In (Markides 1998) it is emphasized that it is changing market and industry conditions that may give rise to such emerging positions in the industry which could be recognized as suitable foundation for strategic innovation development. Whilst the basic strategic innovation notion implies implementation of a 'creative and significant departure form historical practice" (Govindarajan and Trimble 2004), Charitou and Markides took far exceeding point of view by introducing the concept of *disruptive* strategic innovation asserting that not only a different, *new* way of playing the game is required, but the one that enters a *conflict with* the usual way (Charitou and Markides, 2003).

Strategic Entrepreneurship Construct Dimensions

Strategic entrepreneurship (SE) is integration of entrepreneurial (i.e., actions aimed at finding opportunities for development) and strategic (actions aimed at finding competitive advantage) perspectives for the development and implementation of entrepreneurial strategies that lead to an increase in the organization's performance (Shalley et al. 2015). The concept regards different opportunities/new combinations as strategic options whose markets may be thin or even non-existent and put a decision maker into the role of an entrepreneur whose task is at the same time both to sense, scan, create opportunities/new combinations and to seize and exploit opportunities by reconfiguring existing knowledge and other assets. Mathews highlighted that to employ identified opportunities strategic entrepreneur needn't have all required resources available when defined strategic entrepreneurship as "the activity that drives the economy in new directions, through recombination of resources, activities and routines by firms, and the entrepreneur as the economic agent who in principle lacks resources (but knows where to find them), who becomes aware of opportunities that can be turned into profit, and acts to realize these opportunities through resource mobilization and activation in the pursuit of profit" (Mathews 2010).

In (Ireland et al. 2003) contributions of prior research efforts to explicate SE as a single construct were integrated and elaborated so that SE was unfolded in four major groups of distinctive dimensions. The SE underlying dimensions were identified and critically examined using several theoretical perspectives, such as the resource-based view concept, human capital, social capital, organizational learning and creative cognition. The first dimension, defined as entrepreneurial mindset, consists of four components— entrepreneurial opportunities, entrepreneurial alertness, real options, and an entrepreneurial framework. The second SE dimension includes entrepreneurial culture and entrepreneurial leadership as its important aspects. Whereas simultaneous and integrated use of opportunity- and advantage-seeking organization activities can be facilitated if its resource base deployment is managed strategically, the third strategic resource management dimension is concerned with managing organizational resources and capabilities in strategic way. The dimension, in terms of resource-based view, incorporates a set of organization processes required for reconfiguring its resource base and developing and leveraging competencies needed to sense opportunities and successfully exploit them. The fourth dimension consists of applying creativity and developing innovation as critical outcomes of the former three SE dimensions (Ireland et al. 2003).

The present case study uses explication of SE as a construct of distinctive dimensions (Ireland et al. 2003), whose include entrepreneurial mindset, culture and leadership, managing resources strategically and innovativeness. As the purpose of the SE representing in the form of construct comprising some dimensions has been to address how combining and synthesizing opportunity-seeking behavior and advantage-seeking behavior leads to wealth creation, the appropriate processes can be examined by dealing with identification of SE separate construct dimension or even with that of construct key component rather than of the whole SE itself (Kozlov 2018).

MILES AND SNOW STRATEGIC TYPOLOGY

In this paper, to describe organizational transformation for the transition, the approach taken is defining the strategy as a form of adaptive mechanism that coordinates business activity with changes in the external environment in which it operates (Miles and Snow 1978). One of the key premises of literature that investigates the area of strategy is that the latter should align business performance with the environment in which the entity runs. In other words, the most successful organizations are those who have the strategy acting as the most efficient adaptive mechanism for interaction with their environment. In that regard the organization's competitiveness is determined by the quality of its adaptation to substantial changes in the external environment, which must be achieved in such three key areas (or dimensions) as the organization's markets and products, the technologies for their production, as well as the organizational structures and processes created to coordinate and control these technologies (Miles and Snow 1978). Miles and Snow's main research interest, presented in their book *Organizational Strategy, Structure, and Process* (1978), is *why and to what extent organizations within the same industry differ in their strategies, structures and processes*. It is elaborated on empirical findings derived from four industries.

The relative stability of the strategic behavior model developed by the organization to achieve its compatibility with the external environment was noted and examined. Bringing an organization to a state of compatibility with a change in its external environment is called an adaptive selection process or an adaptive cycle (Miles and Snow 1978). Strategic adaptive cycles may be disintegrated for components in such three dimensions as organizational domains of product- market conjunctions, technologies servicing the specified domain and organizational structures and processes developed for coordinating and controlling specific technologies, which the authors called the main problems of a complex and dynamic process of strategic choice.

The authors believe that companies develop their adaptive strategies based on their own perception of the environment in which they compete. Given that different organizational types have a different perception of their environment, they also pursue different strategies. These adaptive strategies allow some organizations to be more adaptable or sensitive to their environment than others, and different organizational types present a range of adaptability to the environment. The authors point out that organizations develop relatively steady patterns of strategic behavior in order to achieve compatibility with environment, and strategic types are differentiated by the level of their adaptation to the competitive environment. The *compatibility* of the organization and environment is referred to as the process of adaptive choice, i.e., adaptive cycle (Miles and Snow 1978). There are three key strategic issues of adaptive cycles, which the authors refer to as *problems of a complex and dynamic process of strategic choice.*

During periods of significant changes in the external environment of incumbent organizations, a combination of the following three problems manifests itself: (1) an entrepreneurial problem, the solution of which comes down to the choice of specific product and market segments; (2) an engineering problem involving the creation of a system that implements the solution of an entrepreneurial problem, and which is solved by choosing the appropriate technology for the production of selected products and their distribution, (3) an administrative problem that provides a successful solution to the organization's entrepreneurial and engineering problems by rationalizing and formalizing its activities.

According to the empirical data analysis outcome, Miles and Snow identified four persistently repetitive types of strategic organization response to environment change. The authors believe that the specifics of the adaptive strategy developed by the firm are based on the typology of its own perception of the nature of the competitive environment. Among these archetypes, known as Defender, Prospector, Analyzer and Reactor, the former two being pure alternatives.

Defender

For the top managers of the Defender, the organization's priority is keeping its strategic stability, achieved through the sealing off a narrow market segment so that to create a stable niche in which only a limited set of products is offered and the entry into which for any potential competitor seems to be an unacceptably cumbersome task. Since the Defender chose growth prospects for himself in the direction of an even deeper penetration into his niche market segment and the production and supply of goods or services in cost-effective manner, he does not consider organizational change at a strategic level as a basic instrument to gain an advantage over competitors. Therefore, the Defender's managers do not need any significant cognitive and dynamic capabilities to change the strategy, the configuration of the resource base and the leverage of new core competencies required to outrun competitors in the fast realization of new opportunities. In case of the need to change the strategy, the level of Defender's available capabilities that this type of organization has to employ to go beyond its niche, identify and use new market segments and business opportunities, manifest itself as rather insufficient. The organizational culture of the Defender and the mentality of its managers are mostly of a formal administrative-bureaucratic type.

Prospector

Prospectors seek to locate and exploit new product and market opportunities while Defenders attempt to seal off a portion of the total market to create a stable set of products and customers. Analyzers occupy an intermediate position by following Prospectors into new product-market domains while simultaneously protecting a stable set of products and customers. The Prospector defines the essence of his extremely proactive approach to the organization development as the search for and use of opportunities related to the creation of new products and the development of new markets. His proactive strategic behavior is deemed not as environmental forces but considered as *the* driver of Prospector performance (Baden-Fuller and Stopford 1994), (Berghman 2006).

It's his capabilities to search for and use the opportunities that constitute the foundation of his competitive advantage. The choice of products and markets by the Prospector is not limited to those located within the competencies and capabilities of the current research and resource potential of his organization.

Several typical features of the Prospector could be demonstrated by analyzing the content of the message to shareholders for 2016 by Jeff Bezos (Bezos 2016), the founder of Amazon, the company with heavily expressed Prospector typology. Because Prospector aims to offer new product/service with higher customer value, and/or do this in a better way than competitors have ever done before, it has been argued that the success of his SI largely depends on a deep understanding of customers' needs and priorities (Markides 1997). The Amazon founder's message confirms that Prospectors are mostly customer-oriented, when creating new products as well as developing core technologies (Slater and Narver 1998) and demonstrate real obsession with customers and with technology that continuously pushes product and market boundaries, rather than with competitor focused: "There are many ways to center a business. You can be competitor focused, you can be product focused, you can be technology focused, you can be business model focused, and there are more. But in my view, obsessive customer focus is by far the most protective of Day 1 vitality. Why? There are many advantages to a customer-centric approach, but here's the big one: customers are *always* beautifully, wonderfully dissatisfied, even when they report being happy and business is great. Even when they don't yet know it, customers want something better, and your desire to delight customers will drive you to invent on their behalf. No customer ever asked Amazon to create the Prime membership program, but it sure turns out they wanted it, and I could give you many such examples" (Bezos 2016).

To be capable of identifying new areas of promising opportunities, the Prospector must develop and maintain absorptive and cognitive capabilities to study a wide range of conditions of the external environment of the organization. The significance of the Prospector's attention to the manifestation of powerful trends is also emphasized by Jeff Bezos: "The outside world can push you into Day 2 if you won't or can't embrace powerful trends quickly. If you fight them, you're probably fighting the future. Embrace them and you have a tailwind. These big trends are not that hard to spot (they get talked and written about a lot), but they can be strangely hard for large organizations to embrace."

To be capable of employing the identified opportunities, the Prospector's managers must develop and maintain dynamic capabilities to change the configuration of its resource base and form the key competencies to outrun competitors in the earliest acquisition of these capabilities. High level of Prospector's decision-making speed, one of the components of managerial dynamic capabilities, may be evidenced again from (Bezos 2016): "To keep the energy and dynamism of Day 1, you have to somehow make high-quality, *high-velocity* decisions. Easy for start-ups and very challenging for large organizations. The senior team at Amazon is determined to keep our decision-making velocity high." The Prospector's organizational culture and managerial mentality are entrepreneurially oriented.

On the positive side, the tendency of the organization to stabilize the type of response of its strategy to changes in the external environment means that the organization has a proven set of mechanisms for responding to changes in the external environment. However, from a negative point of view, such stereotyping means that it becomes more difficult for organizations to accept the need to implement unconventional strategic changes and to be able to implement them (Hambrick 1983). In the conditions of growing dynamism and unpredictability of the competitive environment, inevitably sooner or later such radical strategic disruptive innovation comes in that deprives the organization's current stable strategy of its viability. In the event of such a disruptive innovation, the Defender is forced to respond to this change in the external environment in some proactive way, which would require initiating a process of changing the typology of the strategic adaptation of the organization. Therefore, the task of carrying out the organization's strategic transformations to change its typology of adaptation is becoming increasingly important, especially in respect to the transition from the Defender's typology to the Analyzer's one, which may be represented as a blend of Prospector and Defender archetypes.

Analyzer

Unlike persistent Defender and Prospector archetypes, Analyzers represent more flexible and opportunistic typology in terms of selection of either defensive or prospective strategic response to new market segment occurrence. Some opportunities that Analyzers encounter arise due to their incremental approach to exploiting their position with current product lines and existing markets. Others arise when Analyzers keep track of Prospector's activities. Because of the plurality of opportunities Analyzers can identify in various domains, the most successful of them differentiate prospects thoroughly and pursue either prospective or defensive strategic typology so that they can deploy their resources most effectively.

Customer-oriented and competitor-oriented behaviors, encouraged by their heterogeneous prospective/defensive cultures, are characteristics of high performing Analyzer organizations. To identify opportunities via unattended market segments or potential product improvements, Analyzers must closely monitor not only customer reactions, but also competitors' activities, successes, and failures. In other words, while customers are certainly important to Analyzers, monitoring competitors' actions is equally important to Analyzers' success. Analyzers often observe Prospector's performance at new innovative product market areas so that to be capable of quickly following them in the event of the new market spaces would "grow to capture a large share of the established market" (Markides 1998), (Charitou and Markides 2003), following to the strategy known as that of Fast Second (Geroski and Markides 2005). As fast followers, Analyzers require informal and decentralized structures staffed by marketing specialists; this expedites the process of bringing "new and improved" products to market and helps avoid falling too far behind. This also is consistent with their dual emphases on growth and stability.

Microsoft is regarded as one of the most flourishing organizations pursuing Analyzer archetype strategy. As Slater (Slater et al. 2010: 475) describes, "Microsoft has a very broad product line, with many of its best known products (e.g., DOS, Word, Excel, PowerPoint, Internet Explorer, X-Box) entering the market as second – or, even later – movers." The steady stream of revenue generated by these, and other similar products, has served as the catalyst in funding other company developments. Slater also remarks that "Microsoft expends considerable effort identifying emerging product-market opportunities that have been established by traditional market innovators [Prospectors] – such as Apple, Sony, and Nintendo – and then pursuing sales in the mainstream market." Microsoft has a very broad product line, with many of its best known products (e.g., DOS, Word, Excel, PowerPoint, Internet Explorer, X-Box) entering the market as second——or, even later——movers. While these products have evolved over numerous iterations, the steady streams of revenue they generate are essential to funding development of other products for the company.

Hambrick, in his paper devoted to 25th anniversary of Miles and Snow book release, commented on contradictory nature of top manager's dual position in an Analyzer organization because "they are walking a tightrope, trying to be innovative at the same time they are trying to be efficient and reliable" (Hambrick 2003). Analyzers tend to occupy a more balanced position between exploration and exploitation by simultaneous combining careful monitoring of new product/market opportunities with maintaining of their core skills, products and customers (Slater and Narver 1993), (Sollosy 2013).

Hambrick highlighted advisability of Analyzer further research when suggested "a third [research] opportunity is to address the practical challenges of pursuing the most complicated of Miles and Snow's strategic types: the Analyzer" (Hambrick 2003:118). However, the Miles-Snow typology is purely static in nature and unequipped to describe the transformation of one organizational type of company into another (Murray et al. 2002), (Gnjidić 2014). Next, there is introduced a model for the description of transition of the Analyzer organization adaptation from the defensive typology to the prospective one.

HETEROGENEOUS ANALYZER TYPOLOGY AND STRATEGIC ENREPRENEURSHIP

To develop a model describing the organization's transition from the defensive type of adaptation by Analyzer archetype organization to prospective type, it is advisable to use some of the Miles-Snow typology provisions, amending them with some elements of strategic innovation and SE concepts.

Statement 1

Miles and Snow adaptive selection process or an adaptive cycle can be applied to describe the process by mean of which Analyzer changes his defensive type of adaptation to prospective type in response to appearance of new market segment in the organization environment to bring himself to a state of compatibility with the environmental change and capture the new market segment.

To structure the organizational adaptation of Analyzer, for example in the context of stakeholder driven strategic transformation to capture a new market segment, the model of the adaptive cycle in terms of definition and solution of entrepreneurial, engineering and administrative problems is applied to describe its transformational process in response to appearance of the market segment in the external environment of the organization. In view of Miles and Snow model using for strategy change analysis, the specific environmental change in the form of the emergence of new market segments is regarded as an opportunity to be adopted for the transition to servicing the consumers of the next higher level.

The Analyzer's transition from the defensive to the prospective typology may require reconfiguration of its current organization strategic innovation capacity in the form of organizational strategic disruptive innovation itself rather than the capacity incremental improvement. For example, existing human capital that has been specially selected for defensive typology solution of Analyzer engineering and administrative problems would hardly be relevant one for the solution of those problems after beginning of his transition to prospective typology. Moreover, former Analyzer systems built for resolution of engineering and administrative problems, mediating solution of former product/market entrepreneurial problem of defensive Analyzer, are expected to follow their essentially defensive typology even when Analyzer's management is trying to employ the opportunity and follows prospective strategic typology in regards of entrepreneurial problem definition.

Statement 2

When an organization follows over an extended period of time to a defensive version of Analyzer typology, it may lead to its negative response to the adoption of new strategy initiatives to get to the next strategic level of organizational development, when some of defensive Analyzer's employees and stakeholders tend to resist to the transformation and react by pursuing the Defender strategic typology.

The search of entrepreneurial, engineering and administrative problem solution on the trajectory of the Analyzer transition to strategic innovation is also hampered by the risk of the organization market-sensing capabilities being insufficiently developed for identification of emerging market development (Johnson and Hoopes 2003) and precise selection of the new most lucrative market area option. The type of risk arises from the rejection of new activities and counteracting inclination of the organization to follow the defensive typology, which is exacerbated by the Analyzer and its stakeholder cognitive capabilities constrained and unequipped to the new opportunity recognition because of the novelty and non-standard efforts for the defensive Analyzer to go outside of its niche and make transition to prospective typology.

If any innovative solutions to the entrepreneurial problem in the form of exploiting new opportunities, such as appearance of new product-market domains, have long been rejected by the defensive Analyzer, the Defender's archetypal stability binds the organization within the current market segment. The existing core rigidity precludes defensive Analyzer from starting to solve engineering and administrative problems towards building capabilities and designing a product for a new more promising market segment even in the case of stakeholder-driven strategic change.

The systems may contribute to a contradictory attempt to raise the level of the Analyzer organization competitiveness by more efficiently following the defensive strategic typology, that is, to better serve existing customers of the established market segments, or to build new positions at similar, less distant in cognitive aspect rather than most lucrative, segments. In several works it was uncovered that not every employee is prepared to adopt the strategic transformation. They can also block the process which can take place in two modes at individual behavior level. First, employees may resist changes because, instead of comparing perspectives of defensive and prospective type of adaptation in objective manner, they do it in subjective way, overestimating the risk of a threat to the defensive typology ongoing value and well-established model of Analyzer's operation. This is a fair concern but sooner or later each well-established business model would be invariably imitated by competitors, challenged or commoditized (Kim and Mauborgne 1997). Second, many employees find it difficult for themselves to change their mentality so that to acquire new more advanced and, as a consequence, more complicated competencies and do not see their involvement in a new typology to be oriented towards new market segment. Defender chief executives and long tenure top management teams can cause inertia and resistance to any changes due to their commitment to the established strategy and market-product policies (Boeker 1997).

Statement 3

The persistence of the mentality of managers and the organizational culture corresponding to the defensive Analyzer's engineering and administrative problem solution may be expressed so heavily that it completely excludes any alternatives of leaving current product-market niche, including the exploitation of any identified opportunity for the organization to move to the next level of development for offering new product to a new segment of customers. Even if new strategic directions of development are adopted, they may be selected from the standpoint of the greatest accessibility and correspondence of the product/market niche occupied, rather than of maximal performance potential for gaining competitiveness.

The subject of administrative problem is not only reduced to the Analyzer's internal structure, but also comprises his organizational culture and leadership. The administrative problem solution system is responsible for hiring, employment and leverage of human capital and acquisition of other resources required to solve the entrepreneurial problem. When Analyzer start changing its strategic typology trying to exploit new opportunity, entrepreneurial problem is revisited first by the time of new strategy adoption while organizational systems established for solution of engineering and administrative problems are not. Such heterogeneous composition of prospective entrepreneurial problem with defensive administrative problem means that organization internal structure, leadership, culture may keep on running according to defensive version of Analyzer typology, and its human capital is still selected due to its relevance to the defensive strategic goal rather than to initiating transition to prospective type of Analyzer. Even worse, the obsolete but nevertheless functioning defensive administrative system goes on making the organization strategic typology even less prospective oriented opposed to the newly declared orientation of entrepreneurial problem.

It is proposed to extend the set of Miles and Snow Analyzer's adaptation typology in its original form by introducing a new transitional type of dynamic adaptation to individual specific change in the external environment. This adaptation typology is defined at the space of key strategic dimensions by the extent to which the manifestations of the defensive typology hinder Analyzer's adaptation to the new prospective typology, its readiness to introduce changes in its products, markets and technologies in order to use the opportunity that has arisen due to changes in the external environment in the form of the emergence of a new market segment. Let's define adaptation type as homogeneous if its administrative and engineering problems are solved in compliance with strategic orientation of entrepreneurial problem, and as heterogeneous if the solutions of the administrative and engineering problems are not aligned to the goal of entrepreneurial problem solution. According to Prospector and Defender's definition, they are examples of homogeneous adaptation type. As long as Analyzer may pursue either defensive or prospective version of strategy, this adaptation type is unlikely to remain always homogeneous.

Statement 4

To simulate the restrictive influence of obsolete but still operating systems, designed for the solution engineering and administrative problems under former defensive Analyzer typology, soon after his transition to prospective entrepreneurial problem, extension of the original Miles and Snow typology is proposed. It introduces a transitory Heterogeneous Analyzer strategic typology determined alongside the *key strategic dimensions* as a combination of the newly formulated entrepreneurial problem with mostly defensive systems for the solution of engineering and administrative problems established under former defensive Analyzer typology.

The Heterogeneous Analyzer intrinsic contradiction is that its strategic goal reflects beginning of his transition to the implementation of initial stage of strategic transformation while the conservative mentality of most managers and the organizational culture remain focused on the fuller use of the well-established niche of the current product-market domain.

In contrast to the classic Analyzer in the Miles and Snow typology, who is supposed to possess infinite level of strategic innovation capacity and being capable of switching instantly from defensive to prospective typology, the type of Heterogeneous Analyzer is intended to describe a specific process of his transition to an **organization**'s proactive adaptation model when its current strategic innovation capacity level in respect to solution of new entrepreneurial problem is insufficient to do so. The typology is specially designed to uncover the source of prominent troubles the Analyzer may face when decided to leave his entirely defensive typology because his inherited systems for engineering and administrative problem solution are difficult to transform as fast as entrepreneurial problem is reformulated, so they remain to be essentially defensive. The need to follow such a model may be temporary and exhaust itself upon the completion of a strategic innovation with the acquisition of the features of an ambidexter organization and the capability to react proactively to the competitive environment change.

To significantly increase the level of his capability to respond in prospective way, the defensive Analyzer type needs not just a significant development of his dynamic capabilities and the whole resource base, accompanied by an increase in the performance indicators of the organization. In the Heterogeneous analyzer model this development comes as a result of the coordinated building of such engineering and administrative problem solutions that provide a solution to the entrepreneurial problem during the process of switch from the defensive version of Analyzer typology to the transitory adaptation type.

Following the Heterogeneous Analyzer's typology allows the organization to both reformulate and resolve the problems in other manner more appropriate to new prospective strategic typology and gain competitive positions at new most relevant and demanded market segments, raise the level of financial resources, the customer value of the products or services and attract most capable employees from the external environment worldwide.

The solution of the entrepreneurial problem of transition to the Heterogeneous Analyzer type is mediated by the solution of an engineering problem aimed at launching an organizational learning mechanism to create new competencies in the product market to meet the needs of an identified consumer segment corresponding to the next level of organizational development. Unless new products for the next level were created, and new consumers are trying to offer a product or service that is already available, then such products are unlikely to be competitive against competitors' offers, that is, the potential of the identified opportunities will not be fully utilized.

Since just right after Analyzer's adoption of prospective typology his new market competencies are at a very low initial level, at the first stage of the transition from the defensive typology into the Heterogeneous Analyzer's typology these capabilities must be readjusted and leveraged. The principal issue here is that neither existing system designed for the solution of defensive strategy engineering problem fits for the development of new market competencies nor current system for the solution of administrative problem is suitable for so much needed engineering system rearrangement.

It was demonstrated in (Hess and Hess 2016) that the process of stakeholder-driven strategic renewal is carried out by boundary spanning employees. New engineering system integrates the knowledge and skills of individual boundary spanning stakeholders drawn from the external environment. At the second stage of the transition, in addition to the activities of the boundary spanning stakeholders drawn from the external environment, the process of organizational learning and human capital selection is deployed, which ensures differentiation between fast and slow learners among trained employees and the involvement of best learners, as members of the emerging internal boundary spanner community, in the building of teams for development of products for a new segment of consumers. Therefore, the precondition of Heterogeneous Analyzer engineering problem execution may be defined as selection and hiring of best available external boundary spanners for new product-market domain development and flexible and fast learning of employees inside the organization to support enhancement of next level market competencies. Respectively, the Heterogeneous Analyzer's administrative problem is specially designed to introduce human capital development processes that facilitate employment of teams composed of best hired boundary spanner newcomers and fast learners among organizational employees and then set up new product-market units lead by the people selected from most capable team participants. Protection of the teams from the influence of former defensive administrative system influence is combined with organizational boundaries movement towards new product-market unit development. Thus, it is possible to formulate the following statement:

Statement 5

The solution of engineering problem of Analyzer stakeholder-driven prospective reorientation is enabled by the solution of his administrative problem aimed at launching the mechanism of organizational learning to create new product-market competencies by introducing strategically managed human capital development processes which facilitates productive employment of best hired boundary spanning stakeholders and fast learners, isolates them from negative influence of the former systems set up for resolution of engineering and administrative problems of previous defensive strategic typology and builds alternative systems for resolution of engineering and administrative problems of adopted prospective typology with preferential promotion of most productive boundary spanning stakeholders and fast learners.

To significantly advance in competitiveness, it is not enough for Analyzer just significantly develop its dynamic capabilities and the resource base in general, accompanied by an increase in the performance indicators. The development must be purposefully targeted at the coordinated building of such solutions for engineering and administrative problems that ensure the transition from the defensive into a proactive Heterogeneous typology (referred next as Heterogeneous Analyzer's typology) with respect to the next higher level of organizational development through the identification and exploitation of the opportunity of servicing the new customer segment which will ensure the advanced growth of indicators ahead of competitors.

Therefore, the transition of Analyzer to the opportunity employing strategy is unlikely to be proceeded in an arbitrary form of strategic change or renewal. The transition, shaped in the form of substantial strategic organizational innovation, involves a switch from the adaptive archetype of the defensive Analyzer into Heterogeneous Analyzer's typology to build an alternative solution of entrepreneurial, engineering and administrative problems so that to mitigate effects of formerly established systems for the solution of defensive strategic typology engineering and administrative problems.

To support the defensive Analyzer's adaptation to the new market segment occurrence, the Heterogeneous Analyzer top management needs to provide a high level of SE construction dimensions in reconfiguring the systems for solution of his engineering and administrative problems. The SE acts as a driving force for developing a new combination of the Analyzer's resources and capabilities which leads to an increase in the level of its core competencies required to identify and employ new opportunities associated with the emergence of new market segments in the external environment of the organization. As a result, an organization's increased capability to proactively respond to the emergence of new opportunities in its environment beyond its former strategic innovation capacity niche is achieved by pursuing strategic innovation, increasing the level of dynamic capabilities (Teece et al. 1997) and increasing the resource base based on a new combination of financial, human and social capital entrepreneurial management to identify and use business opportunities. As soon as the defensive Analyzer hasn't developed any adequate cognitive capabilities to identify new opportunities and an incentive to develop them, in absence of strategic entrepreneurship mentality top manager stakeholder there is neither any driver for strategic innovation nor any advance in competitiveness performance indicators.

The decomposition of strategic organizational innovation process is carried out by allotment of its constituent parts such as redefinition and building new solution of the entrepreneurial, engineering and administrative problems in the adaptive cycle model. The executive with SE mentality at the head of the organization solves the entrepreneurial problem by identifying new types of activity, as well as new market segments corresponding to the next level of organizational development. He (or she) also proceeds to the solution of the administrative problem at the initial stage of transformation in the form of restructuring and consolidation of the organizational structure. This allows him (or her) to make the organization more manageable, fill the managerial positions of structural units with entrepreneurial mentality managers, carry out the initial reconfiguration of resources and create new structural units focused on a proactive model of adaptation to the new identified market segments.

The use of a new model of adaptation makes it possible to decompose the dynamic capabilities of an organization from the point of view of clarifying the target orientation of its resource base reconfiguration. In case of departure from the defensive version of Analyzer typology, this reconfiguration is aimed at an alternative definition and solution of its entrepreneurial, engineering and administrative problems in such a way as to circumvent the resistance of the defensive archetype, eliminate the impact of its trajectory dependence in the future and go beyond its niche to the new market segment to use the emerging opportunity.

A strategic entrepreneurship mentality executive at the top position of an organization resolves entrepreneurial problem by identification of new activities as well as new market segments representing next level of organizational development and proceeds with initial stage of administrative problem solution. The top-manager usually carries out an up-front administrative system change in the form of restructuring and enlarging the organizational structure, which makes the organization more manageable, to fill out the managerial positions of structural units with entrepreneurial mentality type managers, initial reconfiguration of resources and set up new separate structural units oriented to the implementation of the adaptive development cycle employing a proactive model for newly identified market segments. The issue here is that it takes much longer time span for organization to articulate engineering and administrative problem and build its solution, so after new strategy pursuing new big opportunity has been adopted and the organization may start to resolve the appropriate entrepreneurial problem, its inherited engineering and administrative solution systems remain to be essentially defensive ones. They were designed before for implementation of former niche strategy and are hardly applicable for the making solution of new strategy entrepreneurial problem.

Human capital, considered to be crucial to organizational success (Hitt et al. 2001), has been comprehensively defined as the "individual capabilities, knowledge, skill, and experience of the company's employees and managers, as they are relevant to the task at hand, as well as the capacity to add to this reservoir of knowledge, skills, and experience through individual learning" (Lumpkin and Dess, 2001). In view of the definition, success in resolution of the Heterogeneous Analyzer's administrative problem may be expressed in terms of the degree of relevance of employee and manager's new individual capabilities, knowledge, skill, and experience grown up with introduced human capital development processes to the problem definition and solution. High level of the human capital development relevance can be provided by managing human capital strategically when its deployment facilitates the simultaneous and integrated use of opportunity- and advantage-seeking behaviors. Managing human, social and financial capital strategically constitutes the third SE construct dimension. While this specific SE construct dimension evidently contributes to the success of administrative problem solution, it seems comprehensible to examine whether influence of another SE construct dimensions for that matter turns out to be positive as well.

The first of the SE construct dimensions, an entrepreneurial mindset, is considered in (McGrath and MacMillan 2000) as a way of thinking about business that focuses on and captures the benefits of uncertainty. It was shown that organizations capable of successfully dealing with uncertainty tend to outperform those unable to do so. Also, recognizing entrepreneurial opportunities, one of the most relevant components of an entrepreneurial mindset and, at the same time, its common outcome, is a key wealth-creation activity (Ireland et al. 2003). Thus, an entrepreneurial mindset is highly likely to affect positively on administrative problem solution.

The administrative problem is not only limited to the Analyzer's internal structure, but also comprises his organizational culture and leadership. Since the second of the SE construct dimensions is composed of entrepreneurial organizational culture and leadership, then the dimension may exert a decisive influence on the administrative problem solution so that to manage resources in strategic manner. An effective entrepreneurial culture is committed to the equal significance of opportunity-seeking and advantage-seeking behaviors and facilitates organization's efforts to manage resources strategically. An entrepreneurial type of leadership is defined as the ability to influence others to manage resources strategically in order to emphasize both opportunity-seeking and advantage-seeking behaviors (Covin and Slevin 2002). Therefore, entrepreneurial organizational culture, as well as entrepreneurial leadership, is highly likely to affect positively on administrative problem solution.

The fourth of the SE construct dimensions, applying creativity and developing innovation, is concerned with the organizational innovation that Heterogeneous Analyzer needs to implement to solve its entrepreneurial problem. Innovations resulting from new combinations of production factors are critical to firms' wealth-creating efforts. To develop its organizational innovation, the entity should be creative. Being critical outcomes of the former three SE dimensions (Ireland et al. 2003) affecting positively on administrative problem solution, creativity and developing innovation is highly likely to affect positively on administrative problem solution either. Thus, it is possible to formulate the following statement:

Statement 6

SE construct dimensions possessed initially by Heterogeneous Analyzer's top-management act as the organizational strategic innovation trigger and its driving force, contributing to the solution of his entrepreneurial and administrative problem where the latter facilitates SE dissemination throughout the organization, its successful opportunity- and advantage-seeking activities in the form of engineering problem solution which has a positive influence on completion of the Heterogeneous Analyzer switch to the prospective homogeneous Analyzer typology and the execution of competitive advantage.

The scheme of organizational strategic innovation process of Heterogeneous Analyzer discussed in the study is as follows:

Formulation of new entrepreneurial problem$\rightarrow$ Formulation of new engineering problem $\rightarrow$ Formulation of new administrative problem $\rightarrow$ Presence of SE construct dimensions $\rightarrow$ Introduction of organizational process of managing human capital strategically$\rightarrow$ Solution of new administrative problem $\rightarrow$ Solution of new engineering problem $\rightarrow$ Strategic innovation and competitive advantage $\rightarrow$ Solution of new entrepreneurial problem.

The administrative problem solution system is responsible for hiring, employment and leverage of human capital and acquisition of other resources required to reach the entrepreneurial problem solution. When Analyzer start changing its strategic typology trying to exploit new opportunity, then entrepreneurial problem is revisited either by the time of new strategy adoption while organizational systems established for solution of engineering and administrative problems are not. Such heterogeneity means that organization internal structure, leadership, culture may keep on operating according to defensive version of Analyzer typology, and its human capital is still selected for following the defensive strategic goal rather than for initiating transition to prospective type of Analyzer. Even worse, the obsolete but nevertheless functioning defensive administrative system goes on making the organization strategic typology even less prospective oriented opposed to the newly declared orientation of entrepreneurial problem.

In another words, when firms structure a resource portfolio, bundle resources to form capabilities and leverage those capabilities flowing from their financial, human and social capital (resources) to simultaneously enact opportunity- and advantage-seeking behaviors and create wealth, they are managing their resources strategically (Ireland et al. 2003).

Analyzer organization could be classified in terms of combination of newly adopted strategic goal of increasing competitiveness with maintaining its inclination to solve entrepreneurial, engineering and administrative problems pursuing its existing set of competencies according the Defender's typology framework. Unlike original Miles and Snow archetype typologies, the Heterogeneous Analyzer's typology is not a stationary one, and in this case the completion of transition from the defensive engineering and administrative problem solutions adaptation typology of the Defender's to the prospective consistent typology can be recognized as soon as new structural units, oriented towards new customer segment, have emerged against the background of the former defensively oriented structural units. Consequently, the Heterogeneous Analyzer's organization takes on the feature of structural ambidexterity, where the defensively oriented units keep on developing products for existing consumers, whereas the new units offer mostly new products for consumers of the next level, acting as the points of future growth.

The solution of the entrepreneurial problem is mediated by the solution of the engineering problem aimed at reconfiguring the product development and market competencies at the macro level through the involvement of such boundary spanner employees who are capable of contributing to integration of their individual capabilities for launch of the organizational capability formation and learning processes and for establishment of new alternative system for the solution of administrative problem. Thus, the inhibitory influence of former defensive strategy systems on the solution of engineering and administrative problems corresponding to the niche strategy and the defensive typology of Analyzer's adaptation, whose managerial and employee dynamic capabilities are inadequate to solve the problems in prospective manner, is bypassed.

As a result, an organization's increased capability to proactively respond to the emergence of new opportunities in its environment beyond its former strategic innovation capacity niche is achieved by pursuing strategic innovation, increasing the level of dynamic capabilities (Teece et al. 1997) and increasing the resource base based on a new combination of financial, human and social capital entrepreneurial management to identify and use business opportunities.

Next case study of EPFL is employed to verify the statements proposed above and present evidences of the changes his defensive type of adaptation to prospective type at the university organizational strategic innovation. Some of EPFL strategic entrepreneurial components and features exhibited in its history of success are investigated in the case structured according to the three following key strategic issues of adaptive cycles, which the Miles and Snow refer to as *problems of a complex and dynamic process of strategic choice* SE construct distinctive dimensions (Miles and Snow 1978):

- entrepreneurial problem,
- engineering problem,
- administrative problem

EPFL Entrepreneurial, Engineering and Administrative Problem Case Study

EPFL Entrepreneurial Problem

In 2001, Patrick Aebischer, the newly appointed president revised former EPFL strategy (Fumasoli 2011). There were introduced the creation of a doctoral school and the introduction of the tenure track system to contribute to the development of the human resource potential of scientific research. As an evidence of entrepreneurial problem reformulation and substantial reorientation of the organization from domestic research market segments towards more lucrative emerging European market, the new strategy presumed the establishment of life sciences faculty and the extension of natural sciences, which became a driver of university development dynamics (Noukakis et al. 2011). It was these two new thematic areas that had been mainly responsible for the success of EPFL in the development of scientific research and brought the lion's share of funding received in the form of European Research Council (ERC) grants.

The orientation of the new faculty to the development of international research activities, the identification and employing of the emerging opportunities for attracting funding on a competitive basis, primarily from the ERC, was then extended to other faculties. As a result, for last decade EPFL has been able to attract 94 ERC grants with a total amount about €220 million (Aebischer 2015). Taking into consideration the receipt by EPFL of significant revenue from the exploitation of a new segment of the emerging European market for scientific research, it seems to be quite probable that its solution of revisited entrepreneurial problem allowed the EPFL University to implement strategic innovation.

EPFL Administrative Problem

The EPFL strategy, revised in 2001, also prescribed on strategic level the creation of "tenure-track assistant professor" position system to foster excellence in research. The operation of the EPFL tenure track system reflects its strategic approach to managing human capital, which is illustrated by another faculty interview. "There isn't any more a chair planning made position by position. The approach now is very different, we say: we have strategic intentions, hence there are fields to be developed, then we recruit, but in a very broad manner; the best academics in the world are recruited, based on very broad profiles, then the real best ones can be selected" (Fumasoli 2011).

The benefits of this strategically oriented process introduction can be illustrated by EPFL outstanding results in winning ERC funding. The EPFL President treats the introduction of tenure track system as the most important reform in EPFL, and the advantage of being surrounded by the best and able to collaborate with them as a secret of good research institutions (Aebischer 2014). Systematic implementation of US-like model of human resources policies allowed EPFL to renew 70 per cent of EPFL's academic positions (Aebischer 2015) and extend its competitive capabilities, as it follows from the interview below (Fumasoli 2011):

> "EPFL positioning depends on rankings. Our competitors are, first, in Europe, like everything, because we are fundamentally European (...) just look at the origin of our typical Master students, a lot of them come from Europe. We also recruit a lot of professors, who are European but who went to the US and want to come back to Europe, profit from a system very close to the US. There aren't a lot (of such systems) in Europe, unless you want to go to the UK, but even there is quite different from US."

Patrick Aebischer believes that the introduction of an assistant professor tenure track system for young scientists turned out to be the most important reform in EPFL. He highlights that the system attractiveness for brightest scientists is mainly due to the independence in selection of research topics it can provide: "Probably, the most important reform we undertook at the EPFL was setting up an assistant professor tenure track system for young scientists. This has attracted the brightest scientists and engineers because they know they can become independent early on in their career. The tenure track system is the strength of the USA compared to Europe. It was an experiment to adapt the US system to European conditions" (Aebischer 2014). Therefore, the system provided freedom and independence in selection of research direction for tenure trackers as protection from negative influence of defensive engineering system. In the case of the EPFL, the administrative problem is solved at the microlevel by preferential assigning to professorships and creating thematically independent units, like laboratories, for those researchers at the tenure track positions, whose capability to develop world-class research has been evidenced by getting ERC grants.

In (Kozlov 2018) it was shown that it is the SE that acts as a driver of strategic innovation, whose presence in the EPFL management mentality allowed top executive and his management team to carry out strategic innovation, which is the content of the solution of the entrepreneurial problem of the adaptive cycle of gaining competitiveness. Thus, it can be concluded that the assistant professor tenure track system adoption may be regarded as the introduction of the specific process of managing human capital strategically which, alongside with the presence of SE construct dimensions, represents most critical condition for the solution of administrative problem, as it evidenced both from the concept developed and from the priority attached to the tenure track system by EPFL top-management as the most important reform. As any other instrument of strategical or entrepreneurial management is unknown to be capable of obtaining the analogous outcome when applied to the solution of the case like that, it may be concluded that the new conceptual framework of Heterogeneous Analyzer has shown its usefulness and comprehensiveness.

EPFL Engineering Problem

The introduction of "tenure-track assistant professor" position system allowed EPFL to solve its engineering problem highly successfully: in 2014, of 390 EPFL academics, 60 were tenure-track. In the EPFL case, the building of solution to the engineering problem was first initiated not on the scale of the whole organization, sooner it was localized near the boundary between the organization and its external environment. The implementation of this decision involved managers of strategically entrepreneurial orientation and engaged researchers from newly created Life Science school: "There was quite some resistance at the beginning. But with time, the faculty saw the advantage at being surrounded by the best, to be able to collaborate with them. That's the secret of good research institutions." The establishment of life sciences faculty and the extension of natural sciences, which became a driver of university development dynamics (Noukakis 2011). It was these two new thematic areas that have been mainly responsible for the success of EPFL in the development of scientific research and brought the lion's share of funding received in the form of European Research Council (ERC) grants.

The process of organizational learning of the capability to develop a new product for the next customer segment was introduced so that the tenure track engaged researcher positive experience in the preparation of ERC grant applications could be further extended to the whole organization, and the pre-existing structural units and thematic areas researchers acceded the ERC grant application preparation.

The orientation of the new faculty to the development of international research activities, the identification and employing of the emerging opportunities for attracting funding on a competitive basis, primarily from the ERC, was then disseminated to other schools.

DISCUSSION, IMPLICATIONS AND LIMITATIONS

The study extends the original work by Miles and Snow (Miles and Snow 1978) by introduction of a new dynamic Heterogeneous Analyzer typology that ensures more comprehensive understanding of an organization's process of its transition from a former defensive strategic orientation into the new one. The typology takes into consideration the fact that it takes much longer time span for organization to articulate engineering and administrative problems and build their solutions than to revisit entrepreneurial problem, so after new strategy pursuing new big opportunity has been adopted and the organization may start to resolve the appropriate entrepreneurial problem, its inherited engineering and administrative solution systems remain to be essentially defensive ones. They were designed before for implementation of former niche strategy and are hardly applicable for the making solution of new strategy entrepreneurial problem. For example, existing human capital that has been specially selected for defensive typology solution of Analyzer engineering and administrative problems would hardly keep his relevance for the solution of those problems reexamined after beginning of his transition to prospective typology.

Using new typology ensures examination of the strategic transformation decomposition in terms of definition and solution of the entrepreneurial, engineering and administrative problems as well as identification of the process stage being most critical to the success of organization's strategic transformation. It follows both from the new Heterogeneous Analyzer framework and case study findings that the introduction of a process of managing human capital strategically is the distinguishing characteristic of administrative problem solution and, eventually, critical condition to the solution of its entrepreneurial problem. The Heterogeneous Analyzer innovation process critical stage determined in that way confirms the empirically observed fact that EPFL's transition from defensive Analyzer to more prospective strategic typology would not have occurred without the introduction of the EPFL tenure track system as an example of a novel strategically oriented process in the sphere of human capital management.

The findings of the study evidence the view that the Analyzer possessing SE construct dimensions has more chances to develop its adaptation capability and solve its new entrepreneurial problem than its competitors do. A strategic entrepreneurship mentality executive at the top position of an organization resolves entrepreneurial problem by identification of new activities as well as new market segments representing next level of organizational development and proceeds with initial stage of administrative problem solution. The top-manager usually carries out an up-front administrative system change in the form of restructuring and enlarging the organizational structure, which makes the organization more manageable, to fill out the managerial positions of structural units with entrepreneurial mentality type managers, initial reconfiguration of resources and set up new separate structural units oriented to the implementation of the adaptive development cycle employing a proactive model for newly identified market segments.

For verification of the proposed conceptual framework case study of the EPFL has been examined by structuring the content of its extensively documented success story of the university transition to prospective Analyzer typology in terms of the entrepreneurial, engineering and administrative problems. The study has demonstrated that, as a conceptual perspective, Heterogeneous Analyzer typology decomposition in the form of its entrepreneurial, engineering and administrative problem dimensions offer a useful instrument due to uncovering the importance of introduction of a process of managing human capital strategically and of SE presence.

This research contributes to the study of the mechanism of the organization transition from one adaptation archetype to another by implementing strategic transformation. Previously, results were obtained (Rindova and Taylor 2002), relating to the macrolevel development of DC and the development of new market competencies in the transition of the organization to the next level of development, which is represented as its transition to servicing a new segment of consumers. In this paper it is shown that the solution of engineering and administrative problems is carried out at the micro level for the sake of growing DC and creating new market competencies. It seems likely that to accomplish such transition organization, as a part of its engineering problem solution, has to launch a product or market innovation and, therefore needs engineering competencies, in case of technology pushed innovation process, and new market competencies, in case of market pulled innovation process, accordingly. Hence, the Heterogeneous typology concept outcomes describing Analyzer's managerial and market/technology capabilities development by new engineering problem solution system correspond in general to the empirical findings of (Rindova and Taylor 2002).

The main limitations of this study are that only one case of Analyzer transition to prospective typology has been explored and that incomplete set of SE construct distinctive dimensions has been considered.

As only single Heterogeneous Analyzer was examined in the case study, there exists a risk that the generalizability of findings from the work may, to some extent, get constrained when the model describing EPFL development will be applied to another Analyzer in different settings. The risk is diminished by proper selecting of a differentiated example of the Heterogeneous Analyzer succeeded transition to prospective typology.

Besides, the study employed mostly secondary data extracted from various sources. The lack of primary information may cause the issue of incongruence between the adaptive cycle dimensions derived using new Heterogeneous Analyzer strategic innovation framework and the real essence of the case study categories due to the absence of confirmation of the findings with the EPFL that has been explored. In view of very good coincidence between Heterogeneous Analyzer entrepreneurial, engineering and administrative problem dimensions and the case study categories this limitation didn't take place, partially because of gathering large volumes of relevant data available from multiple sources.

As at its initial stage of the framework development this EPFL case study is based on available, mostly secondary data, there were considered only those SE construct distinctive dimensions which could be both logically explained and discovered in the case study. The research will be further elaborated to incorporate all SE dimensions, such as entrepreneurial type of organizational culture and cognitive aspects of EPFL top management. It would be comprehensible to carry out replications of the case study with other Analyzer organizations capable of implementing its transition to more prospective typology as well as with Analyzer organizations unable to do it so that to compare the results and see whether innovation process stages would differ. Also, it would be very interesting to observe, how another Analyzer organization specific environment features, like other than ERC "pocket of profitability," may affect the process of its transition to more prospective typology.

First, the conceptual model of the Heterogeneous Analyzer transition to more prospective typology, rather than be exclusively applied for the study of Analyzer strategic transformation, may be generalized to investigation of efforts to transform Defender archetype to employ emerging opportunity in organization environment. In addition to the above rationale for the proposed model of the transition of the Analyzer organization's typology of adaptation from defensive to prospective, it should also be noted that the model more comprehensively notes adaptation typology dynamics and SE construct dimensions as relevant features of known cases of the implementation of such a transformation than prior models do (Markman and Phan 2011). For example, the presence of new, dynamically growing segments of the cloud digital technologies market served as an objective prerequisite for solving the entrepreneurial problem of Microsoft's strategic transformation initiated in 2014 with the goal of entering these market segments from its niche related to Windows/Office products. Indeed, the appointment of the new head Satya Nadella with his strategic entrepreneurial mentality and the support of his reform efforts by shareholders were a subjective prerequisite for solving this problem. The solution to the engineering problem was accompanied by intensive integration of resources from the external environment in the form of acquiring over this time more than 40 startup companies, most of which were developers of cloud technologies (Miller 2017). The solution of the administrative problem required several reorganizations in the form of a change in the structure and appointment of managers with relevant competencies and entrepreneurial mentality to key positions.

One of the consequences of the application of the developed model may be the recommendation for the stakeholder, who decides to change the strategic typology of the organization, to appoint a manager with a strategic entrepreneurial mentality to the top position of its organization. Since the Defender or defensive Analyzer has developed neither adequate cognitive capabilities to identify new opportunities, nor capabilities for their development, in the absence of a top-manager with a SE mentality, there is neither a driver of strategic innovations, nor any significant progress in the level of competence related to proactivity.

REFERENCES

Aebischer, Patrick. 2015. *Swiss Precision*, available at: https://www. timeshighereducation.com/one-hundred-under-fifty-rankings-2015/swiss-precision Accessed November 20, 2018.

Aebischer Patrick. 2014. "Competition is Inherent to Science." *Labtimes*, 4:26-29, available at: http://www.labtimes.org/epaper/LT_14_04.pdf Accessed November 20, 2018.

Baden-Fuller, Charles W. F., and Stopford, John M. 1994. *Rejuvenating the mature business: The competitive challenge.* Boston, MA: Harvard Business School Press.

Berghman, Liselore A. 2006. *Strategic innovation capacity: A mixed method study on deliberate learning mechanisms.* PhD diss., Rotterdam: Erasmus Research Institute of Management.

Bezos, Jeff. 2016. *The Letter to Shareholders*. Available at: https://www.businessinsider.com/read-amazon-ceo-jeff-bezos-2016-letter-to-shareholders-2017-4. Accessed November 20, 2018.

Boeker, Warren. 1997. "Strategic Change: The Influence of Managerial Characteristics and Organizational Growth." *The Academy of Management Journal* 40:152-70.

Charitou, Constantinos D., and Markides, Constantinos C. 2003. "Responses to disruptive strategic innovation." *MIT Sloan Management Review* 44: 55-63.

Covin, Jeffrey G., and Slevin, Dennis P. 2002. 'The entrepreneurial imperatives of strategic leadership,' In *Strategic entrepreneurship: Creating a new mindset*: edited Michael A. Hitt, R. Duane Ireland, S. Michael Camp, and Donald L. Sexton, 309–27. Oxford: Blackwell Publishers.

EPFL. 2011. *EPFL Development Plan 2012-2016*, available at: https://developpement-durable.epfl.ch/files/content/sites/direction/

files/EPFL%20Plan%20d%C3%A9veloppement%202012-2016%2031
0811%20fin.pdf. Accessed November 20, 2018.

Fumasoli, Tatiana. 2011. *Strategy as evolutionary path. Five higher education institutions on the move.* PhD diss., Università della Svizzera Italiana.

Geroski Paul A., and Markides Constantinos C. 2005. *Fast second: How smart companies bypass radical innovation to enter and dominate new markets.* San Francisco: Jossey-Bass.

Gnjidić, Vladimir. 2014. "Researching the dynamics of Miles and Snow's strategic typology." *Management* 19: 93-117.

Govindarajan, Vijay and Trimble, Chris. 2004. "Strategic innovation and the science of learning." *MIT Sloan Management Review* 45:67-75.

Hambrick, Donald C. 1983. "Some tests of the effectiveness and functional attributes of Miles and Snow's strategic types." *Academy of Management Journal* 26:5-26.

Hambrick, Donald C. 2003. "On the staying power of defenders, analyzers, and prospectors." *The Academy of Management Executive (1993-2005)* 17: 115-18.

Hamel, Gary and Prahalad, Coimbatore K. 1994. "Corporate imagination and expeditionary marketing." *Harvard Business Review*, 69:81-92.

Hamel, Gary and Välikangas, Liisa. 2003. "The quest for resilience." *Harvard Business Review* 81:52-63.

Hess, Megan F., and Hess, Andrew M. 2016. "Stakeholder-Driven Strategic Renewal." *International Business Research.* 9:53-67.

Hitt, Michael A., Bierman, Leonard, Shimizu, Katsukiho, and Kochhar, Rahul. 2001. "Direct and moderating effects of human capital on strategy and performance in professional service firms: A resource-based perspective." *Academy of Management Journal* 44:13-28.

Ireland, R. Duane, Hitt, Michael. A. and Sirmon David G. 2003. "A Model of Strategic Entrepreneurship: The Construct and its Dimensions." *Journal of Management* 29:963-89.

Johnson, Douglas R., and Hoopes, David G. 2003. "Managerial cognition, sunk costs, and the evolution of industry structure." *Strategic Management Journal* 24:1057-68.

Kim, W. Chan, and Mauborgne, Renee. 1997. "Value innovation: the strategic logic of high growth." *Harvard Business Review* 75:103-12.

Kozlov Mikhail R. 2018. "Strategic Entrepreneurship Based Model of Latecomer University," *International Journal of Innovation Science* 10:108-24.

Larsen, Erik, Markides, Costas C. and Gary, Shane. 2002. "Imitation and the sustainability of competitive advantage." Best Paper Proceedings, presented at the *Academy of Management Conference*, Denver.

Lumpkin, G. T., and Dess, Gregory G. 2001. "Linking Two Dimensions of EO to Firm Performance: The Moderating Role of Environment and Industry Life Cycle." *Journal of Business Venturing* 16:429-51.

Markides, Constantinos C. 1997. "Strategic Innovation," *Sloan Management Review* 38:9-23.

Markides, Constantinos. 1999. "Six principles of breakthrough strategy." *Business Strategy Review* 10:1-10.

Markides, Costantinos C. 1998. "Strategic Innovation in Established Companies." *Sloan Management Review* 39:31-42.

Markman, Gideon D., and Phan, Phillip H., edited 2011. *The competitive dynamics of entrepreneurial market entry.* Edward Elgar: London, United Kingdom.

Mathews, John A. 2010. "Lachmannian Insights into Strategic Entrepreneurship: Resources, Activities and Routines in a Disequilibrium World." *Organization Studies* 31: 219-44.

McGrath, Rita G., and MacMillan, Ian C. 2000. *The Entrepreneurial Mindset*, MA: Harvard Business School Press.

Miles, Raymond E., and Snow, Charles C. 1978. *Organizational Strategy, Structure, and Process,* Stanford University Press: California

Miller, Ron. 2017. *Microsoft experiences the triumph and tragedy of transformation* https://techcrunch.com/2017/07/10/microsoft-experiences-the-triumph-and-tragedy-of-transformation/ Accessed November 20, 2018.

Murray, John A., O'Driscoll, Aidan and Torres, Ann M. 2002. "Discovering diversity in marketing practice." *European Journal of Marketing* 36:373-90.

Noukakis, Dimitrios, Ricci, Jean-Francois and Detterli, Martin. 2011. "Riding the globalization wave: EPFL's strategy and achievements." In *Paths to a world-class university: Lessons from practices and experiences,* edited Liu Nian C., Wang Qi and Cheng Ying, 177-93. Sense, Rotterdam.

Porter, Michael E., and Heppelmann, James E. 2014. "How smart, connected products are transforming competition." *Harvard Business Review* 92:64-88.

Porter, Michael E., and Heppelmann, James E. 2015. "How smart, connected products are transforming companies." *Harvard Business Review* 93:96-114.

Rindova, Violina and Taylor, Susan. (2002). "*Dynamic capabilities as macro and micro organizational evolution.*" Available at: www.rhsmith. umd.edu/hcit/docs/dynamic.pdf Accessed November 20, 2018.

Shalley, Christina A., Hitt, Michael A., and Zhou Jing, edited 2015. *The Oxford Handbook of Creativity, Innovation, and Entrepreneurship.* Oxford: Oxford University Press.

Slater, Stanley F., Olson, Eric M., and Hult, G. T. M. 2010. "Worried about strategy implementation? Don't overlook marketing's role." *Business Horizons* 53:469-79.

Slater, Stanley F., and Narver, John C. 1998. "Customer-led and market-oriented: Let's not confuse the two." *Strategic Management Journal* 19: 1001-1006.

Slater, Stanley F., and Narver, John C. 1993. "Product-market strategy and performance: An analysis of the Miles and Snow strategy types." *European Journal of Marketing* 27:33-51.

Sollosy, Marc D. 2013. *A Contemporary Examination of the Miles and Snow Strategic Typology through the Lenses of Dynamic Capabilities and Ambidexterity.* DBA diss., Kennesaw State University, Dissertations, Theses and Capstone Projects. Paper 552.

Teece, David J, Pisano, Gary and Shuen, Amy. 1997. "Dynamic capabilities and strategic management." *Strategic Management Journal* 18:509-33.

Van Den Bosch, Frans A. J., Van Wijk, Raymond and Volberda, Henk W. 2003. "Absorptive capacity: Antecedents, models, and outcomes." In: M. Easterby-Smith and M. A. Lyles (Eds.), *The Blackwell Handbook of Organizational Learning and Knowledge Management*: 278-301. Oxford: Blackwell Publishers.

In: The Power of Entrepreneurship
Editor: Daan Dirksen

ISBN: 978-1-53615-114-5
© 2019 Nova Science Publishers, Inc.

Chapter 2

ENTREPRENEURSHIP AND RESEARCH SKILLS IN SMES

Ileana Hamburg[1,], Emma O'Brien[2,†] and Fikret Öz[1,‡]*
[1]IAT, Westphalia University Gelsenkirchen, Gelsenkirchen, Germany
[2]Centre for Teaching and Learning, Mary Immaculate College, Limerick, Ireland

ABSTRACT

An Entrepreneur is a person who identifies a need and starts a business; Entrepreneurship could be defined as a capacity and willingness to develop, organize and manage a business venture (https://searchcio. techtarget.com/definition/entrepreneur). Entrepreneurship and Entrepreneurship Education have an important role in social and economic developments (Zahra and Wright, 2016). The EntreComp framework outlined by the EU commission in 2016 highlights that Entrepreneurship should not be limited to those people setting up businesses, but in all aspects of life. "Entrepreneurship is when you act upon opportunities and ideas and transform them into value for others. The value that is created

---

[*] Corresponding Author Email: hamburg@iat.eu.
[†] Corresponding Author Email: Emma.Obrien@mic.ul.ie.
[‡] Corresponding Author Email: oez@iat.eu.

can be financial, cultural, or social." (http://publications.jrc.ec.europa.
eu/repository/bitstream/JRC101581/lfna27939enn.pdf)

There are more Small and Medium-sized Enterprises SMEs than any other organizations in Europe. Because SMEs are small, and their resources are constrained, their staff need to regularly adapt to changes and learn new competences and skills relatively quickly. To survive, they need to be proactive and look for new opportunities, in addition to the daily operations of the company. Due to limited capacity, owner managers together with employees need to develop an entrepreneurial culture. Slevin and Covin (1990, p. 43) highlight that "a successful firm not only engages in entrepreneurial managerial behavior, but also has the appropriate culture and organizational structure to support such behavior." Most entrepreneurship programs are targeted at new business owners or startups. There is, however, less research on the relationship between entrepreneurial skills of employees in existing SMEs and innovation capacities.

The ongoing Project Reinnovate focusses mainly on providing workplace research skills to encourage all employees in SMEs to develop an entrepreneurial mindset, increasing the chances of the small firm's survival. Reinnovate "Practice based research to enhance the innovation capacity of SMEs through learning and ICT supported collaboration" is an Erasmus + Project, with project partners from five European countries (www.iat.eu). Within the framework of the project, an intense cooperation with SMEs, research organizations, and representatives of higher education is crucial. The provision of a training program and model accreditation will assist employees in SMEs to find/create the knowledge required to become more competitive, to develop a culture of entrepreneurship, and become more innovative. This chapter will explore how the discipline of entrepreneurship has evolved, the role of entrepreneurship education, and how research skills could facilitate the development of entrepreneurial culture and innovation. Finally, it will detail a program being developed by the REINNOVATE project to develop entrepreneurial culture in SMEs through the provision of research skills.

INTRODUCTION

The concept of an entrepreneur and entrepreneurship has evolved significantly over the past twenty years. It was traditionally limited to someone who creates a new organization and bears the risks associated with this (Dees, 1998; Gartner, 1989). Recently, entrepreneurship has expanded into social and everyday life contexts to the active pursuit of opportunities for value creation (not just financial) (Bacigalupo et al., 2016).

Entrepreneurship has been identified as one of the eight key competences for lifelong learning (https://eur-lex.europa.eu/legal-content/EN/TXT/?uri=celex%3A32006H0962). The constant state of change in our economy is defining the need for individuals to take initiative and responsibility, to become proactive rather than responsive to change.

Entrepreneurship education has an important role in social and economic developments, encouraging society to look for opportunities and take initiative, thus creating jobs and economic prosperity and providing social value to citizens (Ribero-Soriano, 2017).

Many educational and training curricula have been developed in this area, these are largely formal programs which focus on increasing the number of new organizations. Those offered by enterprise support offices targeted at new or potential business owners. However, there is little focus on sustaining a business beyond its creation. In the EU, the average birth rate for small companies is 10%, however their growth rate remains quite low, at 2% (Muller et al., 2017). To ensure the survival of new companies which are precious to economic development, Entrepreneurship education needs to extend to all individuals, not just those starting a business.

Fang, 2005, argues that entrepreneurship and innovation are interrelated and should embody everyday work practices not just at a strategic level. Both are required for a company to succeed (Miller 1983). Entrepreneurship sparks the initiative to pursue a new opportunity or idea. However innovation provides sustainability, involving the creation and exploitation of new and existing knowledge (OECD, 2005). To be innovative, research is a core skill which involves the creation of knowledge in a systematic manner (OECD, 2018). Thus, innovation and research are a core component of the skill entrepreneurship.

To facilitate sustained entrepreneurship, it is important that programs expand beyond formal education. In a third level context, universities have introduced experiential and active learning to help students understand how innovation theories can be applied to the real world (Gibb, 1996). However they are not immersive in the working world, and for those already employed in communities and small companies these programs can be limited in terms of the practical application of knowledge. Formal third level programs need to collaborate with industry and social communities; those programs offered by enterprise offices should consider extending them to staff within these organizations to develop entrepreneurial culture.

In these programs it is important that such skills are provided which allow those in a workplace or community setting to become inquiry focused. It should encourage them to continuously look for opportunities to improve the organization - identifying value for stakeholders, gathering the knowledge to enable them to put these ideas into action and reflecting on the success. These skills largely align to research skills which involve identifying a question, collecting information and data to answer that question, developing a solution to this (a short business plan) and observing and reflecting on the solution. And, being oriented to the competencies in the Entrecomp framework defined by the European commission

The project Reinnovate focusses on developing a program that embeds the development of research skills based on a methodology to deliver entrepreneurial education and develop an entrepreneurial culture in the workplace to sustain the survival of small companies. It is expected that this will assist them to find/create the knowledge required to become more competitive, to develop a culture of entrepreneurship and become more innovative.

In the next part of this chapter, we explore the concept of the entrepreneur and entrepreneurship in the future workplace and of future entrepreneurial skills. The second part conducts a critical review of current entrepreneurship education in the context of the future workplace, and part three details workplace learning and how it can be adapted to encourage entrepreneurial thinking.

Part four is dedicated to an example of a program developed as part of the EU project Reinnovate focused on developing workplace research skills to enhance the entrepreneurial capacity of small companies.

THE ROLE OF THE ENTREPRENEUR AND ENTREPRENEURSHIP IN THE FUTURE WORKPLACE

Team working, communication, entrepreneurship and innovation, intercultural skills, adapting to new situations and analytical and problem solving are vital skills in a future workplace (EU, 2010). Furthermore, the EU have categorized many of these as key skills which will form the basis to develop more complex competencies which are 'necessary to drive creativity and innovation and 'cope with complexity and uncertainty' in a fast evolving workplace' (EU, 2016). One of these key skills is entrepreneurship.

Emmanuel (2010) defines entrepreneurship as the ability of a person (the entrepreneur) to create a new investment prospect, develop a venture based on this and manage it effectively for social benefit or making of profit. This traditional view associate's entrepreneurship as an outcome being the development of products and businesses for commercial value; in this perspective it has been argued that the skills required to achieve this outcome could be developed through training.

In contrast, Herbert and Link (1989) describe an entrepreneur as a personality that possesses some comparative advantage due to access to sound information or different viewpoint about a situation or opportunity to enhance his/her decision-making activities. Palich and Bagby (1990) define an entrepreneur as an individual that uses the privilege of turbulence, instability, lack of availability and need to create a new item or service or adjusts an existing one for the sole aim of making profit. However, the behavioral perspective of Entrepreneurship argues that such traits cannot be taught. In this context Entrepreneurship demands decision making across all the facets of a new line of business under uncertainty in a dynamic socio-technical environment. Entrepreneurship is now viewed as a way of thinking and behaving which has wider implications for society and the economy, and such an understanding of entrepreneurship now requires also a different approach to training (Cooney).

Furthermore, the European Commission (2011) view entrepreneurship as both a life-long and life-wide experience and should encompass all stages of education. Being viewed as the fourth element of production, there has been significant interest in Entrepreneurship in policy and research. Recent literature refers to it as the most persuasive economic dynamism ever experienced globally (Kuratko, 2003). Entrepreneurship is concerned with identifying current opportunities and applying the relevant resources in a creative manner to meet a need.

In some contexts, entrepreneurship has been identified as a standalone skill, however in reality it is a competency comprising of multiple skills. A competency is defined more broadly as a *'motive, trait, skill, aspects of one's self image, social role or a body of knowledge which he or she uses'* (Hornby and Thomas, 1989). The classification of Entrepreneurship as a competence ensures both the behavioral and skills perspectives of entrepreneurship as considered

Entrepreneurship has different skills ranging from leadership, innovation, risk taking and management. To overcome ambiguity concerning the competence of entrepreneurship, the ENTRECOMP framework was developed by the EU commission in 2016 (Bacigalupo et al., 2016). It develops an overarching framework encompassing all these skills; its categories entrepreneurship as having three competence categories and 15 different elements which are interrelated.

The skills involved with entrepreneurial activities can be classified as business management, personal and technical entrepreneurial skills (Kuratko, 2003). Kutzhanova et al. (2009) identified four main dimensions of entrepreneur skills:

- Technical Skills - which are those skills necessary to produce the business's product or service;
- Managerial Skills, which are essential to the day-to-day management and administration of the company;
- Entrepreneurial Skills - which involve recognizing economic opportunities and acting effectively on them;

- Personal Maturity Skills - which include self-awareness, accountability, emotional skills, and creative skills.

O'Hara (2011) identified several key characteristics of an entrepreneur which need to be considered when developing entrepreneurial skills:

- The ability to identify and exploit a business opportunity;
- The human creative effort of developing a business or building something of value;
- A willingness to undertake risk;
- Competence to organize the necessary resources to respond to the opportunity.

To develop a competence in entrepreneurship a wide variety of skills are required, some discipline specific and others contextual. This has given rise to the need for more immersive learning approaches which allow learners to develop these skills in an experiential interactive manner

A CRITICAL REVIEW OF CURRENT ENTREPRENEURSHIP EDUCATION

Entrepreneurship education refers to the use of a variety of skills to develop a Culture of Entrepreneurship (Bacigalupo et al., 2016) aimed at the development of behavior, attitudes and capacities that create value. According to Fayolle (2009) issues like creativity, innovation, business start-up and generation of ideas culminate in entrepreneurship education. Entrepreneurship education was developed as a separate discipline by educators in to overcome challenges in the corporate global business environment (Isaac, Visser, Friedrick and Brijlal, 2007).

Chinnoye and Akinlabi (2014) affirm that entrepreneurship education is most successful through active learning approaches such as experiential, team-based project and problem-based approaches.

Given that entrepreneurship is a comprises of several skills, it is important that a pedagogical model for entrepreneurship education encourages personal as well as professional development and takes account of the learners' motivations, objectives and learning needs (Fayolle et al., 2008).

Its main outcomes are generating a learning environment that develops an understanding about the concept, application and practice of entrepreneurship (Gibb and Hannon, 2006) to:

- personal entrepreneurial skills, manners and attitudes,
- personal assurance and capability
- understand an entrepreneurial means of living
- entrench entrepreneurial philosophies in all aspects of life
- stimulate students toward entrepreneurial livelihood
- understand business innovation processes
- appreciate broad entrepreneurial competencies and their application in everyday life
- develop important technical business know-how
- encourage personal relationship and networking skills, to brace-up for self-employment, to have a mind-set for new ventures, and to exploit institutionally-owned IP.

Azizi (2009) proposes that the long-term outcomes of entrepreneurship education are transformations in behavior, support system, culture and impact on business; if this is applied early in a person's education it can lead to the inter-generational adoption of an entrepreneurial culture.

Consideration of the student profile is important in entrepreneurship education (Lonappan et al., 2011) because audiences have different social and economic backgrounds with varying degrees of attachments to entrepreneurial activities. As entrepreneurship is a competency comprising of behavioral as well as performance attributes, programs should differ based on the discipline, educational background and motivations of the students. For example, is the student from Arts, Science, Humanities; do they have a postgraduate or a second level education; do they wish to set up a business, work in an organization or become more proactive. On the other hand, there are practitioners and professionals which may also have an interest in the discipline. In order to achieve its objectives entrepreneurship education should be a creative process rather than a mechanical one; this approach is challenging and problematic and requires new and active teaching methods.

Instructional approaches to entrepreneurship education have been widely researched many of these related the pedagogy of active learning. Oyelola (2013) highlight the importance of metacognition and the process of learning rather than the learning outcome/content-based approach. They recommend encouraging the learner to reflect on the process by which they learn and come to decisions using approaches such as problem and project-based learning and learning from mistakes.

Similarly, Arasti et al. (2012 and Torben (2010) highlight the importance of practical and experiential based learning approaches and encouraging learners to 'study' existing entrepreneurs and businesses.

Emerging entrepreneurship education approaches being advocated by the research are problem orientated, project orientated, simulations, action research, peer learning, group learning, mentoring, gaming/simulation and field visits. Esmi et al. (2015) summarize all the previous studies and methods introduced by different researchers, analyzing methods of entrepreneurship teaching and recognizing their strengths and weaknesses methods. We consider all these recommendations within the teaching and learning methodology in the Erasmus+ project Reinnovate. Some of them are the following:

- Direct teaching-learning methods like discussions with entrepreneurs, mentoring and tutoring
- Interactive teaching-learning methods i.e., chats and group discussions, problem-based learning, active learning
- Practical-operational teaching-learning methods like small work-oriented small research projects, role playing.

However, to determine the applicability of these approaches to the development of workplace research skills in SMEs we need to examine the learning approaches currently adopted in small companies.

SME AND WORKPLACE ORIENTED LEARNING

It is known that the development of employees should be a strategic initiative targeted at improving a firm's competitiveness. This is often difficult for small and medium-sized enterprises due to resource constraints and management priorities which are mainly concerned with the daily survival of the company rather than the long-term competitiveness. However, without strategic planning and encouraging innovation and growth, the long-term survival of the company is at risk. Therefore, approaches that are concerned with developing skills that can be applied in multiple contexts are required. It is important that learning is embedded in the workplace to address the daily operational problems faced by the company but will ensure the long-term sustainability of the company (Matthews, 2007; Della Corte et al., 2013). SMEs must survive and grow by continuous learning – particularly oriented to their ways of practice.

SMEs traditionally adopt informal learning approaches, (O`Brien, Hamburg) using mediums such as on the job, coaching and mentoring (Mazzarol, 2003; Ellinger and Cseh, 2007; Marsick, 2009). Existing studies show that many SMEs do not put themselves in long-term, proactive or formal job/staff planning, but often concentrate on short-term solutions to solve quickly work based problems.

This limits the SME as these are often inward facing approaches which leverage from the internal skills in the company and developing these skills in all staff; their success is largely dependent on the dissemination of good practice internally. Unless external mentors or coaches are used, they do not encourage the employee to look outwards and integrate external knowledge and skills into the company to develop further. In order to be competitive, it is necessary that learning in SMEs should be strategic, related not only to daily work but also to company business grow objectives, structure/

systems/processes, in order to achieve innovative entrepreneurship competence for staff adapted to existing employees' knowledge, skills and abilities. Approaches such as action learning (Clarke et al., 2006) or work-integrated learning are key of success (Panagiotakopoulos, 2011).

Some conclusions from a study conducted by Tam and Grey (2016) are the following:

- SME owners/managers, should encourage both individual and team learning. Team learning can allow individual learning to be disseminated at organizational level, so it aligns with the strategic objectives of a company; however, in SMEs organizational learning is not sufficiently mature.
- Given this weakness, SME owner/managers can still convert employee learning into a strength by developing/maximizing what learning practices are always effective and preferred by their employees – such as individual learning.
- It is also necessary that SMEs train also the inter-organizational level of workplace learning this encourages employees to become outward focused and integrate new knowledge into their company.

Informal and incidental often viewed as inferior, it is difficult to assess and define (Golding et al., 2009), However for SMEs informal learning is more cost effective, timely and contextualized to the needs of the SMEs and their employees (Ellinger and Cseh, 2007; Marsick, 2009).

Matlay (2007) scribes that "it appears that in micro- and small businesses most work-based learning is incidental and it occurs sporadically throughout routine daily tasks." To allow workplace learning to improve competitiveness it is important that it becomes more structured relating to the company objectives and what staff skills and knowledge need to be developed further to achieve such objectives (Marsick, 2006). To facilitate this reflection is key; Marsick discusses the integration of informal and incidental learning single and double-loop learning developed by Argyris and Schön (1978, 1996). This allows the individual learner to reflect on and apply to an organizational level

Jones and Iredale (2010) studied the dynamics of organizational learning in SMEs using Crossan et al.'s (1999) framework and propose four levels of learning that SMEs referring their workplaces – individual, group, organizational and inter-organizational.

Achieving Workplace-Oriented Research Skills - An Example

Research is required for innovation and innovation is needed to generate ideas for entrepreneurship, but it is traditionally limited to academia and pedagogical approaches to developing research skills is limited to doing so in an academic environment. Entrepreneurship programmers are focused more on business creation not to develop innovative skills, however there is an increasing need for research to be applied to practical situations and societal ones.

Workplace-oriented research skills empower the employee to identify and gather appropriate material to their learning needs and it encourages a 'learning to learn approach'. The approach will allow employees to learn the skills to gather data in a systematic manner to fill knowledge gaps in their organization. These skills can be applied to a wide variety of contexts, disciplines and situations. Some situations that demand the entrepreneur research are i.e., to establish the nature of customers' needs, grasp an opportunity or a new business, adapt to changes, and substantiate a judgment, carrying out a feasibility study and evaluation of new products and services that can be introduced.

Learning and teaching process of workplace-oriented research skills focuses on critical thinking about business tasks in order to facilitate the recognition, acquisition and application of individual knowledge, skills and abilities, to achieve specific important outcomes for the learners, their work and the company and to get credentials.

A key to learning research skills for their work is employees understanding of the learning methodology and supporting ICT tools. The contribution of the worker in company is important also due the action involved in accessing data at workplace and then going on to develop and apply the research findings to a work-place oriented business project.

Work-place oriented research projects in cooperation with universities use their expertise of learning, for example, research, evaluation, synthesis and critical thinking to enable practitioners to use the workplace and its resources for development and innovation.

Head (2012) highlighted the importance of information skills in the workplace. In addition, there have been some studies into the development workplace information literacy in recent years. However little research has been done on how to exploit workplace research skills to enhance entrepreneurial culture

In order to exploit research skills as a method of developing entrepreneurial capacity in SMEs a learning method which aligns both the pedagogy of developing research skills and entrepreneurship education is necessary.

The project Reinnovate focusses on using systematic research to facilitate the development of work-place oriented practical research and entrepreneurial skills of employees in SMEs to assist them to find/create the knowledge required to become more competitive, to develop a culture of entrepreneurship and become more innovative.

One of the main activities within Reinnovate is the development of a learning methodology and accredited curriculum to support the development of SME orientated practice-based research skills. This ensure that the research skills are orientated towards the needs. Within this training program the employees will learn to do a bit business research. The purpose of business research is to gather information to add business related decision-making. Business research involves a systematic and objective process of collecting, recording, analyzing and interpreting data for solving managerial problems i.e., for building innovative business models.

In business research it is important to identify opportunities and threats. Often a SME success or failure is dependent on the actions undertaken within conducting research.

For all modules planned in the Reinnovate learning program the methodology should support an active learning and teaching. Active learning involves students directly and engages them actively in the learning process itself. If it's possible students should be involved in all stages of planning, design, execution and evaluation of the learning processes.

The Chinese Proverb: is I hear, and I forget, I see, and I remember, I do, and I understand

Bonwell and Eisan (1991) affirm that "in active learning, students participate in the process when they are doing something besides passively listening." The main benefits associated with this type of learning include:

- Learner and learning focused
- Increases information retention.
- As learning is being applied in practice learners are more motivated.
- Many active learning approaches advocate team work which encourages the development of communication skills.
- Encourages higher order thinking skills.
- Encourages self-directed learning through independent research.
- Active learning employs a wide variety of approaches.

For businesses to survive it is important that all staff are proactive, constantly looking for opportunities and leveraging from these, both at an operational and strategic level. It is important that these opportunities are identified using data driven techniques. First, it is important to learn how to find and collect reliable data and information in one topic connected with the workplace, and how to analyze them, to structure it and use them in a research project.

The methodology of Reinnovate is direct including interviews with guest entrepreneurs, recording videos, counselling, if possible, group discussions, learning from mistakes, process-oriented teaching, practical-operational teaching methods like starting a business, roleplay.

The Reinnovate methodology should help to

- Take into consideration the most common practices in SMEs which are informal learning and workplace learning.

- Take into consideration effective and preferred practices by employees to keep the employees moral at work and extend their employability perspectives.
- Support the inter-organizational level of workplace learning i.e., regardless of life-cycle stages.
- Support not only individual learning but also giving group learning opportunities, since SMEs at high-growth perform more practices at the group level of workplace learning.

CASE STUDY: DEVELOPING AN ENTREPRENEURIAL CULTURE IN SMEs: SMART RESEARCH AS A 21ST CENTURY SKILL FOR BUSINESS

Research skills are a prime way of providing learners with the capacity to gather new knowledge to enable them to adopt new methods of doing business. To reflect the use of research skills to allow learners to adapt to new business demands the programme title *Smart Research as a 21st Century Skill for Business* was agreed within Reinnovate.

Research skills will allow employees in the workplace to adapt to these changes by proactively seeking new opportunities for their company, making data driven decisions to implement these opportunities and evaluating the impact of this on the business performance. The student will also be required to manage the implementation of the workplace research project by leveraging from internal resources readily available to them. They will have to evaluate the value of the project to their organization from a financial, social and cultural perspective. They will also have to identify future opportunities for their organization.

At the end of the programme the employee will have designed, managed and implemented a small-scale research project in their organization, determined its impact on the organization and explored future avenues for research. The programme will comprise of four modules which will align to the the ENTRECOMP framework. Prior to taking the programme the entrepreneurial orientation of the individual (in terms of autonomy) (Hart 1991) and the organization will be measured (Knight, 1997) to determine if the programme impacted the entrepreneurial orientation of the firm. The programme is structured as follows

- Four modules will be offered, each module will be offered over the course of a six-week period, if a learner takes all four modules, they will accumulate credits for a level 7 certificate award
- Modules will be delivered using an active learning pedagogy using a model of inquiry-based learning
- Modules will be delivered online and mentored by an academic and practitioner

The modules align to the competencies identified in the Entrecomp framework

Module 1: Using Research to Identify Future Opportunities

This module will enable learners to conceive and explore the feasibility of different business opportunities using different forms of learning. The new world of work is subject to continuous change, to keep up to date and employees should have the ability to identify and assess the viability of opportunities and skills to realize new opportunities in their workplace.

The business model they must develop should fit in the business environment of the company and when it is ready it should get closer to the business goal chosen by the learner.

In order to understand better a business model, it is recommended besides the text to present examples of business models. These will be specific in each country and choose sectors.

Some of students come to their business model with a clear research/business question to address but others have only some ideas but not specific research/business question. So, it is necessary to help them to choose a business topic and research question.

Entrepreneurship and Research Skills in SMEs 61

It is recommended that the students talk/communicate with others about their ideas and if necessary, build a common business project. Referring to Entrecomp it means to achieve competences to mobilize others (Group 2 Resources) and working with others (Group 3 Into action).

The students should be encouraged to explore if there exist some references in this context, so new learning resources.

In order to do some research how it is required in the Syllabus of the Module 1 they must learn how to look for necessary information to develop their business model.

The methodology for this module should support an active learning and teaching students being engaged actively in the learning process itself. Like the Chinese Proverb the student should learn by doing (EntreComp Group 3 into action). If it is possible a kind of Design Thinking s should be used as a process for problem-solving

Unlike analytical thinking, Design Thinking includes "building up" ideas, with few, or no, limits on breadth during a "brainstorming" phase. This helps reduce fear of failure in the participant(s) and encourages input and participation from a wide variety of sources in the ideation phases.

Design thinking is also now explicitly taught in general as well as professional education, across all sectors of education.

Referring Digital innovation, the students should learn how the business that embrace digital transformation can benefit, so to look at the changes in business models they develop.

Module 2: Smart Methods to Gather and Analyzing Data

One of the major problems of statistics had been the collection of data. It had been time consuming, expensive and even not feasible to collect. This is the main reason most of the statistical procedures focus on small data, based on observations or measures on small number of units of analysis. The problem today differs from the past problems. Today, the question is how to deal with a huge number of data driven from various resources (Text, video, audio etc.). Collection of data has become much easier and cheaper especially due to widespread use of information and communication technologies in various spheres of our life. The amount of data is growing exponentially each year and is set to continue.

Dealing with huge amount of data put new challenges as well as new opportunities for business life. The information lacking or even unknown or unachievable in the past is now available to use. Consumer preferences, feedback, product reputation, consumer needs can be now analyzed via targeted surveys or through analysis of social media. In addition to external data resources, use and analysis of internal data from various resources and instruments within the company means new challenges for the productivity and competitiveness.

In general, Small and medium enterprises are regarded as slow adapters of the new technology of big data analytics. As stated in an scientific article, various factors play a role for the low level of adaption of business and big data analytics by SMEs, mainly: lack of understanding of big data analytics, lack of qualified personal, cultural barriers within the firm, shortage of data analytic expertise, shortage of qualified data analysist on the labor market, shortage of useful and affordable consulting services targeted at SMEs, concern of data protection and data privacy and financial barriers (Coleman at al. 2016).

The use of Data analytics and Big Data is regarded as domain of big and international companies with resources and personal capacities. Despite of the positive prognoses about business volumes, the return of investments for big data analytics lag still behind the expectations, even for big companies. Success stories and best practices dominate the discussions. The connection between innovation and big data and data analytics is still under discussion and there is little research on it.

Nevertheless, the ability of using data can offer new business opportunities to growth and new ideas for innovation for SMEs as well.

This module will enable learners gather and analyze the relevant data to allow them to implement a business opportunity or an innovative idea. Learners will design and implement new ideas in a data driven manner. Meanwhile, there are various training programs from universities and commercial companies which address several aspects of data analysis. Such programs are somehow long-term investments and require 1-3-year training program. Furthermore, the learners should have high school degree and experience in the fields of computer science, mathematics, and statistics and data analysis in general. The training programs are not cheap and for most of the learners interested in not affordable at all.

Within the framework of the project Reinnovate the learners would rather be introduced the techniques and methodologies of data analytics and possibilities of using and interpreting the data for business success, innovation and new business opportunities and ideas. In addition, cooperation and networking with external consulting and IT-companies and their data analytic tools would help SMEs to avoid the gap due to lacking personal resources. In this module, the learners will have an overview how to assess and use such external resources and implement or apply in their own business fields.

Collecting Data (Primary and Secondary)

Analysis of data and developing new business ideas by using findings from data analysis are main targets, but they build up last steps in the research process. At first, there must be any data. In General, the data are driven from various resources (Text, video, audio etc.). It may stem from internal resources, which are collected within the company through instruments, machines, sensors or internal surveys. There may be other external resources as well: social media, official statistics or commercial resources. The students will be introduced to various forms of data and the possibilities of resources. They will learn how to differentiate between data forms and how to find sector specific resources and their relevance in their own business field in the SME.

Data Driven Decision Making

Data-driven decision making involves making decisions that are backed up by hard data rather than making decisions that are intuitive or based on observation alone. The focus in this module lies in the introduction to Data Analytics and its role in business decisions. "Big Data" refers to the large volumes of both structured and unstructured data that exist within and outside a company. The data could be a source of information a business can translate into insights. The students will learn why data is important and how it has evolved. Data Analytics should fit in the business environment of the company.

Design of Implementation Solution or Business Idea

The students will be introduced to a framework for conducting Data Analysis and what tools and techniques are commonly used. They will have a chance to put your knowledge to work in a simulated business setting. Using best-practices and examples from the praxis, they will learn to assess the possibilities which would emerge by dealing with "Big data". This module will provide learners with the analytical insights and overview to use traditional and technology based analytical approaches that are oriented towards the needs of individual users.

The program consists of flexible, tailored coursework based on actual, current business scenarios and case studies.

Module 3: Managing Your Research Project

The methodology within this module will be orientated to the main goals of this module that every participant should manage a research project – alone or in a team, identify performance objectives and communicate the results. To address these needs the students will learn how to leverage off or and mange from internal resources to bring the business opportunity ideas developed in previous modules to implementation stage. If it is possible this last activity should be done within the company where the participant works but it is assumed that learners are also students who finish their entrepreneurship studies or fired employees who look for a job. These participants should be helped by the tutor to find right stakeholders.

Entrepreneurship and Research Skills in SMEs 65

A research projects consists mainly of an introduction, a main body and a conclusion, some form of literature review, investigation in this topic, something original, and analysis of research findings in connection with the business proposed objectives.

Within teaching this module the following structure of a research project should be followed additionally competences that could be achieved - see EntreComp):

1. Choose own research area (EntreComp Vision Group 1) Participants should be advised to choose a field related to an area they already worked or are working/studding since they can better identify potential research topics than in a completely new area. If they work in team, they should discuss the topic with group participants. If the learner does not find a topic he/she should be helped by the course tutor.

2. Conduct preliminary research for the project (EntreComp – Vision Mobilizing Resources, Group 2) This involves surveying current literature, getting advice from the tutor. Key tools that can be relevant and are available like: internet search engines especially ones that offer advanced search features (i.e., http://www.google.com), electronic available journals should be given by tutor

3. Decide own research topic (EntreComp Creativity, Vision Group 1) It is better that the research topic is defined at the start of the project, what should be achieved and how the project should be monitoring to achieve the desired objectives.

4. Decide the methodology for research: experimental, observational (i.e., in the company), more theoretical. If possible, the methods should be justified (EntreComp, Planning and management, Group 3).

5. Submit the research proposal to the tutor for approval this can be a first assessment stage

6. Finalize the topic, the milestones and methodology (EntreComp, Planning and management, Group 3).

7. Conduct own research (EntreComp, Valuing ideas, Group1)

8. Analysis of data/information processing - see module 2 i.e., statistical analysis, generating graphs (i.e., by Design Thinking), charts, tables, organizing information into categories
9. Writing up
10. Submission

Module 4: Evaluating Success & Feature Opportunities

The methodology for teaching and learning within this module will be oriented to the main objective to enable learners to reflect on impact of workplace research (done within a small research project) on the organization and determine opportunities for further workplace research. The students should learn how to evaluate the impact of small research projects, reflect on the findings and learn from these by identifying future opportunities for their workplace. Finally, they will implement an ePortfolio.

It is known that evaluation is an integral component of quality improvement also referring research within SMEs and there is much to be learned from the evaluation of small improvements in the corresponding projects of learners.

Reflection is an integral component of lifelong learning and so is a need for including opportunities for SME employees and students who would like to achieve entrepreneurial competence also within the Reinnovate curriculum to develop these skills.

The methodology within this module should engage students in thinking what they learned in each concept (i.e., to develop a research project) and how they will apply that in future particularly at their workplaces.

The module should help the students to do a critical reflection i.e., to analyze, questioning a reframing an experience (developing a research project) on order to assess it for learning (reflective learning) and to improve practice (reflective practice). Reflective learning improves the professionalism and critical thinking.

The evaluation proposed to be used within this module relates to two main types of learning: learning within the project and generalized learning about the implementation of quality improvements

CONCLUSION AND FUTURE WORK

This chapter has involved a review of different articles and the opinion of the authors about how the discipline of entrepreneurship has evolved, the role of entrepreneurship education and how innovative training methods could facilitate the development of entrepreneurial culture and support SMEs to grow. Finally, it has been established that it is not easy to scale up business from a traditional small enterprise but through new educational practices and a cooperation between HE, research and industry entrepreneurial mind-sets can be supported including achieving competences like described in EntreComp but also new work-oriented research skills. The program being developed by the Reinnovate project to develop entrepreneurial culture in SMEs through the provision of research skills can contribute in this context.

The authors will work further in collaboration with SMEs to make some adjustments towards transformational entrepreneurship and a sustainable socio-economic development of SMEs.

ACKNOWLEDGMENT

This paper describes work within the on-going Erasmus+ project Reinnovate.

REFERENCES

Alberti, A., Sciascia, B., and Poli (2004). Entrepreneurship education: Notes on the ongoing Debate in *14th Annual International Entrepreneurship*

Conference, University of Napoli Federico II, Italy. Academy of Management Learning and Education, 3(3), 258-273.

Arasti, Z., Kiani Falavarjani, M. & Imanipour, N. (2012). A Study of Teaching Methods in Archer L. B. et al. (1979) *Design in General Education*. London: The Royal College of Art.

Azizi, M. (2009). *The study of entrepreneurship education in public universities in Tehran and provision of entrepreneurial training model.* Unpublished PhD thesis, Shahid Beheshti University.

Bacigalupo, M., Kampylis, P., Punie, Y. and Van den Brande, G. (2016). *EntreComp: The entrepreneurship competence framework.* Luxembourg: Publication Office of the European Union.

Bonwell, C. & Eison, J. (1991). *Active Learning: Creating Excitement in the Classroom AEHE-ERIC Higher Education Report No. 1.* Washington, D.C.: Jossey-Bass.

Cedefop (2018). *Insights into skill shortages and skill.*

Chinonye, I.M. and Akinlabi, M. (2014). Entrepreneurship curriculum and pedagogical challenges in captivating students' interest towards entrepreneurship education. *Research Journal of Economics and Business Studies,* 4(1), 1-11.

Clarke, J., Thorpe, R., Anderson, L. & Gold, J. (2006). *It's all action, it's all learning: action.*

Cooney, T.M. and Bygrave, W.D. (1997). The Evolution of Structure and Strategy in Fast-Growth Firms Founded by Entrepreneurial Teams – *17th Entrepreneurship Research Conference 1997*, Babson, Wellesley, MA, April 16 – 19.

Covin, J.G. and Slevin, D.P. (1989). "The strategic management of small firms in hostile and benign environment," *Strategic Management Journal,* Vol. 10 No. 1, pp. 75-87.

Gibb AA and Hannon PD (2006). Towards the entrepreneurial university. *International Journal of Entrepreneurship Education* 4: 73–110.

Della Corte, V., Zamparelli, G. & Micera, R. (2013). Innovation in tradition-based firms: dynamic knowledge for international competitiveness. *European Journal of Innovation Management,* Vol. 16 No. 4. pp. 405-439.

Ellinger, A.D. & Cseh, M. (2007). Contextual factors influencing the facilitation of others' learning through everyday work experiences. *Journal of Workplace Learning,* Vol. 19 No. 7. pp. 435-452.

Eison, J. (1991). *Active Learning: Creating Excitement in the Classroom AEHE-ERIC Higher Education Report No. 1.* Washington, D.C.: Jossey-Bass. ISBN 1-878380-08-7.

Emmanuel, C.L. (2010). *Entrepreneurship: A Conceptual Approach, Lagos:* Concept Publications.

Esmi, K., Marzoughi, R. & Torkzadeh, J. (2015). Teaching learning methods of an entrepreneurship curriculum. *J Adv Med Educ Prof* 2015, 3(4). pp. 172-177.

EU (2010). *Transversal Analysis on the Evolution of Skills Needs in 19 Economic Sectors:* Report prepared by Oxford Research for DG Employment, Social Affairs and Equal Opportunities: Denmark.

EU (2016). *Skills Challenges in Europe* (2016) available at: http:// skillspanorama.cedefop.europa.eu/sites/default/files/2016_Skills_Chall enges_AH.pdf accessed on: 23rd April 2018.

EU Skills Panorama (2014). Employability and skills of higher education graduates. *Analytical Highlight.*

European Commission (2011). *Entrepreneurship education: Enabling teachers as a critical success factor.*

European Commission (2016). *A new skills agenda for Europe,* Brussels, 17th October 2016.

EUROSTAT (2015). *Statistics on small and medium-sized enterprises Dependent and independent SMEs and large enterprises.*

Fang Zhao (2005). *Exploring the synergy between entrepreneurship and Innovation.*

Fayolle, A. and Gailly, B. (2008). From craft to science: Teaching models and learning processes in entrepreneurship education. *Journal of European Industrial Training,* 32(7), 569-593.

Gibb, A.A. (2002). In pursuit of a new 'enterprise' and 'entrepreneurship' paradigm for learning: creative destruction, new values, new ways of doing things and new combinations of knowledge. *International Journal of Management Reviews,* 4(3), 233-269.

Hamburg, Ileana (2015). Learning approaches for entrepreneurship education. In: *Advances in social sciences.*

Hamburg, Ileana/O'Brien, Emma (2014). Using strategic learning for achieving growth in SMEs. In: *Journal of information.*

Hamburg, Ileana/Bucksch, Sascha (2017). Digital skills for eco-innovative entrepreneurship. In: *Advances in social sciences research journal* 4, no. 14, p. 127-136Weblink.

Hamburg, Ileana/O'Brian, Emma/Vladut, Gabriel (2018). Workplace-oriented research and mentoring of entrepreneurs: cooperation university - industry. In: *Archives of business research* 6, no. 6, p. 243-251.

Hamburg, Ileana (2015). Learning approaches for entrepreneurship education. In: *Advances in social sciences research journal* 3, no. 1, p. 228-237.

Hamburg, Ileana (2014). Improving education and training impact on competitive advantages of SMEs. In: *International journal of innovative research in electronics and communications (IJIREC)* 1, nr. 4, p. 54-60 PDF.

Hamburg, Ileana (2014). Improving SME's capacity through learning and new technologies. In: *International journal of education and practice* 2, no. 9, 213-221.

Hornby, D. and Thomas, R., (1989). Towards a better standard of management. *Personnel Management, 21*(1), pp.52-55.

Hart, S. L. (1991). Intentionality and autonomy in strategy-making process: Modes, arche-types, and firm performance. In P. Shrivastava, A. Huff, & J. Dutton (Eds.), *Advances in strategic management,* vol. 7: 97-127. Greenwich, CT: JAI Press.

Hebert, R. F. and Link, N.A. (1982). *The Entrepreneur.* New York: Praeger Publishers, 1982.

Head, A.J., (2012). *Learning curve: How college graduates solve information problems once they join the workplace.*

Honig, B. (2004). *Entrepreneurship education: Towards a model of contingency based business planning.* http://dx.doi.org/10.2801/23250

http://ec.europa.eu/eurostat/statistics-explained/index.php/Statistics_on_small_and_medium-sized_enterprises.

Jones, B. and Iredale, N. (2010). Enterprise education as pedagogy. *Education+ training,* 52(1), pp.7-19.

Knight, Gary A. (1997). "Cross-cultural reliability and validity of a scale to measure firm entrepreneurial orientation." *Journal of business venturing* 12, no. 3 (1997). 213-225.

Kowsari, M. & Norouzzadeh, R. (2009). *An Explanation of the Characteristics of BA Course.*

Kuratko, D.F. (2003). Entrepreneurship education: Emerging trends and challenges for the 21st century. Coleman Foundation White Paper Series for the U.S. Association of Small Business and Entrepreneurship. Learning in SMEs. *Journal of European Industrial Training,* Vol. 30 No. 6. pp. 441-455.

Kutzhanova, N., Lyons, T.S. & Lichtenstein, G.A. (2009) - Skill-Based Development of Entrepreneurs and the Role of Personal and Peer Group Coaching in Enterprise Development - *Economic Development Quarterly,* Vol. 20, No. 10.

Kutzhanova, N., Lyons, T.S. & Lichtenstein, G.A. (2009) - Skill-Based Development of Entrepreneurs and the Role of Personal and Peer Group Coaching in Enterprise Development - *Economic Development Quarterly,* Vol. 20, No. 10.

Lee, L., and Wong, P. (2007). Entrepreneurship education- A Compendium of related issues in Zoltan, J. and David B. Audretsch. *International Handbook Series on Entrepreneurship,* 3. 79-105.

Marsick, V.J. (2009). Toward a unifying framework to support informal learning theory, research and practice. *Journal of Workplace Learning,* 21(4), pp.265-275.

Mazzarol, T., 2003. A model of small business HR growth management. *International Journal of Entrepreneurial Behavior & Research,* 9(1), pp.27-49.

McGraw, P. & Peretz, M. (2011). *HRD practices in local private sector companies and MNC.*

McGraw, P. (2014). A review of human resource development trends and practices in Michaelson, L.K. and Sweet, M. (2008). The essential elements of team-based learning. *New Directions for Teaching and Learning*, 2008(116), 7-27.

Matthews, P. (2007). ICT assimilation and SME expansion. *Journal of International Development,* Vol. 19 No. 6. pp. 817-827.

Mills, B and Cottel, P.G. (1998). *Cooperative learning for higher education faculty.* Phoenix, AR: American Council on Education, Orynx Press. Mismatch: Learning from Cedefop's European skills.

Mojalalchubqlu, M., Abdullahfam, R. & Tamjidtalesh, A. (2011). Pathology of the entrepreneurial process in the university curriculum: a case study in Islamic Azad University. *Management beyond.* 2011, 18. Persian. pp. 167–87.

Mwasalwiba, E.S. (2010). Entrepreneurship education: A review of its objectives, teaching methods and impact indicators. *Education + Training,* 52(1), 20-47.

O'Brien, Emma/Hamburg, Ileana (2014). Supporting sustainable strategies for SMEs through training, cooperation and mentoring. In: *Higher education studies* 4, no. 2, p. 61-69 Weblink.

O'Brien, E., Carroll, L. (2015). *A report on how problem based learning and ICT can support.*

OECD (2005). *Guidelines for Collecting and Interpreting Innovation Data,* Third Edition.

OECD (2018). *Researchers (indicator).* doi: 10.1787/20ddfb0f-en (Accessed on 23 April 2018).

O'Hara, B. (2011). *Entrepreneurship in Ireland* – Gill and MacMillan, Dublin

Oyelola, O.T. ed. (2013). Embedding entrepreneurship education in to curriculum: A case study of Yaba College of technology, Centre for Entrepreneurship Development. *The 1st International Africa Enterprise Educators Conference*, 2013 January. Lagos, Nigeria.

Palich, L.E., and Bagby, D.R. (1990). Using cognitive theory to explain entrepreneurial risk-taking: challenging conventional wisdom. *Journal of Business Venturing* 10(6):424–438.

Panagiotakopoulos, A. (2011). Workplace learning and its organizational benefits for small enterprises: evidence from Greek industrial firms. *The Learning Organization*, Vol. 18 No. 5. pp. 364-374.

Ribeiro-Soriano, D. (2017). *Small business and entrepreneurship: Their role in economic and social development.*

Timmons, J.A., Gillin, L.M., Burshtein, S.L and Spinelli, S. (2011). *New Venture Creation: Entrepreneurship for the 21st Century: A Pacific Rim Perspective*, McGraw-Hill, Sydney.

Tam, S. & Gray, D. E. (2016). The practice of employee learning in SME workplaces: A micro view from the life-cycle perspective. *Journal of Small Business and Enterprise Development,* Vol. 23 Issue: 3. pp. 671-690.

Torben, B. (2010). The camp model for entrepreneurship teaching. *International Entrepreneurship and Management Journal.* 2010, 7(2). pp. 279–96.

Woodruffe, C. (1993) "What Is Meant by a Competency?" *Leadership & Organization Development Journal,* Vol. 14.

Yadollahi, J. & Mirarbrazi, R. (2009). An Examination of the Introduction of Entrepreneurship Education Curriculum in Educational Sciences. *Journal of Entrepreneurship Development.* 2009, 3. Persian. pp. 4.

Zahra, S.A. and Wright, M., (2016). Understanding the social role of entrepreneurship. *Journal of Management Studies*, *53*(4), pp.610-629.

ABOUT THE AUTHORS

Ileana Hamburg worked 20 years as a professor for Mathematics and Computer Science at the University of Craiova, Romania. In Germany, she worked as a software developer for a company and as a researcher within the Faculty of Informatics at the University of Erlangen, Germany. She is a research fellow at the Institute for Work and Technology (IAT), Westfälische Hochschule Gelsenkirchen and lecturer for Informatics at the Open University (FU) of Hagen. She works and coordinates German and

European projects in the field of digitalisation, competence development and knowledge management.

One of the research topics of Ileana Hamburg is entrepreneurship including also methods of improving entrepreneurship education. In the last 10 years, Ileana Hamburg published some papers in this context and presented her research at national and international conferences.

Emma O'Brien, Academic Developer (TEL) is an Academic Developer in Technology Enhanced Learning in Mary Immaculate College, having previously worked as a lecturer and researcher in the University of Limerick, Limerick Institute of Technology and with the Atlantic University Alliance (www.aua.ie). She has lectured in higher education for over thirteen years. Emma has taught across several different disciplines including Business, Humanities and Computer Science, through blended, online and face-to-face mediums. She has taught on undergraduate, postgraduate and professional programmes including several modules in e-learning and instructional design. Emma has a PhD in Technology Enhanced Learning (2005, UL) and a Masters in Computing in Education (2003, LIT).

Emma has been principle investigator on several European projects in the area of technology-enhanced learning, receiving funding of €1.1 million. She has over 30 publications in this area. Emma is currently co-chair of FACILITATE - the national inquiry based learning network and a reviewer for the Journal of Open and Distance Learning.

Her research interests include flexible and informal learning and the use of technology to enhance workplace learning, inquiry and problem based learning through technology, digital information literacy, exploiting technology to enhance the learning experience and graduate employability.

Fikret Öz is a social scientist and has worked for 22 years as a researcher at the Institute for Work and Technology (IAT), Westfälische Hochschule Gelsenkirchen. In addition, he regularly offers statistics courses as a lecturer at the Ruhr University Bochum. His research activities focus on labour market analysis, industrial development, regional and sectoral studies and analysis of occupations, digitalisation, design and conduct of empirical surveys. He works and coordinates several national and international projects. He has experience in quantitative and qualitative analysis. Recently, he has concentrated his research on the fields of digitalisation, effects on labour and qualification, big data usage in SMEs, the impact of digitalisation on work organisation and on qualification of employees in SMSs, as well as measures for skill development with respect to digitalisation are major research interests.

In: The Power of Entrepreneurship
Editor: Daan Dirksen

ISBN: 978-1-53615-114-5
© 2019 Nova Science Publishers, Inc.

Chapter 3

APPLYING THE GLOBAL ENTREPRENEURSHIP DEVELOPMENT INDEX METHODOLOGY TO ASSESS THE ENTREPRENEURSHIP PERFORMANCE IN VIETNAM

Ha Thi Thu Nguyen[*]
Faculty of Economics, University of Economics,
The University of Danang, Da Nang, Vietnam

ABSTRACT

This study mainly aims to measure entrepreneurship performance in Vietnam at the national level through a new approach - the Global Entrepreneurship Development Index (GEDI). The Global Entrepreneurship Development Index (GEDI) consists of three sub-indices, including Entrepreneurial Attitudes, Entrepreneurial Abilities and Entrepreneurial Aspiration, which are divided into fourteen pillars and can

---

[*] Corresponding Author Email: nguyenthithuhaktdn@gmail.com; ha.ntt@due.edu.vn.

be further subdivided into 28 variables. By analyzing these pillars and variables in comparison to two Southeast Asian developing economies - Thailand and Indonesia - which have similar cultural, economic and social characteristics, the study identifies the best and worst performing variables of the Global Entrepreneurship Development Index (GEDI). The research results indicate that in Vietnam, nine bottlenecks of fourteen pillars are poorly performing with very low scores, in which the highest policy priority is given for four pillars, including risk acceptance, opportunity perception, internationalization and technology absorption. Finally, the Penalty for Bottleneck (PFB) methodology, which is considered as the policy application of the Global Entrepreneurship Development Index (GEDI) methodology and a simulation of "optimal" policy allocation are suggested to alleviate the weakest performing pillars, aiming to achieve the greatest improvement of entrepreneurship performance as well as reach the desired five-point increase in Vietnam's Global Entrepreneurship Development Index.

Keywords: entrepreneurship, performance, the global entrepreneurship development index, the penalty for bottleneck methodology, Vietnam

INTRODUCTION

Entrepreneurship offers new and diversified consumer goods and service, job opportunities and enhances national competitiveness, thus promote socioeconomic development (Zahra 1999). The fiercer in competition based on agility, creativity and innovation has led the growing of entrepreneurship wave and entrepreneurship study is growing in many countries (Lee et al. 2006). Entrepreneurship is not well documented factor in the empirical growth literature since it is hard to defined and measured (Stel et al. 2005). Although the conceptualization of entrepreneurship is complex and multidimensional approach, the measurement of entrepreneurship is still limited to single measure such as labour force statistic, business statistic and Global Entrepreneurship Monitor's Total Early-stage Entrepreneurial Activity (TEA) (Szeb, Aidis and Ács 2012). Ács et al. (2017) pointed out that quality matters more than quantity in entrepreneurship, a country is entrepreneurial when it has the best entrepreneurs, not the most. Those studies mentioned above only paid attention on entrepreneurship in term of quantity result while neglected the quality differences across entrepreneurial activity (Szeb, Aidis and Ács 2012). Then Global Entrepreneurship Monitor adopted a multidimensional approach and highlighted more aspects such as attitude, activity and aspiration, but the formal definition of entrepreneurship still not included (Kelley et al. 2011).

Global Entrepreneurship and Development Index (GEDI) developed by the Global Entrepreneurship and Development Institute to measure the health of entrepreneurship ecosystem of research countries and rank their performance in the international context. Global Entrepreneurship and Development Index (GEDI) highlights the contextual feature of entrepreneurship, tests the combined effect of individual and institutional variables, focuses on the quality aspect of entrepreneurial activity, forms entrepreneurial attitudes, activities and aspirations factors into sub-indexes and recommend specific policy alteration to each country based on their strengths and weaknesses (Szeb, Aidis and Ács 2012). On the other hand, the research of Global Entrepreneurship and Development Institute measure only productive entrepreneurship which creates the wealth and society better off (Ács et al., 2017).

Entrepreneurship has been formally accepted in Vietnam since the 1990s and known as the simple view such as business activities, individual level or firm level. Therefore, the traditional approach usually is used by researchers and policymakers when analyzing Vietnam's entrepreneurship (Vietnam Chamber of Commerce and Industry (VCCI) 2014). In fact, entrepreneurship is the complex view based on the multidimensional measure in a country (Iversen, Jørgensen and Malchow-Moller 2008). When discussing entrepreneurship in countries, recent studies follow the National Systems of Entrepreneurship introduced by Ács et al. (2014), which are fundamentally resource allocation systems and driven by both the individual and country-specific institutional characteristics in evaluating the entrepreneurship performance of a country.

The main purpose of this chapter is to measure the entrepreneurship performance of Vietnam at the national level. First, this study employs the Global Entrepreneurship Development Index (GEDI) methodology to analyze Vietnam's entrepreneurship performance through the overall Global Entrepreneurship Development Index (GEDI) level, three Global Entrepreneurship Development Index (GEDI) sub-indices, which are then divided into fourteen pillars and further subdivided into 28 variables, as well as its relative positions at the pillar and variable levels. Furthermore, to have a more detailed and deeper understanding of Vietnam's entrepreneurship performance, this study chooses two developing Southeast Asian countries having similar cultural, economic and social characteristics - Thailand and Indonesia - to compare and identify the best and the worst performing pillars and its corresponding institutional and individual variables of the Global Entrepreneurship Development Index (GEDI) in Vietnam. The Penalty for Bottleneck (PFB) methodology and a simulation of "optimal" policy allocation, which are considered as the policy tools of the Global Entrepreneurship Development Index (GEDI) methodology, is then applied to alleviate the weakest performing pillars or the bottlenecks aiming to achieve the greatest improvement of the Global Entrepreneurship Development Index (GEDI), boost and enhance the entrepreneurship performance in Vietnam.

THE BASIC DESCRIPTION OF THE GLOBAL ENTREPRENEURSHIP DEVELOPMENT INDEX METHODOLOGY

Although entrepreneurship is known as the complex and multidimensional view, most recent empirical researches rely on one-dimensional measures of entrepreneurship in a country to evaluate its entrepreneurship performance (Iversen, Jørgensen and Malchow-Moller 2008). Some popular indicators are used to identify the level and/or dynamics of entrepreneurship such as self-employment, the rate of new business start-up or established businesses and the Total Early-stage Entrepreneurship Activity Index (TEA), which is calculated by the percentage of the working age population engaging in or willing to engage

Applying the Global Entrepreneurship Development Index ... 81

in entrepreneurial activity. Nonetheless, the problem of one-dimensional measures is that it is difficult to distinguish between the quality and the quantity aspects of entrepreneurship (Ács and Szerb 2009; Stephanie and Rafael 2016) and it does not include the impact of national and contextual factors in analyzing the entrepreneurship performance of a country in the different stages of economic development (OECD 2007). Indeed, the one-dimensional measures do not identify differences in the quality of entrepreneurial activity, thus leading to providing policy recommendations concerning only the quantity of entrepreneurship, not its quality.

Because of these problems, it is necessary to adopt a system approach to examine the entrepreneurship performance of a country that not only helps researchers and policy makers think in system and take a broad view when considering individual and country-level indicators, but also is helpful in designing policies to nurture and enhance the entrepreneurship performance for a country's sustainable economic development. Therefore, Ács et al. (2014) introduced a National Systems of Entrepreneurship perspective that emphasized the dynamic interactions between entrepreneurial attitudes, abilities and aspiration by individuals within the institutional context in producing the entrepreneurial action and regulating the quality and the outcome of this action. At the country level, Ács et al. (2014) also mentioned that the Global Entrepreneurship Development Index (GEDI) is the most widely used approach for measuring the output of the multi-faced character of country-level entrepreneurship in countries.

Likewise, Ács et al. (2013) confirmed that the Global Entrepreneurship Development Index (GEDI) is the first complex index concentrating on the multidimensional quality rather than the quantity aspects of country-level entrepreneurship and provides a useful platform for policy analysis. The Global Entrepreneurship Development Index (GEDI) is similar to other indexes having a complex structure with 28 individual and institutional variables that create fourteen pillars and then is divided into three sub-indices: Entrepreneurial Attitudes (ATT), Entrepreneurial Abilities (ABT) and Entrepreneurial Aspiration (ASP). Entrepreneurial Attitudes (ATT) is explained by attitudes on entrepreneurial measures such as perceived opportunities and perceived capabilities to start a business of an economy, the fear of business failure, entrepreneurial intentions. It is influenced by not only geographic and economic factors but also cultural and society issues (Szeb, Aidis and Ács 2012). Entrepreneurship Abilities (ABT) is defined as "what entrepreneurs do" and focuses on the extent to which people start a new business or have an existing business. The Entrepreneurship Abilities (ABT) variable is assessed by measures of Total Early-stage Entrepreneurial Activity (TEA) and Established business ownership (EB). Total Early-stage Entrepreneurial Activity (TEA) is defined as the percentage of the working-age population who is starting a business for less than three months or is willing to run a new business for 3.5 years, while Established business ownership (EB) includes entrepreneurial activities for more than 3.5 years (Reynolds et al. 2005). Motivations to start a business varies depending on the economic development. A higher level of economic growth is, a lower rate of Total Early-stage Entrepreneurial Activity (TEA) is because a high level of economic growth leads to more and better job opportunities, resulting in less probability of individuals starting a business. In other words, Total Early-stage Entrepreneurial Activity (TEA) is shown by new entrepreneurial activities that are related to the economic development. The high Total Early-stage Entrepreneurial Activity (TEA) indicator means that the economy is in the development stage, while the Established business ownership (EB) indicator presents a stable development of business activities in countries (Ács and Szerb 2011). Entrepreneurial Aspiration (ASP) is measured by the growth orientation, innovative orientation of early-stage entrepreneurs who consider their new products in the market and internationalization orientation. In other words, Entrepreneurial Aspiration (ASP) indicates the growth expectations and aspirations of early-stage entrepreneurs that may be connected directly to the top-priority goal for the government (Szeb, Aidis and Ács 2012).

Entrepreneurial Abilities (ABT) and Entrepreneurial Aspiration (ASP) sub-indices show the quality of actual entrepreneurship activities through nascent and start-up businesses, while the Entrepreneurial Attitudes (ATT) sub-index determines the attitudes of the population in a country regarding entrepreneurship. Individual variables are collected from the Adult Population Survey of 79 countries participating in the Global

Entrepreneurship Monitor (GEM), while institutional variables are interaction variables, which are considered as country-specific weighting factors and taken from various surveys of the Global Competitiveness Index, the Doing Business Index or the Index of Economic, or from multinational organizations such as the United Nations and the OECD (Ács and Varga 2005).

However, the Global Entrepreneurship Development Index (GEDI) methodology differs from others in two important respects. First, the Global Entrepreneurship Development Index (GEDI) includes both individual and institutional variables and second, this methodology examines interdependencies of the system by developing a Penalty for Bottleneck (PFB) methodology. The key principles of the Penalty for Bottleneck (PFB) are that the system performance depends on the weakest link and because of having the bottlenecks, the higher scores of pillars cannot show their full influence on the system performance. In this case, the "bottleneck" means a shortage or the lowest level of a particular entrepreneurial pillar as compared to other pillars that vary across country levels, which is critical for policy suggestions. Furthremore, if the weakest indicator improves, the whole Global Entrepreneurship Development Index (GEDI) will be significantly improved (Ács and Szerb 2011).

THE DATA AND RESEARCH METHODOLOGY

The data in this study is collected from various sources, including the World Development Indicators of the World Bank, the Global Entrepreneurship Monitor (GEM) report, the Global Competitiveness Index of World Economic Forum, the Doing Business Index of the World Bamk and the Global Entrepreneurship Development Index (GEDI) from 2011 to 2015 in the entrepreneurship projects of Ács, Autio and Szeb. Furthermore, based on the scores from these surveys and the Global Entrepreneurship Development Index (GEDI) in the Acs, Autio and Szeb's entrepreneurship projects, the authors use the average and statistical methods to calculate the data for the study's purposes.

ENTREPRENEURIAL PERFORMANCE IN VIETNAM

The relationship between the Global Entrepreneurship Development Index (GEDI) and national per capita GDP follows a S shape. High income country tends to have better entrepreneurship ecosystem and vice versa with a correlation of 0.8057. The S-shaped curve show the productive entrepreneurship at different stage of development. It measured the quality of entrepreneurial performance which is positively related to GDP per capita. It shows the effectiveness in explaining long term economic growth but failed to analize short term growth perspective.

On the other hand, the relationship between the Total Early-stage Entrepreneurship Activity Index (TEA) index and per capita GDP follows a U line, when the quantity of entrepreneurship go down when the GDP increase. Global Entrepreneurship Monitor emphasize the quantity of entrepreneurship and announced that a country is low-income when the number of self-employed is high, whereas in wealthier countries, people will work in companies or organizations. Total Early-stage Entrepreneurship Activity Index (TEA) index reflected the prevalence of adults (18-64 years old) that was setting up a new business or the owner or managers of a young firm and the model of Global Entrepreneurship Monitor represented the role of entrepreneurship in national economic growth and adaption (Reynolds et al. 2005). Stel et al. (2005) pointed out that Total Early-stage Entrepreneurship Activity Index (TEA) index has a negative effect impact of entrepreneurship on GDP growth for the developing countries while it has a positive effect for the relatively rich countries. Total Early-stage Entrepreneurship Activity Index (TEA) index does not include qualitative measure, its result fail to capture the intrinsic quality differences between entrepreneurship in countries at very different level of development; therefore, the result is illogical when two countries at the opposite ends of the development spectrum have the same Total Early-stage Entrepreneurship Activity Index (TEA) score (Szerb et al. 2012). Total Early-stage Entrepreneurship Activity Index (TEA) is useful in explaining short term economic growth but can decrease the quality of entrepreneur.

Besides, the consideration of policymakers is how to identify the most important issues affecting entrepreneurship in a country. The Global Entrepreneurship Development Index (GEDI) approach can identify the best and the worst components of the Global Entrepreneurship Development Index (GEDI) of a country before policy priorities are given for this country.

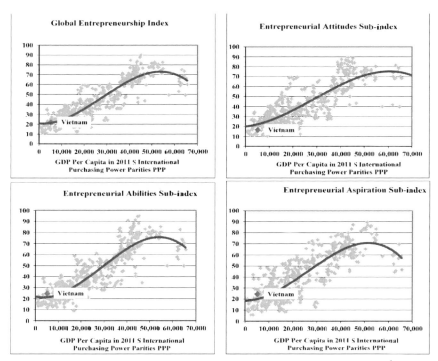

Source: The Global Entrepreneurship Development Index (GEDI) project of Ács, Autio and Szeb.

Figure 1. The relative position of Vietnam at the Global Entrepreneurship Development Index (GEDI) and three sub-index levels, 2011-2015.

The chapter, firstly aims to determine the overall entrepreneurial performance by analyzing Vietnam's entrepreneurial position through its rankings in the Global Entrepreneurship Development Index (GEDI) and three Global Entrepreneurship Development Index (GEDI) sub-indices. The relationship between the Global Entrepreneurship Development Index

(GEDI) values and the economic development, as measured by GDP per capita is shown through the figures above.

Vietnam's overall Global Entrepreneurship Development Index (GEDI) score of 0.222 places it slightly above the development, which is presented by trend-line in Figure 1. This result also indicates that Vietnam's overall entrepreneurial performance is a little higher than would be estimated given its GDP level. It also proved that developed economic is enough to facilitate entrepreneurship. In addition, Vietnam's scores for the Entrepreneurial Abilities (ABT) (do you have proper skills, the abilities to work on entrepreneurship) and Entrepreneurial Aspiration (ASP) (do you want to start-up and build a giant company) sub-indices are 0.249 and 0.248, slight higher than the trend-line or the development, while Vietnam's score for the Entrepreneurial Attitudes (ATT) (how a nation thinks about entrepreneurship) sub-index is below the trend-line. Out of the three sub-indexes, Entrepreneurial Attitudes (ATT) is the worst in Vietnam. This situation also indicates that Vietnam have ideas of start-up, aims at setting up a giant company as well as have enough skills and sufficient knowledge to handle the business. People still doubt about entrepreneurship and its effectiveness. The not so positive attitude toward entrepreneurship leads to not so high start-up rates. The low numbers of people recognize business opportunity affect the supportive environment for entrepreneurship growing.

Table 1 shows the ranking of the Global Entrepreneurship and Development Index (GEDI) in the period 2011 - 2015. No high-income country scores too low, whereas no low-income country scores on the top. Vietnam ranked at 72nd place, out of 93 countries. Compared to other developing countries in Asia (including Philippines, Malaysia, Indonesia, Thailand, China, India, Kazakhstan, Pakistan and Bangladesh), Vietnam's score is lower than almost of developing countries in Asia. It is only slightly better than Indonesia and much higher than Pakistan and Bangladesh. However, because Vietnam is a developing country situated in Southeast Asia, this study chooses Thailand and Indonesia to compare the entrepreneurial performance. The main reason for choosing these developing economies is that both are emerging or transitional economies with similar cultural, economic and social characteristics that can provide comparative insights into the stages of development. Moreover, Vietnam shares the border with Thailand, while Vietnam and Indonesia have similar demographic characteristics with very large populations. As compared to the two countries identified above, the Global Entrepreneurship Development Index (GEDI) score of Vietnam is 0.222, which is slightly better than that of Indonesia (0.212) but is much lower than Thailand's Global Entrepreneurship Development Index (GEDI) score (0.281). Vietnam's low Global Entrepreneurship Development Index (GEDI) score as compared to Thailand indicates Vietnam's sub-par entrepreneurial performance. Entrepreneurship is not the only factor which fosters the economic development, the wealthy of people in a nation (or GDP per capita growing).

In addition to the overall Global Entrepreneurship Development Index (GEDI) score, the study examines Vietnam's entrepreneurial performance by comparing the average scores of the three sub-indices between Vietnam, Thailand and Indonesia, as well as the normalized scores of its components.

As compared to Thailand and Indonesia, out of the three Global Entrepreneurship Development Index (GEDI) sub-indices, Entrepreneurial Attitudes (ATT) is the worst sub-index in Vietnam with the lowest score (0.18), followed by the Entrepreneurial Aspiration (ASP) sub-index and the last is Vietnam's Entrepreneurial Abilities (ABT) sub-index. The low Entrepreneurial Attitudes (ATT) score is because of Vietnam's past small and poor income economy level, leading to low perceived opportunities and capabilities of Vietnamese people to start a business and a big fear of business failure (Vietnam Chamber of Commerce and Industry (VCCI) 2014).

Moreover, the general concept of entrepreneurship has many dimensions, Global Entrepreneurship Development Index (GEDI) analyse both institutional and individual variables, be consistent with the micro and macro level aspect of entrepreneurship. This following part analyses more deeply of the entrepreneurial performance of Vietnam through the detailed analysis of Global Entrepreneurship Development Index (GEDI)'s fourteen pillars. Each pillar is divided into institutional and individual variables to identify the strength and weakness of the entrepreneurship of Vietnam.

Table 1. The Global Entrepreneurship and Development Index (GEDI) overall rank of the countries

Rank	Country	GEDI	Rank	Country	GEDI	Rank	Country	GEI	Rank	Country	GEDI
1	United States	80.9	26	Japan	77.2	51	Kazakhstan	49.2	51	Kazakhstan	30.1
2	Sweden	77.2	27	Portugal	76.5	52	Namibia	46.0	52	Namibia	29.8
3	Canada	76.5	28	Spain	76.3	53	Lebanon	45.7	53	Lebanon	29.6
4	Switzerland	76.3	29	Poland	76.2	54	Macedonia	45.1	54	Macedonia	28.9
5	Denmark	76.2	30	Lithuania	74.5	55	Peru	44.2	55	Peru	28.5
6	Australia	74.5	31	Puerto Rico	70.5	56	Thailand	44.0	56	Thailand	28.1
7	United Kingdom	70.5	32	Turkey	69.7	57	Panama	43.8	57	Panama	27.4
8	Netherlands	69.7	33	Czech Republic	68.6	58	Mexico	43.5	58	Mexico	27.0
9	Ireland	68.6	34	Bolivia	67.6	59	India	21.6	59	India	25.9
10	Finland	67.6	35	Slovakia	65.8	60	Morocco	42.3	60	Morocco	25.7
11	France	65.8	36	Latvia	64.8	61	Russia	41.2	61	Russia	24.8
12	Belgium	64.8	37	Hungary	63.9	62	Georgia	40.6	62	Georgia	24.6
13	Germany	63.9	38	Tunisia	63.5	63	Trinidad & Tobago	38.9	63	Trinidad & Tobago	24.5
14	Austria	63.5	39	Colombia	63.1	64	Philippines	38.7	64	Philippines	23.9
15	Taiwan	63.1	40	Uruguay	60.1	65	Argentina	36.6	65	Argentina	23.7
16	Norway	60.1	41	Italy	59.1	66	El Salvador	36.5	66	El Salvador	23.5
17	Chile	59.1	42	Malaysia	59.0	67	Belize	36.5	67	Belize	23.1
18	Israel	59.0	43	Greece	58.7	68	Ghana	35.7	68	Ghana	23.0
19	Luxembourg	58.7	44	China	57.6	69	Egypt	35.1	69	Egypt	22.7
20	Qatar	57.6	45	Romania	55.2	70	Bulgaria	34.6	70	Bulgaria	22.7
21	Estonia	55.2	46	Botswana	52.2	71	Algeria	34.2	71	Algeria	22.5
22	Singapore	52.2	47	Barbados	51.8	72	Vietnam	33.7	72	Vietnam	22.2
23	Slovenia	51.8	48	South Africa	49.7	73	Nigeria	33.5	73	Nigeria	22.1
24	United Arab Emirates	49.7	49	Croatia	49.4	74	Indonesia	32.2	74	Indonesia	21.2
25	Korea	49.4	50	Costa Rica		75	Brazil	31.1	75	Brazil	21.0

Rank	Country	GEDI	Rank	Country	GEI	Rank	Country	GEDI
76	Iran	20.9	82	Guatemala	17.9	88	Cameroon	14.7
77	Jamaica	20.6	83	Suriname	17.8	89	Uganda	13.8
78	Zambia	20.6	84	Ethiopia	17.8	90	Angola	13.8
79	Ecuador	20.6	85	Libya	17.2	91	Venezuela	13.0
80	Bosnia and Herzegovina	20.0	86	Malawi	16.5	92	Burkina Faso	11.9
81	Senegal	19.7	87	Pakistan	16.0	93	Bangladesh	11.6

Source: the Global Entrepreneurship Development Index (GEDI) project of Ács, Autio and Szeb

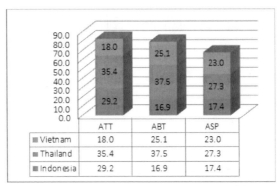

Source: Author's caculation from the Global Entrepreneurship Development Index (GEDI) project of Ács, Autio and Szeb.

Figure 2. A comparison of three Global Entrepreneurship Development Index (GEDI) sub-indices among Vietnam, Thailand and Indonesia.

Table 2. The normalized scores of components of three sub-indices in Vietnam

The normalized scores of components of Entrepreneurial Attitudes Sub-index					
Vietnam	Opportunity perception	Start-up skills	Risk acceptance	Networking	Cultural support
	0.16	0.24	0.07	0.21	0.21
33% percentile	0.32	0.31	0.27	0.36	0.29
67% percentile	0.54	0.58	0.63	0.53	0.57
The normalized scores of components of Entrepreneurial Abilities Sub-index					
Vietnam	Opportunity startup	Technology absorption	Human capital		Competition
	0.21	0.17	0.50		0.22
33% percentile	0.29	0.30	0.33		0.31
67% percentile	0.59	0.60	0.54		0.56
The normalized scores of components of Entrepreneurial Aspirations Sub-index					
Vietnam	Product innovation	Process innovation	High growth	Internationalization	Risk capital
	0.33	0.19	0.22	0.16	0.46
33% percentile	0.31	0.29	0.27	0.34	0.28
67% percentile	0.56	0.60	0.61	0.57	0.60

Source: Author's caculation from the Global Entrepreneurship Development Index (GEDI) project of Ács, Autio and Szeb.

Applying the Global Entrepreneurship Development Index ... 91

Most components of the three sub-indices of Vietnam are not good, with its normalized scores under 0.24, which are presented in red lines in Table 2. For each sub-index, along with the worst score of Vietnam's Entrepreneurial Attitudes (ATT) sub-index, Risk acceptance is the weakest pillar with only 0.07 normalized score. The second weakest pillars are Opportunity perception of the Entrepreneurial Attitudes (ATT) sub-index and Internationalization of the Entrepreneurial Aspiration (ASP) sub-index having the same normalized score (0.16). The last weakest pillar is Technology absorption of the Entrepreneurial Aspiration (ASP) sub-index (0.17).

The Opportunity perception pillar, which is used to measure the "opportunity perception" of a population, defined as the percenatge of the 18-64 aged population that can identify good opportunities to start a business during the next 6 months in the area where they live, is low because Vietnam has experienced a long history of a centrally-planned economy in which private businesses were restricted or even prohibited for decades. Indeed, the history of Vietnam was closely tied with the struggles for national independence, leading to its low income level economy and Vietnam only has transformed to a market driven economy since 1986. The consequence of wars and lack of or limitation of enterprises to access resources and capital in the economy resulted in the low perception level of entrepreneurs regarding opportunities in business, as well as entrepreneurs' big fear of business failure, which causes the low level of the Risk acceptance pillar (Anh and Sullivan 2016). Furthermore, Vietnam only has been a member of the World Trade Organization (WTO) since 2007, and most enterprises in Vietnam are small- and medium-sized with a weak competitiveness. Therefore, economic activities, such as exporting and trading, by small- and medium-sized enterprises (SMEs) in Vietnam are low and below the international average. Hence, it is not surprising the score of Internationalization is low (Anh, Sullivan and Clare 2015). The low score of the Technology absorption pillar indicates the low level of new technology absorption of firms, which is true for Vietnam. Because in emerging economies - especially in stages of transition - entrepreneurs face the same problem of lacking innovation; thus, the ability of firms to absorb new technologies is limited (Dabić et al. 2012).

By contrast, the three best pillars of Vietnam's entrepreneurship are Human capital (the quality of entrepreneurs and this pillar is formed by weighing the percentage of start-ups founded by individuals with higher than secondary education with a qualitative measure of the propensity of firms in a given country to train their staff), Risk capital (is funds invested speculatively in a business, typically a startup. This pillar combines two measures of finance: informal investment in start-ups and a measure of institutional venture capital. Availability of risk capital is considered an important precondition of the ability of new firms to fulfil their growth aspirations. The Risk Capital measure combines the percentage of informal investors in the population aged 18-64, multiplied by the average size of individuals' investment in other people's new businesses) and Product innovation (captures the tendency of entrepreneurial firms to create new products and to adopt or imitate existing ones. This pillar was created by weighting the percentage of firms that offer products that are new to at least some of their customers with a measure that combines private-sector R&D investment, the presence of high-quality research institutions, quality of technology transfer, and the protection of intellectual property) (Reynolds et al. 2005) with normalized scores of 0.5, 0.46 and 0.33, respectively. The first pillar with the highest normalized score (0.5) is a component of Vietnam's Entrepreneurial Abilities (ABT) sub-index, while the two remaining pillars are components of Vietnam's Entrepreneurial Aspiration (ASP) sub-index. The highest level of the Human capital pillar can be explained through a higher rate of Vietnamese entrepreneurs receiving higher education, as well as the government's large investment in the education system in recent years (Vietnam Chamber of Commerce and Industry (VCCI) 2014). Furthermore, the high Risk capital pillar level for Vietnam results from the larger informal investment in startups, which is measured by the liquidity of debt and credit markets and development of the stock market in Vietnam during this period. Finally, Product innovation means the introduction of any improvements in functional characteristics, technical abilities, or ease of use to the existing goods or services of the firm. It also known as the creation and subsequent introduction of a good or service that is either new, or an improved version of previous goods or services. In Vietnam, more investment in Research and Development (R&D) of the private sector, the appearance of high quality research institutions, technology transfer and the attention of government to the intellectual property protection in the period of economic transition has encouraged the enterprises to add value to its products as well as enhance the innovation in production (Enrico and Hien 2013).

To have a more detailed and deeper understanding of Vietnam's entrepreneurial performance, the study continues to analyze the relative position of Vietnam at the pillar level and compare the scores of Vietnam's pillars (which is shown in the inner circle) to that of 93 participating countries in the top one-third (67% percentile) (shown in the outer circle) and bottom one-third (33% percentile) (shown in the middle circle).

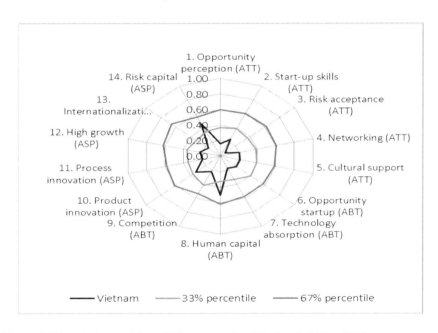

Figure 3. The relative position of Vietnam at the pillar level, 2011 - 2015.

All scores of Vietnam's pillars in Figure 3 are below the scores of the other countries' corresponding pillars in the top one-third. Also, most of Vietnam's pillar scores are below the scores of countries' pillars in the bottom one-third, except for two pillars: Human capital from the Entrepreneurial Abilities (ABT) sub-index and Risk capital from the Entrepreneurial Aspiration (ASP) sub-index.

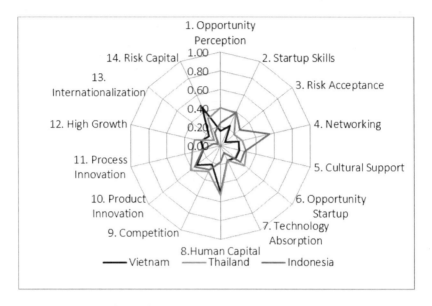

Source: The Global Entrepreneurship Development Index (GEDI) project of Ács, Autio and Szeb

Figure 4. The pillar scores of Vietnam, Thailand and Indonesia, 2011 - 2015.

For the remaining twelve pillars, Vietnam ranks in the bottom one-third, in which the four pillars having the lowest scores are Risk acceptance (determining how much risk people are willing to accept), Technology absorption (firm level technology absorption capability), Internationalization (the degree to which a country's entrepreneurs are internationalised, as measured by businesses' exporting potential and the individual variable export is defined as the percentage of Total Early-stage Entrepreneurial Activity (TEA) business where more than 1% of customers are outside of the home country) and Opportunity perception (refers to the entrepreneur's perceptions about market needs and the means to satisfy those needs).

Applying the Global Entrepreneurship Development Index ... 95

As shown in Figure 4, the performances of Thailand's pillars are the best as compared to the pillar's performances of Vietnam and of Indonesia. Taken alone, Thailand has five strongest pillars out of the fourteen Global Entrepreneurship Development Index (GEDI) pillars, including Opportunity perception, Human capital, Product innovation, Opportunity startup (captures the prevalence of individuals who pursue opportunity-driven start-ups and weights this against regulatory constraints) and High growth (a combined measure of the percentage of high-growth businesses that intend to employ at least ten people and plan to grow more than 50% in five years and business strategy sophistication). In Vietnam there are three best pillars as mentioned above, while the three strongest pillars of Indonesia are Networking (an association of entrepreneurs organized, formally or informally, with the object of increasing the effectiveness of the members' business activities), Product innovation and Start-up skills (the core skills people needed to run a business). The Start-up skills pillar captures the perception if start-up skills in the population and weights this aspect with the quality of human resources available for entrepreneurial processes in the country (Szeb, Aidis and Ács 2012)

It is not surprising the pillar scores of Thailand are higher than those of Vietnam and Indonesia because Thailand now is an upper, middle-income economy (GDP per capita PPP in 2015 was 15346.6 USD), which also has made a remarkable socio-economic development progress with a sustained and strong growth in Southeast Asia (World Bank 2016). Furthermore, Indonesia's pillars performing better than Vietnam's is explained by the higher economic development of Indonesia as compared to Vietnam. In fact, although Indonesia is the world's fourth most populous nation, GDP per capita has steadily increased and now Indonesia is an emerging middle-income country (World Bank 2016). In Vietnam, the population has reached 100 million people, but its economy transferred from a poor income level to enter the low-medium income level in 2008 (Anh, Sullivan and Clare 2015).

All three countries in this study pay more attention to Product innovation in their entrepreneurship development. According to Hoi, Trang and Hoang (2016), in emerging economies, especially in transition stages, entrepreneurs often lack innovation, resulting in their weak foundations of entrepreneurship. Thus, to develop the entrepreneurial performance, it is easy to understand why the first priority is given to the Product innovation pillar for the three countries. Interestingly, the score of the Human capital pillar is high and the same between Thailand and Vietnam. Many studies, such as Jens et al. (2011), Thomas and Dung (2014) in Vietnam and Chuthamas et al. (2011) in Thailand, argued that human capital plays an important role in entrepreneurial success and the entrepreneur's education leads to the business success of small- and medium-sized enterprises (SMEs). More specifically, because of the importance of human capital for Vietnam's economic development, the government invests more in the education system, resulting in a higher rate of entrepreneurs who have a higher education (Vietnam Chamber of Commerce and Industry (VCCI) 2014).

On the other hand, as mentioned above, Vietnam's four worst pillars are Risk acceptance, Internationalization, Opportunity perception and Technology absorption and High growth. Similarly, Indonesia's three worst pillars are Internationalization, Technology absorption and High growth. Two of the three weakest pillars in Indonesia are the same in Vietnam, which is because of the similar demographic, cultural, economic and social characteristics between the two countries. Regarding the weakest pillar of Thailand, only the Internationalization pillar is not good, which is similar to Vietnam and Indonesia and is the main issue not only in these three countries but also in most Asian countries that have to face the global integration process (Pempel 2005).

As previously mentioned, the fourteen pillars can be further subdivided into 28 variables. Each pillar is formed from an institutional and an individual variable. Deeper research on the basic variable is necessary for analyzing Vietnam's entrepreneurial performance.

Table 3 presents the relative position of Vietnam at the variable level, in which Vietnam's scores belong to the upper 33, the middle 33 and the bottom 33 percent of participating countries, which are shown by green, yellow and red colored groups, respectively. The last row in bold shows the Global Entrepreneurship Development Index (GEDI) level and its institutional and individual variable scores.

Table 3. The relative position of Vietnam at the variable level, 2011 - 2015

	Pillars		Institutional variables		Individual variables	
Entrepreneurial Attitudes	Opportunity Perception	0.16	Freedom and Property	0.20	Opportunity Recognition	0.67
	Start-up skills	0.24	Education	0.36	Skill Perception	0.67
	Risk Acceptance	0.07	Business Risk	0.18	Risk Perception	0.27
	Networking	0.21	Connectivity	0.21	Know Entrepreneurs	0.90
	Cultural Support	0.21	Corruption	0.35	Career Status	0.71
	Entrepreneurial Attitudes	**16.9**				
Entrepreneurial Abilities	Opportunity Startup	0.21	Tax and government	0.36	Opportunity Motivation	0.55
	Technology Absorption	0.17	Tech Absorption	0.27	Technology Level	0.40
	Human Capital	0.50	Labor Market	0.57	Educational Level	0.71
	Competition	0.22	Competitiveness and Regulation	0.47	Competitors	0.32
	Entrepreneurial Abilities	**24.9**				
Entrepreneurial Aspiration	Product Innovation	0.33	Technology Transfer	0.46	New Product	0.63
	Process Innovation	0.19	Science	0.34	New Tech	0.79
	High Growth	0.22	Finance and strategy	0.45	Gazelle	0.42
	Internationalization	0.16	Economic complexity	0.32	Export	0.38
	Risk Capital	0.46	Depth of Capital Market	0.66	Informal Investment	0.61
	Entrepreneurial Aspirations	**24.8**				
	GEDI	**22.2**	**Institutional**	**0.37**	**Individual**	**0.57**

Source: Author's caculation from the Global Entrepreneurship Development Index (GEDI) project of Ács, Autio and Szeb.

The overall score of the individual variable is 0.57, which places Vietnam in the middle one-third of the Global Entrepreneurship Development Index (GEDI) countries, is better than the overall level of the institutional variable (0.37). This result also indicates that the individual environment of Vietnam is relatively well developed for entrepreneurial development as opposed to the institutional environment. As can be seen in Table 3, most of the individual variables have high scores. Six individual variables, which receive a score of over 0.65: Opportunity recognition, Skill perception (the percentage of the 18-64 aged population claiming to posses the required knowledge and skills to start a new business), Know entrepreneurs (which is defined as the percentage of the 18-64 year old population who personally know someone who has started a business during the previous 2 years), Career status (the status and respect of entrepreneurs calculated as the average of two variables: NBGOODAV - the avarage percenatage of the population aged 18-64 who say that entrepreneurship is a good carrer choice and NBSTATAV - the avarage percenatage of the population aged 18-64 who say that entrepreneurs enjoy high status), Educational level (the percentage of Total Early-stage Entrepreneurial Activity (TEA) business owner/managers who have post secondary education) and New tech (the percentage of Total Early-stage Entrepreneurial Activity (TEA) businesses using new technology that is less than 5 years old) play a key role in contributing to Vietnam's entrepreneurial performance. However, there also exist five individual variables with a low score of below 0.5: Gazelle (the percentage of Total Early-stage Entrepreneurial Activity (TEA) businesses who expect to employ more than 10 employees in 5 years' time), Technology level (the percentage of Total Early-stage Entrepreneurial Activity (TEA) businesses that are active in technology sectors - high or medium), Export (the percentage of Total Early-stage Entrepreneurial Activity (TEA) businesses where at least some customer are outside their country - over 1%), Competitors (the percentage of Total Early-stage Entrepreneurial Activity (TEA) businesses started in those markets where not many businesses offer the same product) and Risk perception, which place Vietnam in the lowest one-third of the Global Entrepreneurship Development Index (GEDI) countries being considered.

Moreover, the best performing individual variables of Vietnam is Know entrepreneurs (0.90), followed by New tech (0.79), Educational level and Career status (with the same score of 0.71). The last are Opportunity recognition and Skill perception (with the same score of 0.67). According to Acs et al. (2014), the high score of the Know entrepreneurs variable is explained by a better entrepreneurship knowledge or understanding of entrepreneurs. The high score of the New tech variable is a result of an increase in using new technologies in entrepreneurships. For the Education level and Career status variables, these high scores are a result of the development of the education system in providing a good preparation for start-up in the population. Skill perception is known as the percentage of the working-age population having enough knowledge and skills to start a new business. Finally, the high score of Opportunity recognition shows a higher percentage of the working-age population recognizing better opportunities to start a business in the area.

On the other hand, the scores of Vietnam's institutional variables are very low. Only the Labor market variable is green colored, showing it belongs to the top level (33% of the Global Entrepreneurship Development Index (GEDI) countries). This is not surprising because, in recent times, Vietnam has an abundance of young population and cheap labor, which has become the competitive advantage in attracting business startups (Stephanie and Rafael 2016).

Nine Institutional Variables

Freedom and property (which are identified by the efficiency of the government in the regulatory process relating to entrepreneurs starting, operating and closing a business and their ability to access the capital and resources), Education, Business risk (it reflects whether corporate financial information is available and reliable, whether the legal system provides fair and efficient creditor protection, and whether a country's institutional framework is favorable to intercompany transactions. It is a part of the Country Risk Rate), Connectivity (the connection activities among entrepreneurs in the entrepreneurial network), Corruption (the Corruption Perceptions Index (CPI) measures the perceived level of public-sector corruption in a country), Tax and government, Tech absorption (the new technology absorption capability of firms in a country), Science and Economic complexity are coded red, showing that the scores of these variables are in the lowest one-third of Global Entrepreneurship Development Index (GEDI) countries, of which, five out of nine institutional variables with the lowest scores are from the Entrepreneurial Attitudes (ATT) sub-index. Furthermore, out of the nine worst institutional variables, Business risk has the lowest performing score (0.18), followed by Freedom and property and Connectivity with the performing scores are 0.20 and 0.21, respectively, and then Tech absorption with the score of 0.27.

Table 4 shows the four worst pillars and the corresponding influenced individual and institutional variables of Vietnam, which is collected from Table 3. More specifically, the lowest level of Risk acceptance in Vietnam is caused by the low levels of the institutional variable, Business risk and of individual variable, Risk perception. In other words, the lowest level of the Risk acceptance pillar can be explained by the low quality of the business environment in Vietnam and the Vietnamese's fear of failure that prevent them from starting a business (Dang, 2010; Vietnam Chamber of Commerce and Industry (VCCI), 2014). The second lowest score of the Internationalization pillar is affected by the low levels of Economic complexity, represented by the Vietnam's high position in the Economic Complexity Index relative to its low GDP per capita and the limited exporting and trading activities in Vietnam's economy (Ricardo et al. 2013; Anh, Sullivan and Clare 2015). The worst performance of the Technology absorption pillar is because of the limitation of Vietnam firms in new technology absorption (Dabić et al. 2012). Vietnam enterprises mainly rely on low-medium technologies and only two percent of Vietnam's enterprises have high technology (Vietnam Chamber of Commerce and Industry (VCCI) 2014) (which is shown by the Technology level variable). And the low score of the Opportunity perception pillar is mainly explained by the low level of the Freedom and property variable or the low efficiency of Vietnam's government in the regulatory process and the limitation of

Vietnamese enterprises in accessing capital and resources in the economy (Hai 2015).

THE PENALTY FOR BOTTLENECK (PFB) METHODOLOGY

The Global Entrepreneurship Development Index (GEDI) methodology is considered a better policy tool (but not an optimal tool) to identify the weakness inhibiting entrepreneurship development in a country, but it can provide little guidance for policy design. The uniqueness is that this methodology provides a comprehensive analysis of individual and institutional aspects of entrepreneurship derived from the perspective of the system. It helps contextualize the national level entrepreneurial process, thus making it consistent with the study of country-specific features. Indeed, this methodology identifies bottleneck factors, which constitute the weakest link among the pillars and constrain system performance, thereby helping set tangible goals for policies and support initiatives designed to improve the bottleneck identified. In practice, in the Global Entrepreneurship Development Index (GEDI) methodology, the higher pillar values are adjusted to the weakest performing pillar value of the particular sub-index, thus eliminating full, one-to-one substitutability across pillars. However, this methodology does not guide how to measure exactly the penalty; therefore, the solution is not optimal and only provides a better solution (Szerb, Aidis and Ács 2012).

Furthermore, there are some limitations of the Global Entrepreneurship Development Index (GEDI) methodology that require considering a better alternative methodology. First, although the Global Entrepreneurship Development Index (GEDI) is a complex measure of entrepreneurship, we only select 28 variables and fourteen pillars representing the Global Entrepreneurship Development Index (GEDI) that are available in the data reports of countries, thus leading to an imperfect or incomplete selection. Moreover, the policy recommendations do not generalize well. In addition, the fourteen pillars of the Global Entrepreneurship Development Index (GEDI) only reflect a national system of entrepreneurship. Therefore, maximizing the Global Entrepreneurship Development Index (GEDI) of one country does not mean maximizing the entire national system of entrepreneurship of this country.

Second, the Global Entrepreneurship Development Index (GEDI) analysis is not flexible because a perfect configuration that is suitable with all countries and contexts does not exist. More importantly, the Global Entrepreneurship Development Index (GEDI) methodology is the best method to increase the overall GEDI as well as to reduce the disparities between the pillars by improving the weakest Global Entrepreneurship Development Index (GEDI) pillar. Nevertheless, because of the dynamics of the system, the other pillars may become the weakest and restrict a country's entrepreneurship performance. Therefore, the issue of the Global Entrepreneurship Development Index (GEDI) methodology is related to how to allocate additional resources to achieve the optimal outcome of Global Entrepreneurship Development Index (GEDI) (Autio et al. 2012).

Because of the limitations of the Global Entrepreneurship Development Index (GEDI) methodology, and because all pillars are formed as interactions between individual and institutional aspects, the Penalty for Bottleneck (PFB) methodology is considered to be the policy application of the Global Entrepreneurship Development Index (GEDI) methodology, which provides a more realistic analysis of overall entrepreneurial performance of a country, contributing to more insightful policy development and cross country comparison (Szeb, Aidis and Ács 2012).

According to Acs et al. (2014), a bottleneck is defined as the weakest link or the binding constrain in the national entrepreneurial performance. In other words, within a given set of normalized pillars, a bottleneck is a factor with the lowest value. From the policy perspective, the Penalty for Bottleneck (PFB) methodology focuses on the weakest pillar, which is the starting point where policy is generated to achieve the greatest enhancement of the system. The principle of this methodology is that the pillar scores should be adjusted, thereby achieving this concept of balance. After equalizing the scores of all pillars, the value of each pillar is "penalized" by linking it to the value of the weakest performing indicator (that is called the

Applying the Global Entrepreneurship Development Index ... 103

bottleneck) in a given nation. If the bottleneck is improved, the overall Global Entrepreneurship Development Index (GEDI) will be enhanced significantly.

The Penalty for Bottleneck (PFB) methodology also implies that a stable and efficient configuration will be reached if all pillars are the same level. Traditional methods assume full substitutability between indicators of the system, but this assumption is not realistic because the value of substitutability between different components of the system may differ. Based on the approach proposed by Tarabusi and Palazzi (2004) that if the difference between the particular pillar and the corresponding pillar is larger, there requires a higher compensation for the loss of one pillar. Ács et al. (2014) create the penalty function reflecting compensation for the loss of one pillar with an improvement in another pillar. The penalty function is written as follows:

$$h_{(i),j} = \min_{y_{(i),j}} + (1 - e^{-y(i),j) - \min y(i),j)})$$

where: $h_{(i),j}$ is the modified, post-penalty score of pillar j in country i.

$y_{(i),j}$ is the normalized score of pillar j in country i.

$\min y(i),j)$ is the lowest score of $y_{(i),j}$ for country i.

$i = 1, 2,..., n$ = the number of countries.

$j = 1, 2,..., m$ = the number of index components.

In the above function, by adding one minus the base of the natural logarithm of the negative difference between a particular pillar's value and the lowest normalized value of any pillar in country i, we can identify the modified, post-penalty score of a pillar in a country. Therefore, improving the value of the weakest pillar will bring a greater impact on the Global Entrepreneurship Development Index (GEDI) than improving the stronger pillar's value.

For the policy section, this study presents a policy portfolio analysis aiming to increase the Global Entrepreneurship Development Index (GEDI) score by five points. Following the principle of the Penalty for Bottleneck (PFB) approach, once the weakest pillar has been eliminated,

104   *Ha Thi Thu Nguyen*

we add the available resources to improve the next binding pillar and only stop if the additional resources are exhausted.

Table 4. The four worst pillars and the corresponding institutional and individual variables of Vietnam in 2015

Pillars		Institutional variables		Individual variables	
Opportunity Perception	0.16	Freedom and Property	0.20	Opportunity Recognition	0.67
Risk Acceptance	0.07	Business Risk	0.18	Risk Perception	0.27
Technology Absorption	0.17	Tech Absorption	0.27	Technology Level	0.40
Internationalization	0.16	Economic complexity	0.32	Export	0.38

Source: The shorter results from Table 3.

Table 5. A simulation of "optimal" policy allocation to increase the Global Entrepreneurship Development Index (GEDI) score by five points

	Original averaged pillar scores	Required increase in pillars	Percentage of total new effort
Opportunity Perception	0.16	0.08	16%
Start-up Skills	0.24	0.00	0%
Risk Acceptance	0.07	0.17	35%
Networking	0.21	0.03	6%
Cultural Support	0.21	0.02	4%
Opportunity Startup	0.21	0.01	2%
Technology Absorption	0.17	0.07	14%
Human Capital	0.50	0.00	0%
Competition	0.22	0.03	6%
Product Innovation	0.33	0.00	0%
Process Innovation	0.19	0.03	6%
High Growth	0.22	0.00	0%
Internationalisation	0.16	0.05	10%
Risk Capital	0.46	0.00	0%
Sum of Changes		**0.49**	**14.6%**

Source: Author's calculation from the Global Entrepreneurship Development Index (GEDI) project of Ács, Autio and Szeb.

Applying the Global Entrepreneurship Development Index ... 105

To increase the average Global Entrepreneurship Development Index (GEDI) score by five points, the first stage of Penalty for Bottleneck (PFB) methodology is that we increase the weakest pillar's score until reaching the next bottleneck pillar. We assume that the cost of reaching the improvement is the same for all pillars. After that, we continue to add the available resources to improve the next weakest pillar score and so on. Once the desired five-point increase in the Global Entrepreneurship Development Index (GEDI) is achieved, we stop to add further resources.

Table 5 represents the required increase in the particular absolute values and the percentage of total new effort. Vietnam has a relatively low Global Entrepreneurship Development Index (GEDI) score and several bottlenecks. Nine of Vietnam's bottlenecks are Risk acceptance with a 0.07 pillar score, followed by Opportunity perception (0.16), Internationalization (0.16), Technology absorption (0.17), Process innovation (0.19), Networking, Cultural support, and Opportunity startup with the same 0.21 pillar score, and Competition (0.22). Vietnam should allocate the additional resources reasonably among different pillars as well as increase the nine poor performing pillars to 0.24 (up to the level of Start-up skills) to achieve the desired five-point Global Entrepreneurship Development Index (GEDI) increase.

More specifically, Risk acceptance is the weakest performing pillar with the lowest score and is much lower than the scores of other pillars, thus policy priority is given for this pillar. We increase this pillar for Vietnam by 0.17 units to reach the value 0.24 of Start-up skills. The reason for the required high increase in this pillar is that a risk acceptance emphasis is necessary to start up the small- and medium-sized enterprises (SMEs) in a turbulent business environment in Vietnam's transitional economy as well as increase the firm's performance (Swierczek and Ha 2003). More importantly, Vietnam's rate of fear of business failure - a developing country in the first stage of development - is higher than that of other developing countries in the third stage of development. This is because of a decline in economic growth in Vietnam in recent periods, the difficulties of businesses in mobilizing capital and output market, leading to the dissolution of many firms in recent years. The high rate of fear is one of the most important factors blocking an individuals' engagement in entrepreneurship resulting in a low percentage of entrepreneurship in Vietnam (Huan and Tuan 2014).

Once the weakest Risk acceptance pillar has been eliminated, Opportunity perception, Internationalization and Technology absorption become the next weakest pillars. To improve these next binding pillars, we increase a high value for these three pillars 0.08, 0.05 and 0.07, respectively, which is based on the level of required improvement in the context of Vietnam. The policy priority order is a result of a number of issues.

First, because of Vietnam's long history of struggles for national independency, the consequences of a socialist economy and the slow recovery of the economy after the global financial crisis occurred leading to the limitation of economic opportunities to start a business in Vietnam, the percentage of people who perceive an opportunity to start a new business in Vietnam is much lower than that of countries having similar economic development levels of factor-driven economies. As compared to other Asian countries in the same stage of development (Malaysia, Thailand, Indonesia and Philippines), the percentage of Vietnamese who perceive an opportunity to start a new business is lower than that of all four countries. Thus, the second policy priority is given for Opportunity perception, which will receive 16 percent of the total new effort when allocating a 0.08 point increase to this pillar (Huan and Tuan 2014).

Second, Technology absorption is the next important pillar that needs to be enhanced because, like other emerging economies in stages of transition, Vietnam firms now face the problem of lacking innovation and its ability to absorb new technologies is limited, resulting in a low competitive capability of enterprises (Dabić et al. 2012). We allocate 0.07 points to this pillar to reach fourteen percent of the total new effort. After that, a 0.05 point increase is given to the binding pillar Internationalization. The allocation of additional resources for this pillar is necessary because of Vietnam's low level of economic complexity and the low level of Vietnam's enterprises exporting potential (Ricardo et al. 2013; Anh, Sullivan and Clare 2015).

After the Internationalization pillar has been eliminated, Process innovation becomes the next binding pillar with the score of 0.19. In this case, we only allocate 0.03 points to this pillar. The low required increase of this pillar results from more startups' use of new technologies and Vietnam's higher expenditure on Research and Development (R&D) activities as well as a higher potential to conduct applied research in recent years. Businesses in Vietnam make active efforts for process innovation (Anh, Sullivan and Clare 2015).

Networking and Competition are the next binding pillars having the same score as the previous pillar; therefore, we add the same value of 0.03 to these pillars. The important roles of Networking include helping entrepreneurs access and mobilize opportunities and resources as well as improving communication between entrepreneurs. Competition refers to the market uniqueness of start-ups, the market power of existing enterprises and business groups and the effectiveness of competitive regulation (Ács et al. 2014). Therefore, to improve the performance of the Competition pillar, Vietnam must focus on these aspects of entrepreneurship.

Next, we increase the value for the next two binding pillars in Vietnam: Cultural support and Opportunity startup by 0.02 and 0.01 units, respectively. It is worth mentioning that the Cultural support pillar combines how positively a given country's inhabitants view entrepreneurs in term of status and career choice and how the level of corruption in that country affects this view (Szeb, Aidis and Ács 2012). To increase the value of the Cultural support pillar, the Vietnamese culture must appreciate a person's choice of pursuing an entrepreneurial career and also reduce the level of corruption in Vietnam. To improve the Opportunity startup pillar, a country needs to reduce taxes and lessen its bureaucracy while encouraging the consistency of regulations and taxation (Ács et al. 2014).

Finally, we stop to add further resources to reach the desired five-point Global Entrepreneurship Development Index (GEDI) increase. Altogether, a sum of changes (0.49) or 14.6 percent of the existing resources is needed to alleviate the nine binding constraints in Vietnam to improve its Global Entrepreneurship Development Index (GEDI) score from 22.2 to 27.1. The percentage of additional resources in Vietnam is relatively high; therefore, this entrepreneurship improvement is probably an expensive and time-consuming task for Vietnam.

CONCLUSION

The chapter analyzes Vietnam's entrepreneurship performance based on the Global Entrepreneurship Development Index (GEDI) and its sub-indices at the pillar and variable levels, and then utilizes the Penalty for Bottleneck (PFB) methodology to rank policy priorities for entrepreneurship development aiming to improve the Global Entrepreneurship Development Index (GEDI) score by five points for Vietnam.

This chapter first applies the Global Entrepreneurship Development Index (GEDI) methodology in analyzing Vietnam's entrepreneurship performance. To have a deeper understanding of Vietnam's relative position at the Global Entrepreneurship Development Index (GEDI) and sub-index levels, two Southeast Asia developing economies - Thailand and Indonesia - which have similar cultural, economic and social characteristics, are chosen to compare with Vietnam regarding entrepreneurial performance. Indeed, as compared to the overall Global Entrepreneurship Development Index (GEDI) values of 93 participating countries, Vietnam's overall Global Entrepreneurship Development Index (GEDI) only ranks in 72nd place, out of 93 participating countries with a low value of 0.222, which is slightly better than the Global Entrepreneurship Development Index (GEDI) score of Indonesia, but is much lower than Thailand's, indicating Vietnam's poor entrepreneurial performance.

Regarding the three Global Entrepreneurship Development Index (GEDI) sub-indices, Vietnam received the lowest value for Entrepreneurial Attitudes (ATT) and the highest value for Entrepreneurial Abilities (ABT). For the fourteen components of three Global Entrepreneurship Development Index (GEDI) sub-indices, most of these pillars are not good with low normalized scores under 0.24. In particular, Risk acceptance, Opportunity perception, Internationalization and Technology absorption are the four weakest pillars with very low normalized scores because of a long history of the struggles for national independency, the low starting point of Vietnam's economy, most of Vietnam enterprises being SMEs with a low competitive capability in the world market, and the limitation of new technology absorption of enterprises. By contrast, the three best pillars of Vietnam's

Applying the Global Entrepreneurship Development Index ... 109

entrepreneurship are Human capital, Risk capital and Product innovation, which is a result of a Vietnam's rapid economic growth.

It is interesting that there is a similar picture regarding the best and the worst Global Entrepreneurship Development Index (GEDI) pillars in all three countries. As for the best Global Entrepreneurship Development Index (GEDI) pillars, all three countries now pay more attention to Product innovation in their entrepreneurship development. The score of the Human capital pillar is high with both Thailand and Vietnam having the same scores. On the other hand, as for the worst Global Entrepreneurship Development Index (GEDI) pillars, Internationalization is the worst Global Entrepreneurship Development Index (GEDI) pillar in not only the three countries but also in most ASEAN countries facing the global integration process. Indeed, two of the three weakest pillars in Indonesia are the same in Vietnam, including Internationalization and Technology absorption.

The fourteen Global Entrepreneurship Development Index (GEDI) pillars can be further subdivided into 28 institutional and individual variables. In Vietnam, individual variables represent better outcomes than institutional variables. Six out of fourteen individual variables in Vietnam have high scores: Opportunity recognition, Skill perception, Know entrepreneurs, Carrer status, Educational level and New tech, which play a key role in contributing to Vietnam's entrepreneurial performance. However, there also exist the five worst individual variables: Gazelle, Technology level, Export, Competitors and Risk perception. In addition, of Vietnam's institutional variables, only Labor market has a good score, while nine out of the fourteen institutional variables: Freedom and property, Education, Business risk, Connectivity, Corruption tax and government, Tech absorption, Science and Economic complexity, in which five variables with the lowest scores are from the Entrepreneurial Attitudes (ATT) sub-index. These are the main factors explaining the four weakest performing pillars of the Global Entrepreneurship Development Index (GEDI).

The Global Entrepreneurship Development Index (GEDI) methodology is considered a better policy tool (but not an optimal tool) to identify the weakness inhibiting entrepreneurship development in a country. Indeed, this methodology relies on the fourteen Global Entrepreneurship Development Index (GEDI) pillars that reflect a national system of entrepreneurship. Thus, maximizing the Global Entrepreneurship Development Index (GEDI) of one country does not mean maximizing the entire national system of entrepreneurship of this country. The Penalty for Bottleneck (PFB) methodology is then employed, which is considered as the policy application of Global Entrepreneurship Development Index (GEDI) methodology. This provides a more realistic analysis of overall entrepreneurial performance of a country, contributing to more insightful policy development and cross-country comparison. The principle of the Penalty for Bottleneck (PFB) method is that the greatest improvement can be achieved by alleviating the weakest performing pillars - the bottlenecks.

Finally, we suggest a simulation of "optimal" policy allocation to increase Vietnam's Global Entrepreneurship Development Index (GEDI) score by five points. More specifically, we increase the score of the weakest pillar until reaching the next bottleneck pillar. We continue to add the available resources to improve the next binding pillar and so on, and only stop to add further resources once we have achieved the desired five-point increase in the Global Entrepreneurship Development Index (GEDI). In Vietnam, nine bottlenecks with the lowest scores are Risk acceptance, Opportunity perception, Internationalization, Technology absorption, Process innovation, Networking, Cultural support, Opportunity startup and Competition, which are allocated the additional resources reasonably to reach the desired five-point Global Entrepreneurship Development Index (GEDI) increase. Policy priority order in Vietnam is based on the scores of the Global Entrepreneurship Development Index (GEDI) pillars. The highest priority is given for the Risk acceptance pillar, followed by policy priorities for Opportunity perception, Internationalization and Technology absorption. The second policy priority group focuses on the improvement of the Process innovation, Networking and Competition pillars. And the last policy priority group aims to enhance the scores of Cultural support and Opportunity startup. Additional resource allocation is then stopped because the desired five-point Global Entrepreneurship Development Index (GEDI) increase is achieved in this step. However, entrepreneurship improvement is

Applying the Global Entrepreneurship Development Index ... 111

an expensive and time-consuming task for Vietnam because we need a high percentage (14.6%) of the existing resources to alleviate nine binding constraints.

The main limitation is that the data of this study is based only on the Global Entrepreneurship Development Index (GEDI) from 2011 to 2015 in the entrepreneurship projects of Acs, Autio and Szerb. Furthermore, entrepreneurship improvement is an expensive and time-consuming task for any country, especially in Vietnam, which has nine out of fourteen weak pillars. Hence, this topic is critical for Vietnam, in particular and in general for developing countries. Evaluating the entrepreneurship performance at both the individual and national levels and suggesting the approaches as well as a simulation of "optimal" policy allocation will improve the entrepreneurship performance and increase the Global Entrepreneurship Development Index (GEDI) score of a country. Furthermore, this topic will open a new research field for researchers in the future.

REFERENCES

Acs, Zoltán J., Szerb, László. & Autio, Erkko. (2013). *Global Entrepreneurship and Development Index 2013*. Cheltenham: Edward Elgar Publishing.

Acs, Zoltán J., Szerb, László. & Autio, Erkko. (2014). "National systems of entrepreneurship: Measurement issues and policy implications". *Research Policy*, *43*, 476-494.

Acs, Zoltán J. & Szerb, László. (2009). "The Global Entrepreneurship Index (GEINDEX)". *Foundations and Trends in Entrepreneurship*, *5*, no. 5, 341-435.

Acs, Zoltán J. & Szerb, László. (2011). *Global Entrepreneurship and Development Index 2011*. Cheltenham: Edward Elgar Publishing.

Acs, Zoltán J. & Varga, Attila. (2005). Entrepreneurship, agglomeration and technological change. *Small Business Economics*, *24*, no. 3, 323-334.

Acs, Zoltán J., Szerb, László. & Lloyd, Ainsley. (2017). *The Global Entrepreneurship and Development Index 2017*. Washington, D.C: The

Global Entrepreneurship and Development Institute. Accessed December 5, 2017. http://www.thegedi.org/global-entrepreneurship-and-development- index/.

Anh, Quan Nguyen. & Sullivan, Mort Gillian. (2016). "Economic reform and entrepreneurship in Vietnam: A policy perspective". In *Economic Development and Entrepreneurship in Transition Economies: Issues, Obstacles and Perspectives*, edited by Jovo Ateljević and Jelena Trivić, 109-125. Switzerland: Spring International Publishing.

Anh, Quan Nguyen., Sullivan, Mort Gillian. & Clare, D'Souza. (2015). "Vietnam in transition: SMEs and the necessitating environment for entrepreneurship development". *Entrepreneurship and Regional Development*, *27*, no. 3, 154-180.

Autio, Erkko., Cleevely, Matthew., Hart, Mark., Levie, Jonathan., Acs, Zoltan J. & Szerb, László. (2012). *Entrepreneurial profile of the UK in light of the Global Entrepreneurship and Development Index*. London: Victoria & Albert Museum, South Kensington. papers.ssrn.com/sol3/papers2.cfm?abstract_id=2070320.

Chuthamas, Chittithaworn., Islam, Md. Aminul., Keawchana, Thiyada. & Yusuf, Hasliza Muhd. (2011). "Factors affecting business success of small and medium enterprises (SMEs) in Thailand". *Asian Social Science*, *7*, no. 5, 180-190.

Dabić, Marina., Daim Tugrul, U., Aralica, Zoran. & Bayraktaroglu, A. Elvan. (2012). "Exploring relationships among internationalization, choice for research and development approach and technology source and resulting innovation intensity: Case of a transition country Croatia". *The Journal of High Technology Management Research*, *23*, no. 1, 15-25.

Dang, D Anh. (2010). "Trade liberalization and institutional quality: Evidence from Vietnam". Paper presented at the meeting in Munich *Personal RePEc Archive*, Munich, Germany, October 10-12.

Enrico, Santarelli. & Hien, Thu Tran. (2013). "The interplay of human and social capital in shaping entrepreneurial performance: The case of Vietnam". *Small Business Economics*, *40*, no. 2, 435-458.

Hai, Thi Thanh Tran. (2015). "Challenges of small and medium-sized enterprises (SMEs) in Vietnam during the process of integration into the ASEAN Economic Community (AEC)". *International Journal of Accounting and Financial Reporting*, 5, no. 2, 133-143.

Hoi, Vu Quang., Trang, Vuong Thu. & Hoang, Vuong Quan. (2016). "Relationship between past experience, social network participation and creative capacity: Vietnamese entrepreneurship survey." Paper presented at the meeting of Centre Emile Bernheim, *Solvay Brussels School of Economics and Management*, Brussels, Belgium, December 15-17.

Huan, Luong Minh. & Tuan, Nham Phong. (2014). "Understanding entrepreneurial perception and business conditions in Vietnam through the approach of the Global Entrepreneurship Monitor". *VNU Journal of Science: Economics and Business*, 30, no. 2, 13-27.

Iversen, Jens., Jørgensen, Rasmus. & Malchow-Moller, Nikolaj. (2008). "Defining and measuring entrepreneurship". *Foundations and Trends in Entrepreneurship*, 4, no. 1, 1-63.

Jens, M. Unger., Rauch, Andreas., Frese, Michael. & Rosenbusch, Nina. (2011). "Human capital and entrepreneurial success: A meta-analytical review". *Journal of Business Venturing*, 26, no. 3, 341-358.

Kelley, Donna., Bosma, Niels. & Amoros, José Ernesto. (2011). *Global Entrepreneurship Monitor 2010 Global Report*. Accessed August 15, 2017. https://entreprenorskapsforum.se/wp-content/uploads/2011/02/GEM-2010-Global-Report.pdf.

Lee, Sang M., Lim, Seong-bae., Pathak, Raghuvar D., Chang, Daesung. & Li, Weixing. (2006). "Influences on students attitudes toward entrepreneurship: a multi-country study". *The International Entrepreneurship and Management Journal*, 2, no. 3, 351-366.

OECD. (2007). *OECD framework for the evaluation of SME and entrepreneurship policies and programs*. Paris: OECD Publishing.

Pempel, T. j. (2005). *Remapping East Asia: The Construction of a Region*. Ithaca and London: Cornell University Press.

Reynolds, Paul., Bosma, Niels., Autio, Erkko., Hunt, Steve., De, Bono Natalie., Servais, Isabel., Lopez-Garcia, Paloma. & Chin, Nancy.

(2005). "Global entrepreneurship monitor: Data collection design and implementation 1998 - 2003". *Small business economics*, 24, no. 3, 205-231.

Ricardo, Hausmann., Hidalgo, César A., Bustos, Michele Coscia Sebastián., Simoes, Alexander. & Yildirim, Muhammed A. (2013). *The atlas of economic complexity: Mapping paths to prosperity*. Cambridge: The MIT Press.

Shane, Scott. & Venkataraman, MclryIcrnd S. (2000). "The promise of entrepreneurship as a field of research". *Academy of Management Review*, 25, no. 1, 217-226.

Stel, André van., Carree, Martin. & Thurik, Roy. (2005). "The effect of entrepreneurial activity on national economic growth". *Small business economics*, 24, no. 3, 311-321.

Stephanie, Jones. & Rafael, Masters. (2016). *Opening up to international investment and diversification: A case study of Vietnam*. Paper presented at the meeting of Maastricht School of Management, Netherlands, September 15-17.

Swierczek, Fredric William. & Ha, Thai Thanh. (2003). "Entrepreneurial orientation, uncertainty avoidance and firm performance: An analysis of Thai and Vietnamese SMEs". *Entrepreneurship and Innovation*, February, no. 1, 46-58.

Szerb, László., Aidis, Ruta. & Ács, Zoltán J. (2012). *A comparative analysis of Hungary's entrepreneurial performance in the 2006 - 2010 time period based on the Global Entrepreneurship Monitor and the Global Entrepreneurship and Development Index methodologies*. Pécs, Hungary: Carbocomp Ltd.

Tarabusi, Enrico Casadio. & Palazzi, Paolo. (2004). "An index for sustainable development". *BNL Quarterly Review*, 57, no. 229, 185-206.

Thomas, Gries. & Dung, Ha Van. (2014). "Institutional environment, human capital and firm growth: Evidence from Vietnam". Paper presented at the meeting of *CIE Center for International Economics*, Paderborn University, Germany, January 10-12.

Thu, Phan. & Thuy, Thanh. (2017). "Only 2 percent of enterprises have high technology". *Customs news*, December 22, 2016. Accessed August 18.

customsnews.vn/only-2-of-enterprises-have-high-technology-2068. html.

Vietnam Chamber of Commerce and Industry (VCCI). (2014). *Global Entrepreneurship Monitor Vietnam Report 2013*. Ha Noi: Vietnam News Agency Publishing House.

World Bank. (2017). "Indonesia overview." *The World Bank*. Accessed August 15. www.worldbank.org/en/country/indonesia/overview.

World Bank. "Thailand overview." 2017. *The World Bank*. Accessed August 16. www.worldbank.org/en/country/thailand/overview.

Zahra, Shaker A. (1999). "The challenging rules of global competitiveness in the 21st century". *Academy of Management Executive*, *13*, no. 1, 36 - 42.

BIOGRAPHICAL SKETCH

Nguyen Thi Thu Ha

Affiliation: Faculty of Economics, University of Economics, The University of Danang,

Education:

- PhD, Business Administration, 2019
  University of Pécs, Hungary.
- MSc, International Human Resource Management, 2013
  Sheffield Hallam University, the United Kingdom
- BSc, Labour Economics, 2007
  University of Economics, The University of Danang, Vietnam.

Researcher: January 2008 - Present

- Leader in the project: "The factors affecting the income of employees in Da Nang city, Vietnam".

Source of funds for research: The Ministry of Education and Training, 2008.

- A member in the Ministry-level research project: "The impact of human capital on the income of employees in central coastal provinces"
  From January 2009 to June 2010, Code number: B2009-ĐN04-37
  Source of funds for research: The Ministry of Education and Training
- Research title: "The reality of material and spiritual life of employees in industrial zones in Da Nang city"
  From March 2011 to August 2012, Code number: T2011-04-04
  Source of funds for research: The University of Danang.
- A member in the National-level research projects: "The impact of population change on socio-economic development in Vietnam"
  From June 2014 to June 2016, Code number: II.6.2-2013.08
  Source of funds for research: Nafosted (Vietnam National Foundation for Science and Technology Development).
- A member in the National-level research projects: "The relations between emotion and reason in the law culture in Vietnam (Research from the practice of South Central Province).
  From January 2018 to December 2019, Code number: XHNV-37
  Source of funds for research: The Ministry of Education and Training, the Vietnam government budget.

Honors and Awards:

- The second prize in the scientific research, The Ministry of Education and Training of Vietnam, 2008.
- Rector's award, University of Economics, The University of Danang with excellent achievements in science research, 2008, 2010, 2014, 2015, 2017.
- Full scholarship of KDI School of Public Policy and Management, Korea, 2011.

Applying the Global Entrepreneurship Development Index ... 117

- Full scholarship of The Ministry of Education and Training of Vietnam, 2012.
- Full scholarship of the Stipendium Hungaricum Scholarship Program, The Hungarian Government, 2015.

Publications from the Last 3 Years

Journals

Nguyen, Thi Thu Ha. (2015). The effects of demographic and work variables on job satisfaction of teachers in Danang University of Economics. *Journal of Economic Studies*, 3(03), 88-95.

Nguyen, Thi Thu Ha. (2015). Employee's commitment and the effective ways to ensure the commitment. *Journal of Economic Studies*, 2(06), 53-58.

Nguyen, Thi Thu Ha. (2015). Industrial solid waste control in Da Nang city. *Journal of Science and Technology*, 8(81), 65-69.

Nguyen, Thi Thu Ha. (2015). State governing of non-state enterprises in Danang city. *Journal of Science and Technology*, 2(87), 102-107.

Nguyen, Thi Thu Ha. (2015). Identifying the factors affecting the population change in Da Nang city, *Journal of Science and Technology*, 4(65), 36-41.

Nguyen, Thi Thu Ha. (2015). The role of government and investment for the development of cooperatives: Theoretical meaning and experience lessons. *Journal of Economic Studies*, 4(08), 10-18.

Nguyen, Thi Thu Ha. (2016). Achievements and limitations of the export-oriented industrialization policy in Vietnam. *Journal of Theoretical Studies*, No. 1(134), 53-58.

Nguyen, Thi Thu Ha. (2016). The role of labor in the economic growth in Danang city. *Journal of Science and Technology*, 2(99). 2016, 14-19.

Nguyen, Thi Thu Ha. (2016). Policy recommendations from the status quo of elderly population in population ageing process in Vietnam. *Journal of Science and Technology*, 4(101).2016, 107-111.

Nguyen, Thi Thu Ha. (2016). Challenges of population ageing for the economic development in Vietnam today. *Journal of Economic Studies*, *4*(04).2016, 119-125.

Nguyen, Thi Thu Ha. (2016). Identifying factors affecting the early retirement decisions of employees: Meaning for Vietnam to reduce the potential labour shortages due to the population ageing. *VNU Journal of Social Sciences and Humanities*, Vol. *2*, No. 5, 587-598.

Thi, Thu Ha Nguyen., Quang, Binh Bui. & Nguyen, Chuong Ong. (2016). Internal migration in the context of trade liberalisation in Vietnam. *Malaysian Journal of Economic Studies MJES*, Vol. *53*, No. 2 (December 2016), 195-209.

Nguyen, Thi Thu Ha. (2017). Linkages underlying the influence of population ageing on economic growth and policy implications to Vietnam. *Hue University Journal of Science: Economics and Development*, Vol *126*, No 5B (2017), 69-81.

Nguyen, Thi Thu Ha. (2017). A Wal-Mart's successful integarted supply chain and the necessity of establishing the Triple-A supply chain in the 21st century. *Journal of Economics and Management*, Poland, Vol. *29*(3), 102 - 117.

Nguyen, Thi Thu Ha. & Lam, Ba Hoa. (2018). Evaluating the entrepreneurship performance in Vietnam through the Global Entrepreneurship Development Index approach. *Journal of Developmental Entrepreneurship*, USA, Volume *23*, Number 01. https://doi.org/10.1142/S1084946718500061.

Nguyen, Thi Thu Ha. & Lam, Ba Hoa. (2018). On the causality relationship between demographic changes, economic growth and domestic savings in Vietnam. *Jurnal Ekonomi Malaysia*, Volume *52*(2), 1-12.

Conferences

Nguyen, Thi Thu Ha. (2015). "The issues faced by a leader when try to develop employee commitment during the economics recession", *The 1st international conference proceedings for young researchers in economics and business (ICYREB 2015): Economics, management and* *business in global society*, Hanoi: Vietnam, December 2015, Volume *3*, p. 203 - 220.

Nguyen, Thi Thu Ha. (2016). "Building the theoretical framework of the impact of population ageing on economic growth and some policy implications to Vietnam", *The 2nd international conference: Policies Regulations of Relations Between Population and Development: International Experiences and Solutions for Vietnam*, Hanoi: Vietnam, May 2016, p. 121-134.

Nguyen, Thi Thu Ha. (2016). "Supply chain management of Wal-mart - experiences and suggestions for Vietnam's retail enterprises to achieve sustainable competitive advantage", *The 5th International conference on Emerging Challenges: Partnership Enhancement (ICECH2016)*, Hanoi: Vietnam, 11th November, p. 590-597.

Nguyen, Thi Thu Ha. (2016). "Population Ageing: Opportunities and Challenges of Population Ageing for Sustainable Development in Vietnam", *International Conference of University of Economics Ho Chi Minh City: Policies and Sustainable Economic Development (ICUEH2016)*, Ho Chi Minh, Vietnam, November 2016, p. 168-178.

Nguyen, Thi Thu Ha. & Lam, Ba Hoa. (2017). "Evaluating the entrepreneurship performance in Vietnam through the GEDI (the Global Entrepreneurship Development Index) approach", *International Conference for Young Researchers in Economics and Business (ICYREB): Vietnamese enterprises with the Fourth Industrial Revolution*, Da Nang, Vietnam, 30 October, p. 522-534.

Nguyen, Thi Thu Ha. (2017). "Reviewing supply chain approaches and suggesting an excellent supply chain for enterprises in the context of global competition". *The 6th International Conference on Emerging Challenges: Strategic Integration (ICECH2017)*, Ha Noi: Vietnam, 1-3 December, p. 529-535.

Nguyen, Thi Thu Ha. (2016). "Contribution of human resources in economic growth of Danang city in the period 2010 – 2015", *The National Conference on Applied Statistics and Informatics (NCASI)*, Da Nang, Vietnam, 11-12 November, p. 174-183

In: The Power of Entrepreneurship
Editor: Daan Dirksen

ISBN: 978-1-53615-114-5
© 2019 Nova Science Publishers, Inc.

Chapter 4

LOCAL ECONOMIC DEVELOPMENT THEORY AND PRACTICE IN SOUTH AFRICA: FORCING SQUARE PEGS INTO ROUND HOLES?

Danie Francois Toerien[1] and Johannes Wessels[2]

[1]Centre for Environmental Management, University of the Free State, Bloemfontein, South Africa
[2]Enterprise Observatory of South Africa, Bloemfontein, South Africa

ABSTRACT

Two decades of disappointing South African local economic development (LED) outcomes are possibly due to inattention to quantitative research of entrepreneurial dynamics. Brief reviews of the evolution of LED policies and practices and of quantitative entrepreneurial research are followed by a case study to reflect the value of such analyses. It reflects on proportional relationships between demographics, entrepreneurial development and economics; provides evidence that entrepreneurship in South Africa is not limited; explains the concept of entrepreneurial space and the LED implications of its quantification;

presents evidence that the churn rate of enterprises in South African towns should be considered in LED policies; provides evidence that the enterprise richness (i.e., the number of different enterprise types) of towns is linked to productive knowledge, the lack of which plays a role in poverty and unemployment; examines the link between poverty and entrepreneurial development and its implications for pro-poor LED policy; and explains why officials and academics involved with the development and consideration of LED policies and practice in South Africa have ignored the quantification of the characteristics of human settlements in the United States and South Africa. The analysis concludes that the paradigms underlying South African LED policies and practices should be reconsidered and debated in-depth.

Keywords: local economic development, LED policy, enterprise orderliness, entrepreneurship, entrepreneurial space, enterprise richness, power laws; productive knowledge, wealth/poverty; paradigm paralysis

INTRODUCTION

Locally-driven development is important (Christensen and Van der Ree, 2008: 2) and has been enhanced by globalisation (Rodriguez-Pose and Fitjar, 2013: 356). Local economic development (LED) is receiving increased attention internationally (Nel and Rogerson, 2016: 109). In Sub-Saharan Africa, and particularly in South Africa, LED was identified as a critical challenge in the fight against poverty and inequality (Cohen, 2010: 8; Rogerson and Rogerson, 2012: 41). Hoogendoorn and Visser (2016: 95-108) reviewed South African research on small towns. They argued that the South African government's policy support for sustainable LED provides a strategic vantage point from which to analyse small towns in South Africa. They mentioned that government policy and its relevance to small towns stresses community planning, economic restructuring and governance. As a consequence, economic development and job creation are priorities. South Africa was initially regarded positively with regard to LED policy and strategy development (Ndlovu and Makoni, 2014: 503). However, after two decades of LED practice, the outcomes of South African efforts were largely disappointing (Nel and Rogerson, 2016: 110).

Local Economic Development Theory and Practice in South Africa 123

Nel and Rogerson (2016: 109-123) examined the 'congested trajectory' of applied local economic development in South Africa and focused on the LED strategies of 278 municipalities. Their desk-top survey covered nine metropolitan councils, 54 district municipalities and 215 local municipalities. They reported that the focus of a LED Fund, created to support LED activities, had gradually narrowed to being a government-led intervention in which poverty relief projects are the priority. Accordingly, government's directives for pro-poor LED planning contributed to disappointing LED performance (Nel and Rogerson, 2016: 120).

A pro-poor focus was understandable given the high levels of poverty and inequality in the country (Cohen, 2010: 3) but institutional responses differed in different areas. In larger metropolitan areas LED officials: adopted approaches that to some extent focussed on creating a more supportive and competitive business environment; focused on investment in infrastructure that reduced the cost of business, the regeneration of inner city and township areas; and focused on research about institutional support to new sectors with high growth and employment potential. In smaller centres the focus was: on increased service delivery; extension of the social grant system; public works; initiatives to stimulate small, medium and microenterprises (SMMEs); and income generating projects.

Ideological resistance of government to market related strategies resulted in conflict between the public and private sectors and contributed to weak performance (Nel and Rogerson, 2016: 111). A 'disconnect' between business development and LED planning had developed (Rogerson and Rogerson, 2012: 41). The promotion of SMMEs, co-operatives and informal businesses has been favoured by government but some local governments lacked complete understanding of their economies and competitive advantages, which resulted in ineffective LED strategies and projects (Cohen, 2010: 20). A surprising small number of business sectors dominate the strategic thinking of municipalities and their LED strategies (where these have actually been developed) (Nel and Rogerson, 2016: 114). In particular, tourism, agriculture and mining have been considered to be important. The infrastructure development support of all levels of government is often inadequate and the collection of reliable economic data to track local economic trends also limit success (Rogerson, 2008: 307). Disappointingly, the South African National Development Plan (National Planning Commission, 2011) touches upon local development only briefly and in no detail.

Are the disappointing results of South African LED policies and practices (Nel and Rogerson, 2016) also experienced elsewhere? Bartik (1991: 1-14) questioned if the U.S. benefits from state and local economic development policies. His answer is a tentative yes. Some empirical evidence indicates that state and LED competition may increase productivity, redistribute jobs towards the high-unemployment areas that need jobs the most, and increase national employment by using previously unemployed labour. However, a large body of empirical evidence supports the proposition that state and local governments' economic development policies have less influence on firms' location and investment decisions than economic variables such as available markets, characteristics of the labour force, and other direct costs of production (Feiock, 1991: 643). The evidence for positive outcomes of LED policies elsewhere is mixed.

Why have LED policies and approaches that were initially favourably received, been largely disappointing over two decades of LED practice? Bettencourt and West (2010: 913) suggest that the difference between 'policy as usual' and policy led by a new quantitative understanding of cities may well be the choice between creating a "planet of slums" or finally achieving a sustainable, creative, prosperous, urbanized world expressing the best of the human spirit. A series of studies since the early 2000s under the auspices of the Santa Fe Institute have led to the understanding that cities are complex systems whose infrastructural, economic and social components are strongly interrelated (West, 2017). Research on South African towns and local authorities has also revealed strong regularities (proportionalities) in and predictability about the enterprise dynamics and other associated characteristics of South African towns and municipalities (Toerien, 2012, 2014, 2015a, 2015b; Toerien and Seaman, 2010, 2011, 2012a, 2012b, 2012c, 2014). This echoes the findings of the Santa Fe Institute.

Local Economic Development Theory and Practice in South Africa   125

No evidence has been found that quantitative data of enterprise dynamics were considered in the development of LED policies or plans by any South African authority except the Western Cape Provincial government. Recent academic reviews of LED policy development and practice (Nel and Rogerson, 2016) and of research on South African towns (Hoogendoorn and Visser, 2016) paid scant attention to the quantitative research. Given the above dire warning of Bettencourt and West (2010), the prime purpose of this contribution is to examine a postulate that the lack of attention to quantitative information (international and South African) of human settlements is a significant contributing factor to the two-decades of disappointing LED outcomes in South Africa.

Evidence for acceptance of this postulate is pursued in the following manner: Firstly, a brief overview of the evolution of LED policies and practices in South Africa is presented. This is followed by a brief overview of the quantitative research on cities of the Santa Fe institute and of the enterprise dynamics of South African towns. Then a case study is used to sketch the importance of quantitative research on human settlements for the development of LED policies and plans. The case study draws upon enterprise information of towns of the Free State Province of South Africa. In the process, the case study: reflects on the relationships between demographics, entrepreneurial development and economics in the Free State; considers evidence that the oft-stated views about entrepreneurship in South Africa might be incorrect; explains the concept of entrepreneurial spaces and what its quantification reveals; presents evidence that the churn rate of enterprises in South African towns should be considered; explains the term enterprise richness of towns (Toerien and Seaman, 2014) and its link to what is called productive knowledge (Hausmann et al., 2017); examines the link between poverty and entrepreneurial development; explains a possible reason why officials and academics involved with the development and consideration of LED policies and practice have ignored the quantified findings of the Santa Fe Institute and of South African enterprise dynamics. To do this the research of Kuhn (1970) is used to consider the possibility that paradigm paralysis occurred. Finally, the original postulate is revisited

126   *Danie Francois Toerien and Johannes Wessels*

and a call is made that the paradigms underlying LED policy and practice in South Africa be reconsidered and debated in-depth.

Local Economic Development (LED) Policies and Practices in South Africa

After 1994, the definition, substance and practice of LED have been widely debated in South Africa (e.g., Rogerson, 2009: 16; Cohen, 2010: 3; Nel and Rogerson, 2016: 110). However, no common approach to LED strategy development had appeared and a large body of policy and legislative documents contributed to confusion. It was not always clear exactly how practitioners in local authorities were meant to prioritise, interpret and apply the various policies (Cohen, 2010: 4). Over the years and after various guiding documents were produced on policy and practice, the following was promoted: a national effort to focus on poverty, inequality and unemployment; the deepening and enhancing of the economic importance and centrality of effectively functioning local economies to grow the national economy; developing greater awareness of the significance of localities, regions and metropolitan municipalities as nodes of economic growth and generators of national prosperity; intensification of support of local economies to build their economic potential; strengthening intergovernmental coordination of economic development and between government and non-governmental sectors (Department of Provincial and Local Government, 2006: 7). LED in South Africa was anchored on the defined principle of 'developmental local government' (Nel and Rogerson, 2016: 110). The South African Municipal Systems Act 32 of 2000 (Republic of South Africa, 2000) legally determines that integrated development planning is a compulsory activity of all municipalities and legislates a number of key LED functions and responsibilities. Municipalities are required to prepare annually a five-year Integrated Development Plan (IDP) that should contain an LED strategy (Cohen, 2010: 3).

Over time a number of weaknesses were identified. The focus of the LED Fund, created to support LED activities, had gradually narrowed to

Local Economic Development Theory and Practice in South Africa 127

being a government-led intervention in which poverty relief projects were the priority. Government's directives for pro-poor LED planning contributed to disappointing LED performance of LED (Nel and Rogerson, 2016: 120). A pro-poor focus was understandable given the high levels of poverty and inequality in the country (Cohen, 2010: 3) but institutional responses differed. As explained earlier, the approaches to LED of larger metropolitan areas and smaller centres differed. There was also an ideological resistance of government to market related strategies, which resulted in conflict between the public and private sectors (Nel and Rogerson, 2016: 111). A disconnect between LED policy and business considerations (Rogerson and Rogerson, 2012: 41) contributed to weak performance. Some local governments do not fully understand their economies and competitive advantages, resulting in ineffective LED strategies and projects (Cohen, 2010: 20). In addition, the infrastructure development support of all levels of government is often inadequate and the collection of reliable economic data to track local economic trends also limit success (Rogerson, 2008: 307). Disappointingly, the South African National Development Plan (National Planning Commission, 2011) touches upon local development only briefly and in no detail.

Some remedies for poor LED performance have been proposed. Rogerson (2009: 3-5) suggested: there is a need for a clearer balance between the competitive and welfare focuses of LED and clarification of the meaning of LED in order to guide the activities and planning of especially small towns and less well-resourced municipalities. He recommended that the Department of Provincial and Local Government should reconsider its „one-size-fits-all" thinking about LED practice, promote a clearer balance and clarify the meaning of LED in order to guide the activities and planning of especially small towns and less well-resourced municipalities. Policymakers and legislators have also realized that having an LED plan does not automatically mean that LED will occur (Cohen, 2010: 3). In the light of the strong pro-poor focus of the South African government's LED policies and the levels of poverty and inequality in the country, the links between poverty and enterprise development need further examination. This forms part of the case study that follows later.

The Santa Fe Institute Quantitative Research on Cities

There is an obvious analogy between social network systems and urban and corporate structures. This analogy led to a project early in the new millennium at the Santa Fe Institute in the U.S. that investigated if the same sort of analyses used to understand biological network systems could be used for studying cities and companies (West, 2017). Investigation of the relationship between patenting activity and the population size of metropolitan areas in the United States soon showed that new patents were granted disproportionately in larger urban centres. In other words, there are increasing returns in inventing activity with respect to population size (Bettencourt et al., 2007b: 107). The relationship was quantitatively described by a power law with a super-linear exponent (i.e., larger than one). Further empirical evidence indicated that the processes relating urbanization to economic development and knowledge creation are very general, being shared by all cities belonging to the same urban system and sustained across different nations and times (Bettencourt et al., 2007a: 7301). Power laws indicated that many properties of cities scale with population size and the scaling exponents fall in distinct universality classes. Quantities reflecting wealth creation and innovation have exponents larger than unity (showing increasing returns) whereas those accounting for infrastructure have exponents smaller than unity, showing economies of scale (Bettencourt et al., 2007a: 7301). The Santa Fe research further showed that, despite appearances, cities are approximately scaled versions of one another: New York and Tokyo are, to a surprising and predictable degree, nonlinearly scaled-up versions of San Francisco in California or Nagoya in Japan. These extraordinary regularities opened a window on underlying mechanism, dynamics and structure common to all cities (Bettencourt and West, 2010: 913). Cities are remarkably robust: success, once achieved, is sustained for several decades or longer, thereby setting a city on a long run of creativity and prosperity (Bettencourt and West, 2010: 913).

An obstacle to effective policy is the lack of meaningful urban metrics based on a quantitative understanding of cities (Bettencourt et al., 2010: 1). Typically, linear per capita indicators are used to characterize and rank

Local Economic Development Theory and Practice in South Africa   129

cities. However, these implicitly ignore the fundamental role of nonlinear agglomeration in the life history of cities. Agglomeration nonlinearities are explicitly manifested in the super-linear power law scaling of most urban socioeconomic indicators with population size. The predictability resulting from these observations enabled the Santa Fe researchers to develop new urban metrics that disentangle dynamics at different scales and provide true measures of local urban performance (Bettencourt et al., 2010: 1). Youn et al., (2016: 1) reported that there is a universal structure common to all cities, which manifests in self-similarity in internal economic structure as well as aggregated metrics (GDP, patents, crime). They also determined the relative abundances of business types as a function of city size, which shed light on the processes of economic differentiation with scale.

No evidence has been found that the research results of the researchers of the Santa Fe Institute has ever been considered by South African officials involved with LED policies or practice or academics reviewing LED in South Africa.

Quantitative Information/Research about South African Towns

The Western Cape Provincial government in South Africa is the only provincial government that practiced in-depth consideration of quantitative data about towns. Upon request from the provincial government and based on a comprehensive development analysis, Van der Merwe et al. (2005) developed a typology of towns in the Western Cape. The methodology for the study was structured within an interdisciplinary context, the core of which comprised urban-geographical concepts and methods. This was later followed by studies to determine the growth potential of Western Cape municipalities (Donaldson et al., 2012a) and to develop generic interventions to stimulate growth in small towns in the Western Cape (Donaldson et al., 2012b; Van Niekerk et al., 2016). The Municipal Economic Review and Outlook (MERO) of the Western Cape is an annual research publication produced by the Provincial Treasury (Western Cape Government, 2017). The overall aim of MERO is to unpack regional development and sectors that feature in the Provincial Economic Review and Outlook (PERO) and other available economic literature for use by local policymakers across the Western Cape. There is no evidence that government officials involved in LED policy development elsewhere in South Africa considered these results. Recent academic reviews of LED (Nel and Rogerson, 2016) and research on South African towns (Hoogendoorn and Visser, 2016) also did not consider these quantitative analyses in any depth.

The officials and academic reviewers also paid scant attention to research about the enterprise dynamics of South African towns and municipalities (Toerien, 2012, 2014, 2015a, 2015b; Toerien and Seaman, 2010, 2011, 2012a,2012b, 2012c, 2014). Similar to the research of the Santa Fe Institute, these studies identified regularities (proportionalities) in enterprise development and dynamics of South African towns. Statistically significant correlations were recorded between entrepreneurial (e.g., total number of enterprises in towns or number of enterprises in certain business sectors in towns), economic (e.g., gross regional value added [GRVA], total regional personal income and regional employment) and demographic (e.g., town populations) characteristics of South African towns. This orderliness confers quantitative predictive powers about enterprise development and dynamics of South African towns and municipalities (e.g., Toerien, 2015a, 2015b) and adds to understanding. This potential has not yet been used in LED policy development and LED plans.

An economic systems model that links these regularities was proposed in 2012 by Toerien and Seaman (2012d). It assists an understanding of how demographic, economic and entrepreneurial characteristics in South African towns and municipalities are interlinked. This understanding has also been broadened by later studies that quantified the development of entrepreneurial spaces (the precise meaning of the term is presented later) in towns (Toerien and Seaman, 2014). The power law that describes the relationship between the total enterprise numbers and number of enterprise types in South African towns has endured for at least 70 years (Toerien, 2017) and there is no reason to think that it will change in the future.

The implications of the orderliness in enterprise dynamics challenge some long-held tenets about LED and job creation in South African towns. In other words, the existing paradigm/s underlying LED policies and practice might be inadequate. This contribution examines by way of a case study of towns of the Free State if the orderliness in enterprise dynamics: offers new quantified insights that could add to the understanding of entrepreneurship in South African towns; reveals the impacts of poverty on the enterprise dynamics of South African towns; can be used to make predictions that could support improved LED policy development, the planning of LED strategies and LED implementation.

CASE STUDY TO ILLUSTRATE THE IMPORTANCE OF ENTERPRISE ORDERLINESS

Selection of an Illustrative Case Study and Approach Used

The Free State Province was selected for the illustration because it is still the only South African province for which enterprise analyses have been completed for all of the provincial towns and municipalities (Toerien 2014, 2015b). The enterprises of all of the 78 towns (Table 1), which include Bloemfontein, the main settlement that is now in conjunction with the towns of Botshabelo, Thaba Nchu, Dewetsdorp and Wepener recognized as a metropole, were: identified by using telephone directories (supplemented by internet searches where necessary); classified into 19 different business sectors; and enumerated according to the methods of Toerien and Seaman (2010, 2011). The type of each enterprise was determined from a database of more than 700 enterprise types hitherto encountered in South African towns and according to the methods of Toerien and Seaman (2014) and Toerien (2017).

The purpose of the case study is not to provide a comprehensive review of all studies about the enterprise orderliness of South African or Free State towns. Instead, specific examples based on characteristics of Free State towns will be used to illustrate the power of quantitative information that could influence thinking about and planning of LED in South Africa. In the process earlier (Toerien, 2014; Toerien, 2015b) and more recent analyses of Free State towns will be used.

Table 1. The Free State settlements used in the case study

Town			
Allanridge	Ficksburg	Marquard	Thaba 'Nchu
Arlington	Fouriesburg	Memel	Theunissen
Bethlehem	Frankfort	Odendaalsrus	Trompsburg
Bethulie	Gariep Dam	Oranjeville	Tweeling
Bloemfontein	Harrismith	Parys	Tweespruit
Boshof	Heilbron	Paul Roux	Ventersburg
Bothaville	Hennenman	Petrus Steyn	Vierfontein
Botshabelo	Hertzogville	Petrusburg	Viljoensdrif
Brandfort	Hobhouse	Philippolis	Viljoenskroon
Bultfontein	Hoopstad	Phuthaditjhaba	Villiers
Clarens	Jacobsdal	Reddersburg	Virginia
Clocolan	Jagersfontein	Reitz	Vrede
Cornelia	Kestell	Rosendal	Vredefort
Dealesville	Koffiefontein	Rouxville	Warden
Deneysville	Koppies	Sasolburg	Welkom
Dewetsdorp	Kragbron	Senekal	Wepener
Edenburg	Kroonstad	Smithfield	Wesselsbron
Edenville	Ladybrand	Soutpan	Winburg
Excelsior	Lindley	Springfontein	Zastron
Fauresmith	Luckhoff	Steynsrus	

The Relationship between Demographics and Entrepreneurial Development

There are direct and statistically significant positive relationships between the populations of towns and municipalities and their respective enterprise numbers in South Africa (Toerien and Seaman, 2012a). This is also true for the Free State towns (Bloemfontein, by far the largest

Local Economic Development Theory and Practice in South Africa 133

settlement, was excluded to prevent registering a spurious correlation) as shown by relating the 2011 populations to the 2012/13 enterprise numbers:

$$\text{Enterprises numbers} = 0.0061(\text{Population numbers}) - 7.1 \tag{1}$$

with $r = 0.82$, $n = 78$ towns and $P < 0.01$. There is approximately one enterprise for every 164 persons in Free State towns and this is irrespective of the size of towns. The total number of business establishments of metropolitan statistical areas in the U.S. are also linearly proportional to their population sizes (Youn et al., 2016). Their proportionality constant is approximately 21.6 and indicates that there is approximately one business establishment for every 22 people. The difference in the proportionality constrants of the U.S and Free State probably reflects higher general poverty in the Free State.

Such relationships have predictive value. Daniel Kahneman, economics Nobel Prize laureate, illustrated the predictive powers of simple algorithms and promoted their use (Kahneman, 2011). Regression equations such as equation 1 are simple algorithms that can be used to make predictions about the impact of population growth/decrease on the enterprise numbers of specific municipalities. Demographic-enterprise relationships could be usefully applied in LED policy and implementation considerations, something that is not yet done in South Africa.

The Relationship between Demographics and Economics

The previous section raises a new question, namely what drives the size of populations in towns? Toerien and Seaman (2012d) mentioned that there are statistically significant relationships between economic value addition, employment opportunities and populations of South African towns. Because economic data such as economic value addition and employment figures are not available at the level of individual towns but at the level of local and district municipalities, the relationships between 2010 economic value addition, 2010 employment numbers and 2011 population size of 20 Free State local municipalities are presented here (Table 2).

All three the variables are significantly correlated with one another. In U.S. metropolitan statistical areas (MSAs), the number of employees also scale approximately linearly with the population size and there are approximately 7.9 employees per business establishment (Youn et al., 2016).

Whilst the above correlations do not necessarily indicate causality, Toerien and Seaman (2012d) suggested that such correlations are indicative of a systems model, which is (at least partly) driven by the economic value produced in a municipality or town. The model links the economic, demographic and entrepreneurial characteristics of South African towns. The relationships of Table 2 are in line with the above suggestion and suggests that economic value addition and resulting employment opportunities might be driving the population sizes of Free State municipalities.

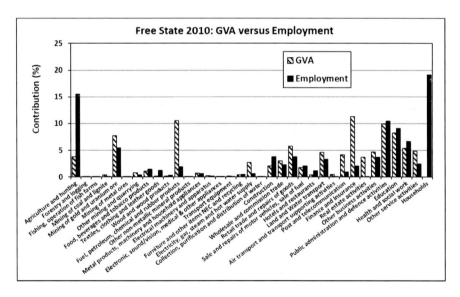

Figure 1. The relative contributions of different business sectors to gross value addition (GVA) and employment creation in Free State municipalities in 2010.

In turn, this raises questions such as: in which business sectors is economic value created; in which sectors is employment created; and are

Local Economic Development Theory and Practice in South Africa 135

there mismatches. Such an analysis is illustrated in Figure 1 for a detailed 2010 economic analysis of the Free State municipalities. There are clear imbalances. For instance, agriculture and hunting creates much more employment relative to the value that is added by this sector. This illustrates that balances of value addition versus employment creation of specific economic sectors should be considered in LED planning. There is little evidence that this is being done anywhere in South Africa.

Table 2. The relationships between 2010 Gross Value Added (GVA), 2010 employment and 2011 population size of Free State municipalities. First mentioned characteristic was used as independent variable

Relationship	Correlation	% variation explained	Regression coefficient	Intercept	n
GVA-Population	0.86	74.6	0.0217	48946.2	20
GVA-Employment	0.91	82.6	0.00463	9431.1	20
Employment-Population	0.97	94.7	4.79	1705.8	20

Are the Often-Stated Views about Entrepreneurship in South Africa Flawed?

New democratic South Africa faces numerous economic, political and social challenges. A key challenge is that of massive and growing unemployment in South Africa (Herrington et al., 2010: 12). In late 2017, the youth (ages 15-34) unemployment rate was 38,6%. This was 10,9% above the national average (Statistics South Africa, 2017). The National Development Plan (National Planning Commission, 2011: 30) stresses the importance of entrepreneurial development, especially for youth development. South African entrepreneurial activity although being very low, increased marginally between 2004 and 2014, but then the early entrepreneurial activity rate dropped by a staggering 34% (Herrington

136 *Danie Francois Toerien and Johannes Wessels*

et al., 2014: 5). Can the disjunct between the stated importance and dismal success of entrepreneurial development be due to flaws in the understanding of entrepreneurship in South Africa? This contribution suggests this is the case.

The argument for this statement is based on two lines of reasoning: the availability of entrepreneurial spaces, and, the implications of the relationship between total enterprises and number of enterprise types [referred to as enterprise richness by Toerien and Seaman, (2014)] in/of South African towns.

Entrepreneurial Spaces

The total entrepreneurial space of a town is the maximum number of enterprises that can be 'carried' in the specific town. A number of studies of towns in South Africa (e.g., Toerien, 2014; Toerien and Seaman, 2012a, 2012b) have demonstrated highly significant (P < 0.01) correlations between the total enterprises in towns and the enterprises of most of the business sectors investigated. In other words, there are strong proportionalities (regularities) involved in the entrepreneurial spaces of towns. Because of the above-mentioned proportionalities, the total entrepreneurial space of a town can be divided into the fractions occupied by different business sectors (e.g., construction, traders, personal services, etc.) or in the fractions occupied by different entrepreneurial types (e.g., new and existing entrepreneurs, concepts that will be explained later). Such proportionalities were also observed for the Free State towns (Table 3).

For nine business sectors in Table 3 more than 90% of the variation and for another five more than 75% of the variation was explained by the regression equations. This indicates extraordinary orderliness and proportionalities in the major part of the enterprise structures of Free State towns.

Important implications for LED policy and plans are: (i) the development of enterprises in the villages and towns of the Free State province, but also elsewhere in South Africa, is orderly and structured. The number of enterprises in most business services sectors form very constant proportions of the total enterprises over a wide range of settlement sizes (see example in Figure 2), and, (ii) the high values of the recorded correlations (Table 3) suggest that the 'entrepreneurial spaces' of most business sectors in towns are fully utilised at all times.

Table 3. The relationships between total enterprises of 77 Free State towns and the number of enterprises in different business sectors of these towns

No	Business sector	Correlation	Variation (%) explained	Regression coefficient*	Intercept
1	Trade services	0.99	98.5	0.2487	-0.1
2	General services	0.99	97.9	0.0700	-1.3
3	Personal services	0.99	97.3	0.0662	1.3
4	Construction services	0.99	97.0	0.0771	-2.3
5	Health services	0.98	96.9	0.0926	0.1
6	Vehicle services	0.98	96.3	0.1054	-2.1
7	Financial services	0.98	95.7	0.0667	1.1
8	Professional services	0.95	90.9	0.0464	-1.6
9	Telecommunication services	0.95	90.8	0.0107	-0.4
10	Transport & earthworks services	0.95	89.7	0.0233	-0.2
11	Legal services	0.94	88.3	0.0186	0.3
12	News & advertising services	0.94	87.5	0.0048	-0.2
13	Engineering & technical services	0.92	84.7	0.0419	-1.6
14	Real estate services	0.87	75.7	0.0164	0.1
15	Tourism & hospitality services	0.84	70.2	0.0462	2.4
16	Factories	0.80	64.5	0.0167	-0.1
17	Processors	0.79	62.2	0.0082	0.7
18	Mining services	0.78	60.3	0.0176	-1.3
19	Agricultural products & services**	0.55	30.1	0.0226	5.0

* The regression coefficient quantifies the fraction of all enterprises occupied by a specific sector; ** Includes enterprises servicing the agricultural sector, not farms.

If this was not the case, much more variation would have been observed in the data rather than the extraordinary closeness-of-fit for data from 77 towns, each analysed independently (see example in Figure 2). There is, therefore, no lack of entrepreneurs in most business sectors in Free State towns and the available entrepreneurial spaces are fully utilized. This is probably also the case for most, if not all, South African towns. This means that the first unstated assumption in South African LED policies and practices (see earlier), namely that there are no limits or factors controlling entrepreneurial opportunities in towns, is incorrect. A lack of entrepreneurs cannot be the reason for dismal LED outcomes.

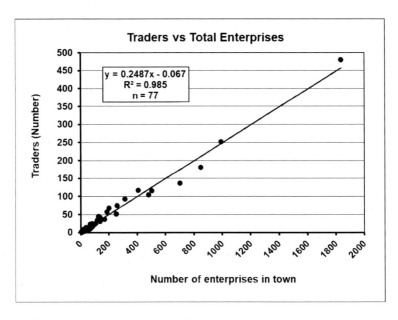

Figure 2. Illustration of the closeness-of-fit of the relationship between total enterprises and traders in Free State towns.

LED plans and strategies generally aim to increase the number of enterprises and employment, to reduce poverty and to influence enterprise ownership profiles (Neumark et al., 2006). Developing LED policies and plans without taking the entrepreneurial regularities of towns and the factors that control them into account, deals in 'strategies of hope' rather than 'strategies of reality.' For instance, plans to train more entrepreneurs in trade services when the entrepreneurial spaces for traders are fully occupied (Figure 2) can only result in a 'musical chairs' result: a successful new entrepreneur will either replace an existing entrepreneur or will not be able to gain a business foothold. There will be no net increase in the number of enterprises and probably no increase in employment.

No evidence was found that officials involved with LED policy development and plans or academics such as Herrington et al., (2010), Rogerson and Rogerson (2012), Herrington et al., (2014), Hoogendoorn and Visser (2016) and Nel and Rogerson (2016) have considered entrepreneurial spaces and the factors that control them. Yet, as shown in the examples above, entrepreneurial space determines what is possible and what not in enterprise development and associated issues such as creation of employment. The lack of such considerations probably signals a weakness in the paradigm/s underlying LED theories and practices in South Africa.

Enterprise Churn Rates

Does Figure 2 indicate there is no room at all for new entrepreneurs in trade sectors of Free State towns? The answer is negative because the turnover (churn rate) of enterprises also needs to be considered. Using the methods of Toerien and Seaman (2010) to identify and classify the enterprises of South African towns, it is possible to: follow the fate of individual enterprises in a town over a number of years, develop a 'numbers balance' and calculate the 'churn rate' of enterprises (the disappearance of existing enterprises and the founding of new ones relative to total enterprise numbers). Figure 3 illustrates the enterprise dynamics of four Free State towns: Bethulie on the banks of the Gariep Dam and in a semi-arid area primarily suitable for animal production (Erasmus, 2004), Bothaville, a large agricultural town in the north-western Free State (Erasmus, 2004), Clarens, a town heavily dependent on tourism (Campbell, 2016) and Koffiefontein, a diamond mining town in the southern Free State that has been challenged to develop a future beyond mining (Marais and Atkinson, 2006).

Over a six-year period (2004/05 to 2009/10), the enterprise numbers of Bothaville stayed relatively constant, those of Bethulie and Koffiefontein declined (by 10% and 33% respectively) and those of Clarens increased by 33%. This has to be contrasted with churn rates that at maximum reached 16% per annum in Bethulie, 22% per annum in Bothaville, 33% per annum in Clarens and 28% per annum in Koffiefontein (Figure 3). Despite the high churn rates, the enterprise numbers remained relatively constant.

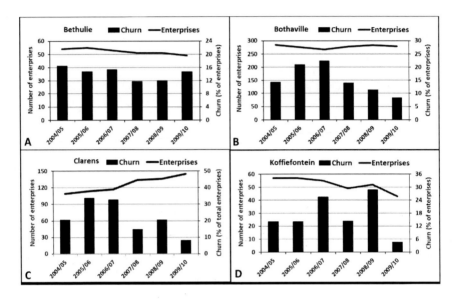

Figure 3. The number of enterprises and the enterprise churn rates over a six-year period of four Free State towns: Bethulie, Bothaville, Clarens and Koffiefontein.

Table 4. Pair-wise comparisons by means of correlation coefficient calculations of the enterprise profiles of Bothaville between the years of 2004/5 to 2009/10. Enterprise profiles are expressed as sector percentages of total enterprise numbers and 19 different sectors are used

Year	2004/5	2005/6	2006/7	2007/8	2008/9	2009/10
2004/5	1.00					
2005/6	1.00	1.00				
2006/7	0.99	1.00	1.00			
2007/8	0.99	0.99	1.00	1.00		
2008/9	0.98	0.99	0.99	0.99	1.00	
2009/10	0.98	0.99	0.99	1.00	1.00	1.00

When the enterprise profiles of each town for the different years are compared pair-wise, the correlation coefficients are initially near unity and reduce only slowly over time as illustrated for Koffiefontein in Table 4. The disappearance of existing and founding of new enterprises seem to happen in the same business sectors, something that is predictable from Schumpeter's description of the process of creative destruction (Schumpeter, 1942: 81-86) and its implication of the survival of the fittest enterprises. For instance, restaurants compete with other restaurants and if one wins, the other loses, typical of a zero-sum game. The churn in different business sectors presents opportunities for black economic empowerment. However, the competitive advantages, if any, of such enterprises have to be considered in LED policies and plans.

The Relationship between Enterprise Types (Enterprise Richness) and Total Enterprises

There is a very strong power law relationship between the number of enterprise types (referred to as enterprise richness) and the total number of enterprises in 134 South African towns (Toerien and Seaman, 2014). The power law is:

$$\text{Enterprise richness} = 1.8086(\text{total enterprises}^{0.7164}) \qquad (2)$$

with $r = 0.99$ and $n = 134$. Enterprise richness scales sub-linearly in relation to total enterprises, indicating that larger towns have proportionally fewer enterprise types and, therefore, relatively more replicates of enterprise types already present. In large towns there are, thus, proportionally more opportunity for entrepreneurs to become successful by starting more enterprises of types that are already present in the town. The opposite is true in small towns.

Equation 2 also reveals that when a town has double the number of enterprises than another town, it has 64.3% more enterprise types. In other words, for every doubling of the total enterprises (i.e., 100% increase), the enterprise richness will increase by 64.3%. Entrepreneurial spaces for enterprise types that have not yet been present in specific South African towns, therefore, develop in a regular way as towns grow. When towns regress they steadily lose enterprise types. This is further proof of orderliness in the enterprise dynamics of South African towns.

The enterprise richness power law of towns in South Africa also extends over space and time (Toerien, 2017). For instance, the 2012/13 power law for the Free State towns (Figure 4) is very similar to equation 2 and suggests that the enterprise richness in Free State towns will increase by 58.9% for each doubling of the number of enterprises. Conversely, halving of the number of enterprises in Free State towns will reduce their enterprise richness by 62.9%.

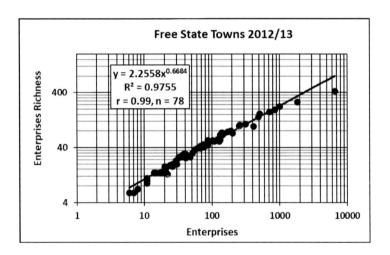

Figure 4. The power law relationship between enterprise richness (i.e., the number of enterprise types) as a function of total enterprises of 78 Free State towns.

The enterprise richness power law (Figure 4) indicates that the expansion of enterprise numbers (and hence creation of employment) in Free State towns requires two processes: establishment of more enterprises of types already present (referred to as existing entrepreneurs) and establishment of some enterprise types that are not yet present (referred to as new entrepreneurs) (Figure 5). For example, new enterprise type formation might be the establishment of the first firm to provide veterinary services in a town. Enterprise type replication takes place when more businesses are established of types that have already been successfully founded, e.g., the second medical practitioner or second attorney in a town.

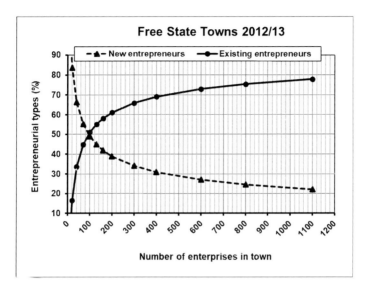

Figure 5. The relative entrepreneurial spaces of new and existing entrepreneurs as functions of the total enterprises in towns. New entrepreneurs start enterprises of types not yet present in a town. Existing entrepreneurs start enterprises of types already present in a town.

In general, new entrepreneurship plays an exceedingly important role in small South African towns. This is also true for Free State towns with fewer than 100 enterprises (Figure 5). A critical challenge in these towns/villages is that there must be entrepreneurs who can identify business opportunities that are not yet present in the town/village. That is a huge challenge for entrepreneurs who often has had limited exposure to business practices and can only draw upon their experiences in their often-impoverished surroundings. For example, one can ask how can a would-be entrepreneur who has never been a tourist be able to discern a business opportunity linked to tourism? Even in very large towns, enterprise and employment growth still needs entrepreneurs that can identify business opportunities not yet present in these towns.

There is no evidence that the existence of the above power laws and their implications have figured in LED policy development, planning and implementation or in academic LED reviews (e.g., Rogerson and Rogerson, 2012; Hoogendoorn and Visser, 2016; Nel and Rogerson, 2016). LED policies and strategies that are out of sync with these regularities have a strong possibility of failing.

Enterprise Richness, Productive Knowledge and the Impact of Poverty on Enterprise Dynamics

The National Development Plan (National Planning Commission, 2011: 1) mentions that too many people in South Africa are trapped in poverty, contributing to a highly unequal society. The elimination of poverty remains a national goal. A question arises whether quantification of enterprise dynamics can assist in an understanding of how poverty impacts upon enterprise dynamics? This is indeed the case.

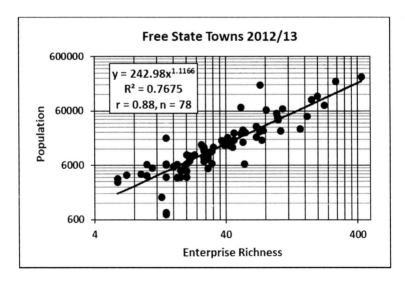

Figure 6. The relationship between enterprise richness (measure of productive knowledge and used as independent variable) and the population size (dependent variable) of Free State towns.

Local Economic Development Theory and Practice in South Africa 145

Firstly, a theoretical argument is provided. Thereafter the issue of productive knowledge (Hausmann et al., 2017) is considered. Secondly, the relationship between population numbers and total enterprise numbers (equation 1) is graphically linked with the relationship between total enterprise numbers and enterprise richness (Figure 6) in an analysis of the Free State towns.

Theoretical Argument

The regression coefficient (slope) of equation 1 is:

$$b = \text{(Enterprises in town/municipality)/}$$
$$\text{(Population in town/municipality)} \tag{3}$$

The inverse of the regression coefficient is:

$$1/b = \text{(Population in town/municipality)/}$$
$$\text{(Enterprises in town/municipality)} \tag{4}$$

$$= \text{Enterprise Dependency Index (EDI)} \tag{5}$$

The EDI is a wealth/poverty measure that measures the number of people needed to 'carry' the average enterprise in a municipality or town. If more people are needed to 'carry' the average enterprise, the EDI is higher and is indicative of greater poverty, and vice versa.

Equations 4 and 5 can be rewritten as:

$$\text{Enterprises} = \text{(Population in town/municipality)/}$$
$$\text{(EDI of town/municipality)} \tag{6}$$

The enterprise numbers in a town/municipality are, therefore, a function of the population size of the town/municipality and the wealth/poverty status of its population.

The Link with Productive Knowledge

Hausmann et al. (2017) pointed out that countries tend to converge to the level of income that can be supported by the know-how that is embedded in their economies; i.e., their so-called productive knowledge. More prosperous countries have more productive knowledge than poor countries, and vice versa. These differences are expressed in the diversity and sophistication of the things that each of these nations makes. Productive knowledge is not book learning but knowledge stemming from practice and experience to produce products or deliver services.

Hausmann and Klinger (2008) argued that producing new things is quite different from producing more of the same and Florida (2002) remarked that human creativity in terms of new ideas and better ways of doing things is ultimately what raises productivity and living standards.

If the level of the productive knowledge of countries determines their economic fates, the same should be true for local economies and populations of towns. The quantification of enterprise richness (such as in Figure 4) provides a measure of the productive knowledge (i.e., the knowledge to produce a specific product or deliver a specific service not yet present, or in other words a 'new thing') in South African towns.

Does more productive knowledge influence the number of people in human settlements? The ability to quantify enterprise richness in relation to total enterprise numbers (Figure 4) and the relationship between total enterprise numbers and population numbers (equation 1), enable the successful linking of enterprise richness (measure of productive knowledge and independent variable) and population numbers (as dependent variable) in Free state towns (Figure 6).

Because the coefficient of the power law in Figure 6 is higher than unity, it indicates that population numbers of towns scale super-linearly relative to enterprise richness. Towns with larger enterprise richness numbers, i.e., more productive knowledge, can progressively 'carry' more people. The results of the Free State towns are in step with the observation that there are relatively more inventors in larger metropolitan areas in the U.S. (Bettencourt et al., 2007b). These observations suggest that money allocated

Local Economic Development Theory and Practice in South Africa 147

to LED projects in South Africa could be applied more effectively in larger towns than smaller towns.

Contrary to the closeness of fit between total enterprise numbers and enterprise richness (Figure 4), the relationship between enterprise richness and population numbers (Figure 6) has a much larger spread. For instance, the populations of towns with an enterprise richness between 12 and 16, can range from about 800 to 18000 (Figure 6). What is the likely cause of this large spread? Equation 6 links the enterprise numbers of towns/municipalities with population numbers and their wealth/poverty statuses (i.e., EDIs). Consequently, the above large spread could be due to differences in the wealth/poverty statuses of towns.

To test this possibility, the Free State towns were ranked in terms of their EDIs and binned into three groups (richer towns with EDIs < 100; intermediate towns with EDIs of 100-300; poorer towns with EDIs of >300). The power law relationship between enterprise richness (independent variable) and population numbers (dependent variable) for each of the three groups was determined (Figure 7).

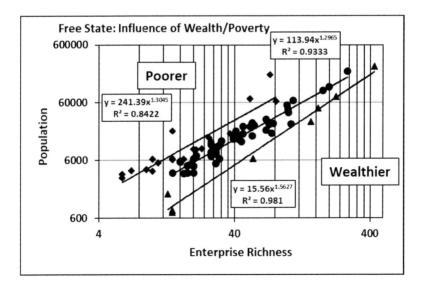

Figure 7. The relationship between enterprise richness and population numbers for three groups of Free State towns (triangles EDI < 100; dots EDIs 100-300; diamonds EDIs > 300). Higher EDIs indicate more poverty, and lower EDIs more wealth.

Each of the groups had a statistically significant power law linking the enterprise richness and population numbers of the towns in the group. The exponential coefficients and slopes of the lines were roughly similar (Figure 7). However, increased poverty statuses (i.e., higher EDIs) moved the lines increasingly higher in Figure 7. Stated differently, more prosperous small towns could 'carry' as many enterprises as less prosperous large towns. This finding has potentially serious implications for pro-poor LED policies. A scenario analysis illustrates this point.

Scenario Analysis

Scenarios can be used to examine the impact of wealth/poverty on the dynamics of enterprise development over time. It was used here to project the influence of poverty on the enterprise dynamics of Free State towns. Two annual population growth rates, namely 2% and 4%, and two town sizes, i.e., 8000 persons (indicative of smaller Free State towns) and 40000 persons (indicative of larger Free State towns) are used. Five issues are obvious. Firstly, poverty has a devastating impact on enterprise development. Poorer towns (EDI > 300) initially have fewer than 10% of the enterprises of equally-sized (in terms of population) richer towns (EDI < 100). After five and 10 years, these differences widen further (Table 5). The potential impacts of this on the planning and implementation of LED plans are clear. Pro-poor investment of LED funds into poorer towns cannot lead to large-scale increases in enterprises and creation of employment. Equation 6 indicates that the total number of enterprises of a town is a function of the population and its wealth/poverty status, the combination of which defines the entrepreneurial space or size of the local market. The entrepreneurial spaces of most sectors of the local markets are fully occupied by existing entrepreneurs (Table 3). Investing money in entrepreneurs with limited productive knowledge to compete in highly competitive markets, local or elsewhere, would be catering for disaster. Wessels and Nel (2016) demonstrated how investment in cooperatives in poverty-stricken areas of the Free State was spectacularly unsuccessful.

Local Economic Development Theory and Practice in South Africa 149

Table 5. Projections five and ten years into the future of the influence of poverty (measured as EDI) on the enterprise dynamics of Free State towns

EDI	Population growth rate p.a.	Characteristic	Year		
			Initial	5	10
<100 (richer)	2	Enterprises	205	226	249
		Population	8000	8833	9752
		ER	70	75	80
	4	Enterprises	205	249	303
		Population	8000	9733	11842
		ER	70	79	90
	2	Enterprises	1023	1129	1247
		Population	40000	44163	48760
		ER	198	211	225
	4	Enterprises	1023	1245	1514
		Population	40000	48666	59210
		ER	198	225	255
100-300 (intermediate)	2	Enterprises	66	73	80
		Population	8000	8833	9752
		ER	34	36	38
	4	Enterprises	66	80	97
		Population	8000	9733	11842
		ER	34	38	43
	2	Enterprises	329	363	401
		Population	40000	44163	48760
		ER	95	101	108
	4	Enterprises	329	400	487
		Population	40000	48666	59210
		ER	95	108	123
>300 (poorer)	2	Enterprises	10	11	12
		Population	8000	8833	9752
		ER	10	11	11
	4	Enterprises	10	12	15
		Population	8000	9733	11842
		ER	10	11	13
	2	Enterprises	50	56	61
		Population	40000	44163	48760
		ER	28	30	32
	4	Enterprises	50	61	75
		Population	40000	48666	59210
		ER	28	32	36

Two population growth rates (2% and 4% p.a.) and two populations sizes (8000 and 40000) are used. EDI = population/enterprises and ER = enterprise richness

Secondly, the population growth rate and size of towns significantly impact the future enterprise dynamics of richer and poorer towns. For instance, a large rich town with a population growth of 4% will in five years add significantly more enterprises (i.e., 222 enterprises) than the total enterprises of a large poor town growing at 4% for five years (i.e., 61 enterprises) (Table 5). A small rich town will also add more enterprises in five years than the total enterprises of a small poor town. If employment creation is an overarching goal, LED funds should be invested in larger and/or richer towns. This reality should be considered in LED planning and implementation.

Thirdly, LED planning in South Africa appears to simultaneously pursue conflicting goals, e.g., employment creation and poverty relief. To create employment, it makes little sense to direct investments to pro-poor relief projects or to business ventures in poor towns where the prospects of economic growth are limited (Table 5). Strategically it would make more sense to invest such funds into projects in richer towns with higher growth rates and more employment prospects. Scenarios of LED investment in Free State towns (Table 5) confirmed this conclusion.

Fourthly, there are three unstated assumptions implicit in the paradigms underlying official policies and practices about IDPs and LED in South Africa:

- *Assumption 1*. There are no limits or factors controlling entrepreneurial opportunities in towns and/or the viability of their enterprises. In other words, if money is made available to would-be entrepreneurs in poverty-stricken places, successful founding of enterprises and subsequent job creation will automatically follow. Table 5 refutes such an assumption.
- *Assumption 2*. What holds for municipalities, as the foundation of LED planning, also holds for the towns included in specific municipalities. In other words, in a municipality with multiple towns, all towns are similar and a single IDP (that includes a single LED plan) is adequate. Table 5 also refutes such an assumption.

- *Assumption 3.* LED practice can successfully integrate activities that will simultaneously reduce poverty, increase employment and enhance black ownership in local economies of South Africa, particularly those of rural areas. Table 5 also shows that optimized investment of LED funds for employment creation would not necessarily simultaneously create black economic empowerment. A recommendations of an international panel of experts that black economic empowerment should be adjusted to be more growth friendly and the emigration of white skills should be prevented as much as possible (Hausmann, 2008) has been ignored by the South African government.

Fifthly, the title of this contribution implies that LED practice in South Africa might be seeking ineffective solutions and the evidence presented supports this contention. This implies that the paradigm(s) underlying South African LED theory and practice could be flawed, and some, if not all, of the flaws are not appreciated. This issue is addressed in the following section.

THE POSSIBILITY OF A FLAWED LED PARADIGM

South African LED theory and practice have been based on international experience as interpreted by local professionals, officials, and academics. Political dogma and wishes of a ruling political party have also played influencing roles. Is it possible that despite the numerous inputs, the prevailing LED theory and practice could be flawed?

The research of Kuhn (1970) helps to unravel this issue. He famously stated that mature science experiences alternating phases of normal science and revolutions. According to him, science does not develop through the accumulation of individual discoveries and inventions but through changes in the values and beliefs of scientists, i.e., their 'paradigms,' which typically resist evidence-based change until sufficient evidence has accumulated to tip the balance of beliefs. He referred to 'normal' and 'revolutionary' science and used puzzle-solving as an analogy to explain the differences between them. Normal science permits the cumulative generation of puzzle-solutions and the puzzle-solvers expect to have reasonable chances of solving the puzzles. They depend on their own abilities, the puzzles and the methods to solve them are known and they generate a growing number of successful 'puzzle-solutions.' Scientific revolutions result in the revision of disciplinary matrices in order to provide solutions for the more serious anomalous puzzles of preceding periods of normal science. Revolutionary science is not cumulative and involves revisions of existing scientific beliefs and/or practices.

The two decades of disappointing South African LED outcomes are indicative of a LED paradigm/s that cannot solve the unemployment and poverty 'puzzles' of South Africa. The quantitative research of the group at the Santa Fe Institute (Bettencourt and West, 2010; West, 2017) and the group in South Africa (e.g., Toerien and Seaman, 2010; 2012a, 2012b, 2012c, 2012d; 2014) probably signalled the arrival of a new paradigm (i.e., revolutionary science) in development science. Bettencourt and West (2010) warned that ignoring the new quantitative understanding of cities (i.e., human settlements) could lead to a "planet of slums" instead of achieving a sustainable, creative, prosperous, urbanized world.

Argyris (1977) provides guidance on a possible solution. He states that organizational learning is a process of detecting and correcting errors, i.e., features of knowledge or knowing that inhibit learning. The process is called single loop learning and forms the basis of normal science. Argyris commented: "Single loop learning can be compared with a thermostat that learns when it … is too hot or too cold and then turns the heat on or off. The thermostat is able to perform this task because it can receive information (the temperature of the room) and therefore take corrective action." The disappointing outcomes after more than two decades of LED practice in South Africa suggest that the same set of solutions (i.e., the prescribed ways in which LED should be done) have been used over and over again, largely without success. LED theory and practice in South Africa has become trapped in a particular paradigm or set of paradigms that advocate a given set of ineffective solutions. In other words, South African LED theory and practice are in paradigm paralysis.

Questioning the underlying approaches, policies and goals provides a second and more comprehensive inquiry, called double loop learning (Argyris, 1977). He added to his thermostat example: "If the thermostat could question itself about whether it should be set at 68°F, it would be capable not only of detecting error but of questioning the underlying policies and goals as well as its own program." The unemployment and poverty problems in South Africa remain dire. Given South Africa's continuing need to expand employment, double loop learning approaches are urgently required to improve the South African LED paradigm and to enhance employment creation. The time has come to revisit the South African LED policies and practices and to have fundamental debates about them.

CONCLUSION

A brief review of the evolvement of LED policy in South Africa indicated it is now basically pro-poor and community-based. Brief reviews of quantitative research on the enterprise dynamics of South African towns indicated that the latter information is ignored in the development of LED policies in South Africa.

A case study of Free State towns was used to illustrate that the proportionalities and regularities between demographic, economic and entrepreneurial characteristics of the ignored quantitative information have many and significant implications for LED policies and implementation in South Africa:

- there is proportionality with predictive potential between the sizes of town populations and their enterprise numbers (see equation 1),
- there are proportionalities with predictive potential between economic value addition, population numbers and employment in municipalities (Table 2),

- the balance between economic sectors where value is added to local economies and sectors where employment is created should be considered (Figure 1),
- the strong proportionalities observed between total enterprise numbers and the numbers of enterprises of different business sectors (Table 2 and Figure 2) indicate that contrary to general beliefs there is no shortage of entrepreneurs in South African towns,
- the churn rate of South African towns (Figure 3) should be considered in LED policies and implementation because it might be important in the identification of opportunities for black economic empowerment,
- the enterprise richness of towns is a power law function of their total enterprise numbers. The power law has a sub-linear exponent (e.g., equation 2, Figure 4). Every doubling (i.e., 100% increase) of the enterprise numbers of Free State towns results in an 64.3% increase in the enterprise richness of these towns. The implications in terms of opportunities for different entrepreneurial types resulting from the proportionality implicit in this relationship (Figure 5) should be considered in LED policy development and implementation,
- enterprise richness serves as a proxy for the level of productive knowledge in towns. The level of productive knowledge links with the wealth/poverty status of Free State towns (see equations 1 and 6, and Figure 6). This is probably true for all South African towns,
- the enterprise numbers of towns and municipalities are functions of the population size of the town/municipalities and the wealth/poverty status of their populations (e.g., Figure 7). Population numbers of towns scale super-linearly relative to enterprise richness. Towns with larger enterprise richness numbers, i.e., more productive knowledge, can progressively 'carry' more people,
- poverty has a devastating impact on enterprise development (Table 5). Pro-poor investment of LED investment funds into poorer towns cannot lead to large-scale increases in enterprises and the creation of employment,

Local Economic Development Theory and Practice in South Africa 155

- the population growth rates and sizes of towns hugely impact the future enterprise dynamics of richer and poorer towns (Table 5). For instance, large rich towns with population growth of 4% per annum for five years add significantly more enterprises and jobs than the total enterprises and jobs of large poor towns growing at the same rate. These realities should be considered in LED planning and implementation as well as in rural development programmes,
- LED planning in South Africa appears to simultaneously pursue conflicting goals. It makes little sense to direct investments towards business ventures in poor towns in order to simultaneously grow the number of enterprises, reduce unemployment and poverty, and to have black economic empowerment. The prospects of economic growth in poor towns are limited (Table 5). From an employment creation viewpoint, it would strategically make more sense to invest such funds in projects in richer and larger towns. The price paid for avoiding the best opportunities for enterprise growth and employment creation could lead to the waste of large amounts of LED-earmarked funds,
- three unstated assumptions implicit in the existing LED paradigm/s underlying official policies and practices about IDPs and LED in South Africa, namely there are no limits or factors controlling entrepreneurial opportunities in towns and/or the viability of their enterprises; what holds for municipalities, as the foundation of LED planning, also holds for the towns included in specific municipalities; and LED practice can successfully integrate activities that will simultaneously reduce poverty, are all refuted by the scenario evaluation in Table 5.

The case study illustrates that the postulate that the lack of attention to quantitative information could be a significant contributing factor to the two decades of disappointing LED outcomes in South Africa can be accepted.

By applying the research of Kuhn (1970), it becomes clear that the paradigms underlying LED policies and plans are outdated. Based on the research of Argyris (1977), a comprehensive inquiry, in other words double loop learning, should be used for in-depth debates on the paradigms underlying South African LED policies and practices.

ACKNOWLEDGMENTS

The Centre for Environmental Management, University of the Free State provided general support. Alumnus services of the Massachusetts Institute of Technology provided online scholarly journal access. Marie Toerien and Estelle Zeelie provided technical assistance.

REFERENCES

Argyris, C. (1977). Double loop learning in organizations. *Harvard Business Review* (September-October 1977): 115-124.

Bartik. J. (1991). *Who benefits from state and local economic development policies?* Report: W. E. Upjohn Institute for Employment Research, Kalamazoo, Michigan.

Bettencourt, L. M. A., Lobo, J., Helbing, D., Kühnert, C. and West, G. B. (2007a). Growth, innovation, scaling, and the pace of life in cities. *PNAS* 104(17): 7301–7306.

Bettencourt, L. M. A., Lobo, J. and Strumsky, D. (2007b). Invention in the city: Increasing returns to patenting as a scaling function of metropolitan size. *Research Policy* 36: 107–120.

Bettencourt, L. M. A., Lobo, J., Strumsky, D. and West, G. B. (2010). Urban scaling and its deviations: Revealing the structure of wealth, innovation and crime across cities. *PLoS ONE* 5(11): e13541. doi:10.1371/journal.pone.0013541.

Bettencourt, L. and West, G. (2010.) A unified theory of urban living. *Nature* 467: 912-913.

Campbell, M. (2016). A great place and not yet another declining small town: The case of Clarens, South Africa. *Urbani Izziv* 27(2): 138-148.

Local Economic Development Theory and Practice in South Africa   157

Christensen, J. D. and Van der Ree, K. (2008) Building inclusive local economies through promoting decent work. @local.glob 5: 2-8.

Cohen, D. (2010). *Key issues in local economic development in South Africa and a potential role for SALGA.* Pretoria. Report for the Department of Cooperative Governance and Traditional Affairs, Pretoria.

Department of Provincial and Local Government. (2006). *Stimulating and developing sustainable local communities: National framework for local economic development in South Africa (2006 – 2011).* Report, Department of Provincial and Local Government: Pretoria.

Department of Economic Development. (undated). *Black Economic Empowerment.* Report accessed at: http://www.economic.gov.za/ about-us/programmes/economic-policy-development/b-bbee.

Donaldson, R., Van Niekerk, A., Du Plessis, D. and Spocter, M. (2012a). Non-metropolitan growth potential of Western Cape Municipalities. *Urban Forum* 23: 367–389. DOI 10.1007/s12132-011-9139-4.

Donaldson R, Spocter M, Du Plessis D and Van Niekerk A (2012b). Towards generic interventions to stimulate growth potential in small towns of the Western Cape Province, South Africa. *South African Geographic Journal* 94(2): 120–136.

Erasmus, B. P. J. (2004). *Op pad in Suid-Afrika.* (in *Afrikaans: On the road in South Africa*) 2nd Ed. Johannesburg: Jonathan Ball.

Feiock, R. C. (1991). The effects of economic development policy on local economic growth. *American Journal of Political Science* 35(3): 643-655.

Florida, R. (2002). *The rise of the creative class.* New York: Basic Books.

Hausmann, R. (2008). *Final recommendations of the International Panel on Growth.* Accessed at: http://www.treasury.gov.za/comm_media/press/ 2008/Final%20Recommendations%20of%20the%20International%20 Panel.pdf.

Hausmann, R., Hidalgo, C. A., Bustos, S., Coscia, M., Chung, S., Jimenez, J., Simoes, A. and Yıldırım, M. A. (2017). *The atlas of economic complexity: Mapping paths to prosperity.* Report, Center for International Development, Harvard University, Cambridge.

Hausmann, R. and Klinger, B. (2008). South Africa's export predicament. *Economics of Transition* 16(4): 609-637.

Herrington, M., Kew, J. and Kew, P. (2010). *Tracking entrepreneurship in South Africa: A GEM perspective.* Accessed at: https://www. researchgate.net/profile/Jacqui_Kew/contributions.

Herrington, M., Kew, J. and Kew, P. (2014). South Africa: *The crossroads – a goldmine or a time bomb?* Accessed at: https://www.research gate.net/profile/Jacqui_Kew/contributions.

Hoogendoorn, G. and Visser, G. (2016). South Africa's small towns: A review on recent research. *Local Economy* 31(1): 95-108.

Kahneman, D. (2011). *Thinking, fast and slow.* Kindle Edition. Amazon Digital Services LLC.

Kuhn, T. S. (1970). *The structure of scientific revolutions.* 2nd ed. Chicago: University of Chicago Press.

Marais, L. and Atkinson, D. (2006). Towards a post-mining economy in a small town: challenges, obstacles and lessons from South Africa. Presented at: *Desert Knowledge Conference*, Alice Springs, Australia, 2-4 November 2006.

National Planning Commission. (2011). *Our future - make it work. National Development Plan 2030.* Pretoria: National Planning Commission.

Ndlovu, M. and Makoni, E. N. (2014). The globality of the local? A decolonial perspective on local economic development in South Africa. *Local Economy* 29(4-5):503-518.

Nel, E. and Rogerson, C. M. (2016). The contested trajectory of applied local economic development in South Africa. *Local Economy* 31(1-2): 109-123.

Neumark, D., Zhang, J. and Wall, B. (2006). *Where the jobs are: Business dynamics and employment growth.* Academy of Management Perspectives 20(4): 79-94.

Republic of South Africa (2000). Act No. 32, 2000: Local Government: Municipal Systems Act. *Government Gazette* 425, no. 21776.

Rodriques-Pose, A. and Fitjar, R. (2013). Buzz, archipelago economics and the future of intermediate and peripheral areas in a spiky world. *European Planning Studies* 21(3): 355-372.

Rogerson, C. M. (2008). Consolidating local economic development in South Africa. *Urban Forum* 19(3): 307-28.

Rogerson, C. M. (2009). *Strategic Review of Local Economic Development in South Africa.* Final Report, Department of Provincial and Local Government, Pretoria.

Rogerson, C. M. and Rogerson, J. M. (2012). Business development and local economic development in South Africa: addressing the disconnect. *Acta Academica* 44(2): 41-69.

Schumpeter, J. A. (1942). *Capitalism, socialism and democracy.* Third Ed. New York: Harper Colophon.

Statistics South Africa (2017). *Quarterly labour force survey – QLFS Q3:2017.* Accessed at: http://www.statssa.gov.za.

Toerien, D. F. (2012). Enterprise proportionalities in the tourism sector of South African towns. In: M. Kasimoglu, (Ed), *Visions of global tourism industry: Creating and sustaining competitive strategies.* Rijeka: Intech. pp. 113-138. http://dx.doi.org/10.5772/37319.

Toerien, D. F. (2014). *The enterprise architecture of Free State towns.* Technical Report 2014, DTK. Accessed at: https://www.rescarch gate.net/profile/Daan_Toerien/publications.

Toerien, D. F. (2015a). New utilization/conservation dilemmas in the Karoo, South Africa: potential economic, demographic and entrepreneurial consequences. In: G. Ferguson, (Ed), *Arid and semi-arid environments: Biogeodiversity, impacts and environmental challenges.* New York: Nova Science Publishers.

Toerien, D. F. (2015b). Economic value addition, employment, and enterprise profiles of local authorities in the Free State, South Africa. *Cogent Social Sciences,* 1: 1054610 http://dx.doi.org/10.1080/233118 86.2015.1054610.

Toerien, D. F. (2017). The enduring and spatial nature of the enterprise richness of South African towns. *South African Journal of Science* 113(3/4), Art. #2016-0190, 8 pages.

Toerien, D. F. and Seaman, M. T. (2010) The enterprise ecology of towns in the Karoo, South Africa. *South African Journal of Science* 106(5/6): 24–33.

Toerien, D. F. and Seaman, M. T. (2011). Ecology, water and enterprise development in selected rural South African towns. *Water SA* 37(1): 47–56.

Toerien, D. F. and Seaman, M. T. (2012a). Proportionality in enterprise development of South African towns. *South African Journal of Science.* 108(5/6):38–47. http://dx.doi.org/10.4102/sajs.v108i5/6.588.

Toerien, D. F. and Seaman, M. T. (2012b). Regional order in the enterprise structures of selected Eastern Cape Karoo towns. *South African Geographic Journal* 94(2):1–15. http://dx.doi.org/10.1080/03736245. 2012.742782.

Toerien, D. F. and Seaman, M.T. (2012c). Evidence of island effects in South African enterprise ecosystems. In: A. Mahamane, (Ed.) *The functioning of ecosystems.* Rijeka: Intech; pp. 229–248. http://dx.doi.org/10.5772/36641.

Toerien, D. F. and Seaman, M. T. (2012d). *Paradoxes, the tyranny of structures and enterprise development in South African towns.* Presented at: *Strategies to Overcome Poverty and Inequality: Towards Carnegie3;* Sep 3–7; Cape Town, South Africa. Accessed at: http://carnegie3.org.za/docs/papers/269_Toerien_Paradoxes,%20the% 20tyranny%20of%20structures%20and%20enterprise%20development %20in%20SA%20towns.pdf.

Toerien, D. F. and Seaman, M. T. (2014). Enterprise richness as an important characteristic of South African towns. *South African Journal of Science* 110(11/12). Art. #2014-0018, 9 pages. http://dx.doi.org/10.1590/ sajs.2014/20140018.

Van der Merwe, I., Ferreira, S. and Zietsman, L. (2005). An investment strategy for effective town development in the Western Cape, South Africa. *Urban Forum* 16(4): 295-312.

Van Niekerk, A., du Plessis, D., Boonzaaier, I., Spocter, M., Ferreira, S., Loots, L. and Donaldson, R. (2016). Development of a multi-criteria spatial planning support system for growth potential modelling in the Western Cape, South Africa. *Land Use Policy* http://dx.doi.org/ 10.1016/j.landusepol.2015.09.014.

Wessels, J. (2016). *Cooperatives: has the dream become a nightmare?* Accessed at: http://www.econ3x3.org/sites/default/files/articles/Wessels%202016%20Cooperatives%20-%20FINAL.pdf.

Wessels, J. and Nel, E. (2016). A new co-operative revolution in South Africa? Reflections on the outcomes of state support in The Free State Province. *Local Economy* 31(1-2): 187-203.

West, G. (2017). *Scale: The universal laws of life and death in organisms, cities and companies.* London: Weidenfeld & Nicolson.

Western Cape Government (2017). *Municipal Economic Review and Outlook 2017.* Report, Provincial Treasury: Cape Town.

Youn, H., Bettencourt, L. M. A., Lobo, J., Strumsky, D., Samaniego, H. and West, G. B. (2016). Scaling and universality in urban economic diversification. *Journal of the Royal Society Interface* 13: 20150937.

In: The Power of Entrepreneurship
Editor: Daan Dirksen

ISBN: 978-1-53615-114-5
© 2019 Nova Science Publishers, Inc.

Chapter 5

WHO IS AN ACADEPRENEUR? TOWARDS A CONCEPTUAL FRAMEWORK OF ACADEPRENEURSHIP

Raouf Jaziri, PhD*

College of Business, University of Jeddah, Saudi Arabia
Researcher, LAREMFIQ-University of Sousse, Tunisia
Researcher, COSTECH-
University of Technology of Compiègne, France

ABSTRACT

"Academic entrepreneurship" is a polyphonic concept. Therefore, there is no precise definition adopted unanimously by researchers within the field of entrepreneurship research. However, the emergence of the neologism of "acadepreneurship," seeks the transcription of an entrepreneurial logic within the university mainly in its extrapreneurial and intrapreneurial dimension. This article emphasises the dilemma proposed by the new concept of "acadepreneurship" especially its two facets of *intrapreneuring* (intrapreneurship) and *extrapreneuring* (extrapren-

---

* Corresponding Author Email: raouf.jaziri@uc.rnu.tn.

eurship). In fact, we want to stress boundaries of the "academic entrepreneurship" and to draw a conceptual framework of the neologisms of both "acadepreneurship" and "acadepreneur."

Keywords: acdepreneurship, acadepreneur; academic entrepreneurship, entrepreneurial university, intrapreneurship, extrapreneurship

1. INTRODUCTION

It is increasingly recognized that the University is an essential vector of nations' development (Aligaweesa, 1987; Bramwell & Wolfe, 2008; Mosha, 1986; Cooper, 2009). The vast number of challenges facing universities in the 21st century imposes their contribution to the economic development as a "third mission" in addition to learning and research (Etzkowitz et al., 2000). In fact, new concepts have emerged such as "entrepreneurial university" (Etzkowitz, 1989; 1998; 2000; 2002; 2004; Clark, 1998), "Intellectual Entrepreneurship" or "academic capitalism" (Slaughter & Leslie, 1997).

The university became an entrepreneurial organization, a "quasi-firm" (Etzkowitz, 2003) or even inevitable "academic enterprise" (Marginson & Considine, 2000; Gingras, 2003), having as quest profitability and performance (Hébert, 2001; Giroux, 2006; (Haeussler & Colyvas, 2011). According to this model university, academic institutions are becoming increasingly dynamic and serve as a basis for innovation and regional development (Van Vught, 1999; Bramwell & Wolfe, 2008; Barnett 2000; Brennan et al., 2005; Jaziri & Paturel, 2010).

According to Etzkowitz et al., (2000), "The entrepreneurial academic paradigm has normative as well as analytical components. To be active, rather than merely formal innovation agents, universities must undergo a first academic revolution, the incorporation of research as an academic mission". They added that universities should reach the second revolution play a crucial role in economics development through the extension of their research and teaching models.

Based on this perspective that the university continues to have an effect in attracting entrepreneurial action insofar as it allows their actors (students, teachers, researchers, administrative staff, etc.) and project leaders to benefit from the actions of the latter in the field of entrepreneurship (Van der Sijde et al., 2008; Kirby, 2011). Seeing these considerations, it is clear that the university and entrepreneurship have been separated for a long time. However, the two subjects became gradually concubines and their alliance took place officially in the United States in the 80s after the signing of the Bayh-Dole Act known also as "University and Small Business Patent Procedures Act" December 12, 1980 . Already, university and entrepreneurship have become inseparable (Stankiewicz, 1986; Schmitt & Bayad, 2001). Strengthening the relationship between university and indenture entrepreneurship has grown considerably and has steadily become more widespread in the societies in which we operate. In fact, we are witnessing the development of an "entrepreneurial capitalism" which is, according to these authors, the third generation of industrial capitalism still described by Armand Hatchuel (2005) as "Entrepreneurial Revolution".

In this chapter we will review the research literature on both entrepreneurial university and academic entrepreneurship, in order to underline the bounderies of new concepts of acadepreneurship and acadepreneur.

2. GENESIS OF THE "ENTREPRENEURIAL UNIVERSITY"

According to David Kirby (2011), the concept of the "entrepreneurial university" was used for the first time by the sociologist Henry Etzkowitz in 1983 to describe universities have implemented several mechanisms, through their research, in order to contribute to regional development and to increase their own resources in terms of revenue. Therefore, several terms have been used by different authors to designate these universities as "University Technology Transfer" (Dill, 1995), "Innovative Universities" (Clark, 1998; Van Vught, 1999) and "university-market" (Slaughter and Leslie, 1997).

Table 1. Key definitions of the entrepreneurial university

Authors	Definitions
Etzkowitz (1983)	Universities are considering new sources of funds such as: patents, concluding research contracts and entering into a partnership with a private company
Chrisman et al. (1995)	The Entrepreneurial University is "the creation of new businesses by university professors, technicians and students
Dill (1995)	University technology transfer is defined by the formal efforts made to focus on academic research by exploiting the results of research through the creation of business ventures. Formal efforts are in turn defined as organizational units with explicit responsibility to promote technology transfer
Clark (1998)	Entrepreneurial university seeks to innovate in how it goes for businesses. It seeks to work on a substantial organizational change in order to achieve a more promising posture for the future. Entrepreneurial universities seeking to become "stand-up" universities, which are important players in their own words
Röpke (1998)	An entrepreneurial university can mean three things: (1) the university itself as an organization is entrepreneurial, (2) members of the university (faculty, students, employees) become themselves a entrepreneurs in some way, and (3) the interaction between the university environment and "structural coupling" between the university and the region, following a entrepreneurial pattern
Subotzky (1999)	The entrepreneurial university is characterized by strong university-industry partnerships, a greater responsibility and ability to access external sources of funding and a mangement ethics of corporate governance, leadership and planning.
Kirby (2002)	At the midst of entrepreneurial culture, entrepreneurial universities have the capacity to innovate, identify and create opportunities, work in teams, take risks and meet the challenges
Etzkowitz (2003)	Just as the University that trains students and sends them into the professional world, the entrepreneurial university is a natural incubator, providing support structures for teachers and students to initiate new intellectual, commercial and joint *projects*
Jacob, et al. (2003)	An entrepreneurial university based both on marketing (education courses, consulting services) and standardization (patents, licenses or creation of star-up by students)
Jaziri (2014)	The entrepreneurial university is an innovative academic institution that improves both intrapreneurial and extrapreneurial action among its members (teachers, researchers, students, employees).

The literature shows the existence of several definitions of "entrepreneurial university", and the absence of a consensus around this concept (see Table 1). Kirby (2011) added that there are some similar factors that influence these "entrepreneurial universities", as:

- the strong relationship between universities, government and industry;
- their different sources of income;
- a strong entrepreneurial potential among members of the university (students, academics and teachers);
- implementation of strategies and actions leading to encouraging the creation of new businesses.

Referring to the pioneering work of Henry Etzkowitz (1989, 1996, 1998, 2000, 2002, 2003), Burton Clark (1998, 2000, 2001, 2002, 2003) and David Kirby (2002, 2011), an entrepreneurial university is able to seize opportunities, to innovate, to mobilize collective action and take risks. Thus, the entrepreneurial university is a "natural incubator" that guarantees support structures and support for members of the university (faculty, students.) to set up new intellectual and commercial projects.

3. SCOPE AND LIMITS OF THE CONCEPT OF "ACADEMIC ENTREPRENEURSHIP"

Since 1970 until today, the entrepreneurial culture that began in American universities seems prevalent in many countries or regions, including Canada (Milot, 2005) and Europe (Jones-Evans, 1998).

Some European authors have conducted pioneering research on "academic entrepreneurship", for example Dylan Jones-Evans has prepared a report for the European Commission (1998) entitled "Universities, technology transfer and spin-off activities: academic entrepreneurship in different european regions. "This report presents a detailed examination of the process of technology transfer from European universities to industry. This study was conducted in seven different regions of Europe, Spain, Finland, Ireland, Northern Ireland, the Wales, Portugal and Sweden. Emphasis was placed on five distinct points with:

- factors affecting the development of academic entrepreneurship in seven regions of the European Community;
- policies and practices pursued by the university towards the university corps and the development of the entrepreneurial spirit, focusing in particular on university-industry liaison;
- the identification of "good institutional practices" of the university in each region, and the analysis of their initiatives in developing closer links with industry;
- analysis of profiles of entrepreneurs (the type of activities created, the influence of personal and professional university, etc..) from universities in different studied regions, in order to emerge an idea of the degree involvement of entrepreneurs in the phenomenon of academic entrepreneurship;
- the elucidation of specific activities created by academics. Activities include academic entrepreneurship case of contract research, consulting activities, patenting and registration of inventions, as well as the creation of spin-offs from members of the university (Table 2).

Stankiewicz (1986, p : 93) said that "Entrepreneurship is more than a constellation of skills or an individual aptitude. It is a way of life, a culture. It thrives in some groups, and is almost wholly absent in others. Many academic communities, particularly in Europe, have traditionally belonged to the second category. It is hard to see how this state of affairs can be changed without transforming the academic monoculture into a more pluralistic one"

For their part, the authors Henrekson & Rosenberg (2000) have considered the concept of "academic entrepreneurship" as a term used to mean hypernym marketing knowledge produced starting university.

Table 2. Activites of the Academic Entrepreneurship

Activities	Descriptions
Large scale science project	Get research projects funded largely from outside or through public subsidies or through resources from industry
Contracted research	Undertake specific research projects within the university system to external organizations
Consulting	The sale of a scientific or technological expertise to solve a personal problem specific
Patenting /licencing	The use of patents or licenses, from the results of research by industry
Spin off firms	The creation of a new business or organization through the use of the results of university research
External teaching	Organization of short courses for non-academic staff and external organizations
Sales	Commercialization of products developed within the university
Testing	Testing and calibration of dedicated individuals and organizations external

"We use this term in a broad generic sense to refer to a variety of ways in which academics go beyond the production of potentially useful knowledge. They also undertake a variety of initiatives to facilitate the commercialization of that knowledge, that is to say, they become active participants in designing new marketable products and take some sort of leadership role in ensuring successful commercialization."

In the same order of ideas, several definitions have been proposed by various authors (Stankiewicz, 1986; Bird and Allen, 1989; Chrisman, Hynes and al, 1995; Slaughter and Leslie, 1997; Henrekson and Rosenberg, 2000; Franklin and al, 2001; Rasmussen, 2004; Shane, 2004a; Mendes., Kehoe, 2007; Van Der Sijde 2008), while using generic terms as close to :

- Industry-university collaborations;
- university-based venture funds;
- university-based incubator firms;
- start-up founding by academicians;

- double appointments of faculty members in firms and academic departments.

Louis, Blumenthal, Gluck, and Stoto (1989: 110) distinguish five activities of the "academic entrepreneurship" as follows:

1) engagement in science scale (externally placed);
2) gain of additional income;
3) support the industry to fund research at the University;
4) obtaining patents or production of trade secrets;
5) an ownership form of contribution in industry, in the capital of companies established on the basis of research from academics.

Bird and Allen (1989) focused their definition of " academic entrepreneurship " on "consulting activity and involvement in new venture creation as entrepreneurial faculty behaviour"

Chrisman, Hynes and al. (1995: 268), in turn, defined "Academic entrepreneurship" in a more narrow way, holding : "the creation of new business ventures by university professors, technicians or students"

Scott Shane (2004a: 4) includes in the "academic entrepreneurship": "the creation of a new company to exploit a piece of intellectual property created in an academic institution."

Brennan and al. (2005, p 308) confirmed that "many academics and students are increasingly involved in academic entrepreneurship activities through consultancy, procurement, contracts with the private sector, joint ventures, spin-out, spin-in and management of intellectual capital. "

The empirical study by Wright et al., (2008), on "academic entrepreneurship" in universities "mid-range" from Germany, Belgium, the United Kingdom (UK) and Sweden showed that these

mid-range universities can contribute to industrial change through the transfer of tacit and codified knowledge in the areas of spin-offs; licensing and patents; contract research, consultancy and reach-out; and graduate and researcher mobility.

Philpott and al. (2011) have, for their part, held that the entrepreneurial paradigm, within the university can take nine activities namely: " nine activities that span across the traditional academic paradigm to the entrepreneurial paradigm, namely: producing highly qualified graduates; publishing academic results; grantsmanship; consulting; industry-training courses; contract research; patenting and licensing; spin-off firm formation; and creation of technology parks ".

It is clear from all the above studies and definitions that the concept of "academic entrepreneurship", has limitations that make us move toward a neologism that is more accepted by the entrepreneurship research community which can serve as "appetizer" for further research on this emerging phenomenon. These limits are reduced to three that seem very relevant for the rest of our analysis, including: focusing on the aspect of extrapreneurial action, and the reduction of the phenomenon to the business creation ex nihilo and marginalizing the overtaking dimension.

4. Towards a Definition of "Acadepreneurship" and "Acadepreneur"

Conceptual boundaries, already mentioned, which undermine the notion of "academic entrepreneurship" in its meanings in French and Anglo-Saxon, and the absence of a definition of the phenomenon led some authors to advance alternative definitions of general application (Chrisman et al., 1995). Rasmussen, in 2004, said that:

> "Obviously, entrepreneurship in universities can take many forms. However, the study of university spin-offs is only one form, and is by definition limited to new firm creation."

According to Mendes and Kehoe (2007, p:6),

> "The most common definition of entrepreneurship in an academic context that emerged was 'encouraging faculty, students, and

administrators to work, act and think differently about opportunity recognition and identification of resources to pursue new ideas."

Sample definitions offered by the administrators were:

- Being innovative in the classroom;
- Applying problem solving and creativity to all academic disciplines;
- Being innovative in research; transferring intellectual capital into ideas and products that are either marketable or that can be applied in new settings;
- Managing careers entrepreneurially;
- Encouraging students, faculty, and administrators to work, act and think differently.

For his part, Van Der Sijde (2008, p: 33), defines more clearly the academic entrepreneurship. He argues that:

> "Academic entrepreneurship is the creation of an environment for (active support of) knowledge exploitation, stimulation of entrepreneurial behavior among all the members of and institutional structures in the academic community."

In this point of view, it should be noted that a minority of french researchers regard universities as entrepreneurial organizations in at least some of their activities (Pirnay, 2001; Emin, 2003; Jaziri, 2007; 2009; 2014), or intrapreneurial (Champagne & Carrier, 2004, Paturel, 2005, 2007, 2008; Jaziri, 2007; Jaziri and Paturel, 2008a, 2008 b, 2009, 2010; Saffu, 2003; Anu, 2007). But few, however, the work focused on intrapreneurship in non-profit organizations, particularly in universities (Jaziri, 2007). Champagne & Carrier (2004) stipulated that "a renewed interest seems to emerge over the past two years [with] intrapreneurship in an academic context." These authors asked the following question: Have our universities need intrapreneurs, whether to create institutes or research chairs, develop new programs and innovative teaching approaches? Champagne and Carrier

Who Is an Acadepreneur?

(2004) have proposed a line of research whose aim was to encourage action "acadepreneurs." Paturel (2006), stated that

> "an official of the National Education training institute creating a non-existent so far in the region where the university or laboratory based research useful for the local economy, is unambiguously entrepreneurial situation."

In his study in 38 Australian universities on teaching entrepreneurship, Saffu (2003) defined the acadepreneur in a unique way as a university "*academic champions*" for the establishment of a curriculum of entrepreneurship within academic institutions. The main purpose was to analyze what will be the role that the academic champion can play inside the entrepreneurship programs. His study led to results that shown that well-established and organized entrepreneurship programs in both grade and undergrad are deeply associated with the "academic champions" or the acadepreneurs who envisioned the programs. *"It is noteworthy that rank appears to be important in the entrepreneurial role played by these academic champions."* (Op. Cit, 2003. p. 2).

Similarly to Saffu (2003), Anu (2007), for its part, has defined the acadepreneur as:

> "an academic champion within a university setting who envisions, starts and grows a program irrespective of whether he/she has the resources. Implicitly, the process not only leads to the creation of new academic offerings, but also to other creative activities."

Based on our review of the literature, it seems that only three francophone authors have specifically used the concept of "acadepreneurship" in their researches (Carrier, 2000; Paturel, 2005; Jaziri, 2007; Jaziri & Paturel, 2008; 2009; 2010; Jaziri, 2013; 2014), however only two Anglo-Saxon authors have used the term "acadepreneur" (Saffu, 2003; Anu, 2007).

Therefore, the pioneers in advancing a definition of this neologism are Jaziri & Paturel (2008a). In fact, they define acadepreneurship as:

174   *Raouf Jaziri*

the phenomenon by which a member of the university (student, employee, researcher, teacher) creates or takeover a new or an existing activity administratively or financially dependent on the university without leaving it (Intrapreneurship action). Similarly, he may create or takeover a legally independent organization of the university while dropping (possibly temporarily) it (Extrapreneurship action). To use the term acadepreneur, he must undergo (alone or with a team) an intense change in his position, profession, geographic or organizational location. He must create a new value (in case of creation ex nihilo) or obtain an existing value (in case of overtake) from the entity that he try to impulse it.

According to this definition that the phenomenon of acadepreneurship reflects two great entrepreneurial dimensions: extrapreneurship and intrapreneurship.

It seems that this definition is highly instructive insofar as it is generating an original typology. Accordingly, the acadepreneur or "academic entrepreneur" can have four different configurations as shown in the following table 3.

Table 3. Different types of Acadepreneurship

	Ex-nihilo Creation	Takeover
Intrapreneurship (intrapreneuring action)	Type-1 Acadepreneur Intrapreneur-Founder Creating a new academic activity dependent from University (Institute, laboratory, etc.)..	Type-2 Acadepreneur Intrapreneur-Takeover Takeover the management of an existing academic activity dependent from university (Institute, laboratory, etc.)
Extrapreneurship (extrapreneuring action)	Type-3 Acadepreneur Spinoff-Founder Creation of spin-off university (Shane, 2004a; 2004b).	Type-4 Acadepreneur Spinoff-Takeover Takeover an existing business and independent from university.

Source: Jaziri, 2014 (p: 97).

The first horizontal reading of the table, particularly focusing on the dimension of the intrapreneurial acadepreneurship allows us to distinguish Type I and II acadepreneurs as follows:

- *Type-1 acadepreneur (Intrapreneur-Founder):* he begins by creating a new activity or organization financially or administratively dependent on the university (new academic institution, new laboratory or research unit, new diploma, new national or international cooperation, etc.) without leaving it. That is to say, he retains his status as an employee. The purposes of our analysis, we consider Type I acadepreneur : *Any intentioned academic practicing full time in university that creates or contributes actively to the creation of a new intra-university activity, under the administrative or financial authority of the university in question.*

- *Type-2 acadepreneur (Intrapreneur-Takeover):* he begins and takes an activity or academic organization administratively or financially dependent on existing public university (institutions, laboratory or research unit, etc.) without leaving it. We see that this called acadepreneur intrapreneur-takeover; since it takes, an academic activity that has been assigned previously to another can be acadepreneur itself as founder or buyer. In this regard, we consider Type II acadepreneur: *Any intentioned academic practicing full time in the university took over the management of an existing intra-university activity (laboratory, research unit, department, etc.), under the administrative or financial authority of an university, while remaining constant as an employee in higher education sector.*

However, the second horizontal reading of the table on the extrapreneurial dimension shows that acadepreneur can take two forms especially Type III and IV:

- *Type-3 acadepreneur (a spinoff-founder)*: He is a person who undertakes to create spin-off (Extrapreneurship) as a new organization or company legally independent of the university, while leaving the latter (spin off organization) in order to invest on its own account, through an academic idea or not. It opts for the creation ex nihilo of a spin-off university through the exploitation of an academic (Pirnay, 2001) or not (Jaziri et Paturel, 2009). In this sense, we can propose the following definition of Type III acadepreneur: *Any member of the University who, as intentioned actor deliberately deciding to leave his university in the context of a spin-off policy, while exploiting an academic idea or not, to create a new business or an economic activity, legally and financially independent from the university. The spin-offs university are only one facet of the Type III acadepreneurship insofar as this academic entrepreneur operate an academic idea.*

- *Type-4 acadepreneur (a spinoff- takeover)*: He takes an organization-offs or existing business legally independent of the university. This begins by an acadepreneur extraprise while leaving the organization in particular spin off university. However, this dimension of spin or university spin-offs has not been addressed in recent work on the university spin-offs (Jaziri & Paturel, 2008, 2009, 2010, Jaziri, 2014). In this context, we define as Type IV acadepreneur: *Any member of the University or intentioned stakeholder deliberately decided to leave his home university within a university spin-off policy in order to acquire a business or economic activity for profit, existing, with individuals.*"

It should be noted that acadepreneurs of Types I, II and IV have not been addressed by researchers in entrepreneurship. However, analysis of both Shane (2004a) and Pirnay (2001) can serve as a basis to explain the process and the development of a class of Type III acadepreneurs through the creation ex nihilo of university spin-offs exploiting an idea and to identify academic, at least in part, the acadepreneurship. Figure 1 illustrates different facets of acadepreneurship.

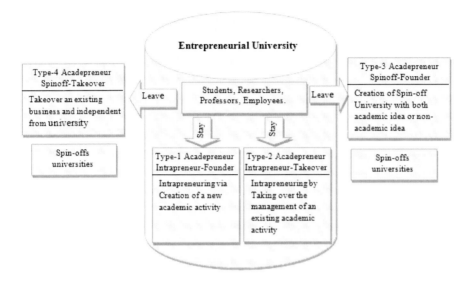

Figure 1. Different types of acadepreneurs.

5. THE ESSENTIAL CHARACTERISTICS OF THE ACADEPRENEUR

Leadership is the driver and engine of innovation and entrepreneurship attitude. The entrepreneurial action starts from an idea that university make it strong and rich by providing a helpful atmosphere which can lead students and professors to be more motivated to invest and create companies. The educational system doesn't show a high integration of this potential. Leadership is taught in different ways but the stimulation of the entrepreneurship behavior missed the way at least in many of the academic programs. The entrepreneurial orientation of the academic stuff and students can be solo or by the creation of group work and intelligence investment coalition inside universities. Few of startup started from the university and the cooperation between industry and academic stakeholders especially in developing countries is suffering from a lack of serious initiative. From this point we believe that universities should review their programs to make them more aligned with their capacity of preparing future entrepreneurs and enhance their cooperation models with the industry and investment word more seriously and deeply. Leadership is the key point that can allow this marriage between the two elements that lead to a real acadepreneur creation. Social activity and entrepreneurial labs and organization inside the university will be the start point of this leadership development. The new models of teaching in entrepreneurship and innovation will help the stimulation of the faculty and students' entrepreneurial attitudes through emulating a climate that helps creativity and innovation to flourish.

Within a motivating entrepreneurial atmosphere inside universities an acadepreneur will not only learn how to do, but he will study, learn, and do. Moreover his interaction with the industry key stakeholders will allow to the acadepreneur enhancing his leadership style and switching the knowledge received from the theoretical side to implement it in the real business world. By doing virtually or really the acdepreneur from the different level presented in Figure 1 will add value and contribute to the crafting and executing of part or the whole sides of business. We think that acting in such environment the acadepreneur will get the chance to test his capacity and capability of being an effective entrepreneur in the future. Generating and brainstorming ideas not only enhance the capacity of investing, but excel the acadepreneur behavior in term of innovation and creativity. Another important character that the academic environment provides to the acadepreneur skills is the attitude and capability of problem solving. The understanding of multiple business case studies will serve as bridge that prepare the acadepreneur to act efficiently in a fragile and changeable business environment. The academic program should show more inspiring model of acadepreneur and keep in touch with success stories that can help to develop fresh students and motivated faculty to follow their investing models. The idea that we provide at this level is to give university actors more chance to behave as entrepreneur especially student by giving them more responsibilities in term of leading projects and running business cases inside their courses. A partnership relation between the professors and students will allow better understanding of the leadership capacity of students and push them to think as investors who have to solve daily issues and interact with other classmates and faculties as suppliers and customers. The main purpose inside the course won't be just learning and grade, but a win/win business strategy. This kind of interaction will create a natural and implicit work environment inside the university based on problem solving and opportunities detection. Such situation is empowering the quality of education and lead to more investing attitude between students and faculty members. Beside this, the remodeling of the teaching styles and academic programs provide a concept of entrepreneurial culture that takes in consideration all the key success factors. In this case, the innovation and creativity will be the result of the differentiation between classes, universities, and fields of study. Acadepreneurs will take advantage of the culture and values spread inside their academic environment then develop their "right & rich vision" of what their business will be. To ensure this situation, universities should make the acadepreneur comfortable and self-confident. For this to happen, Universities must be well organized and open to innovation and new conceptualization of what business can be. A standard and typical courses that campus offer today seems basic and ordinary, thing that can kill innovation and more than this it can be a barrier to be entrepreneurial oriented or motivated. Otherwise, entrepreneurship must be a top priority in the educational programs whatever the field is.

Through the analysis of the majority of academic programs we detected that few of them enhance the entrepreneurship attitude inside students- the majority of the programs that invested in this philosophy are MBA programs provided by prestigious colleges and universities- no shortage in academia shown people able to adept decision making, interpretation, and enforcing rules. A huge lack of this initiative is especially notice in the undergrad programs where universities focus more in providing the "Know" and not the "Know how."

Jaziri & Paturel define an acadepreneur as:

> "any person who can get the responsibility while studying or teaching in his academic environment, shows leadership, decision making and

capacity of running business during his studies curses or after finishing his degree that finalized by establishing a small or big business by himself or in partnership with other stakeholders from inside the academia or outside of it. In other word, the acadepreneur is the person who study, learn, and do and who can get back to learn by doing then study again. More than this, the acadepreneur is the one who get inspired and serve as a source of inspiration for entrepreneurs based on his academic skills, and knowledge sharing culture."

At a regular biweekly meeting chaired by a newly appointed dean of the College of Arts and Sciences and attended by all of her senior lieutenants, one senior associate dean gave a long explanation about a set of rules that prohibited a particular course of action. The dean asked, "Well, who made these rules anyway?" After a long silence someone said, "Well, I guess we did." "Precisely," the dean replied, "and we can also change them." The story of this encounter has been retold countless times, most recently by the new dean of the same college in describing her approach to the job. She said she used to think the dean's job was to help people understand the rules and, where necessary, work around them. She now thinks the job is to evaluate the rules and, where appropriate, change them.

Strong leaders understand the viral effects of a story like this. Such stories help people understand that rules can be changed if necessary to achieve institutional priorities. Effective leaders see opportunities to impact university culture in virtually every action they take, from how they organize their office to how they conduct meetings — and especially in how they spend their time. If they stay at the job long enough, the culture will come to reflect their own personalities and views of the world. A leader with an informal style who has a habit of asking questions and enough humility to welcome advice will create a very different culture from that of a leader with a formal personality. Good leaders are clear both about their role in creating a culture and about the culture they seek to create.

Efficient acadepreneur typically have a business culture and academic backup to his decision making, a respectful capacity of solving complex and nuanced problems, beside a willingness to face and challenge the new businesses assumptions. While problem solving, culture, and decision making are characters of any ordinary entrepreneurs, acadepreneurs are distinguished with their academic orientation and dependence on the university culture and mentality of doing based on study and learning process. In this case the analysis and gathering process will give them an added value comparing to the ordinary entrepreneurs.

In the light of the definition of acadepreneurship we proposed earlier, its essential characteristics can be listed as follows.

5.1. The Acadepreneur Is a Member of the University

All members of the academic community are likely to create or resume an activity dependent or independent of the university, regardless of the status they occupy and functions that they perform. In fact, acadepreneurs are internal stakeholders of the university (see Chapter 2). They are also members and actors of this social organization. They can be:

- *Students*: within the meaning of Pirnay (2001), students can create business after leaving the university, in the form of spin-offs students in a research project operator or the content of a dissertation studies. However, in our view, they can also take existing businesses (e.g., a family), while leaving the university or lead in this project of intrapreneurial culture, arts, associations, scientists, etc.
- *Employees:* they can leave school temporarily or permanently to create or acquire a business, and if that fails, they regain their original position due to the characteristics of the spin-off policy of their home university;
- *Researchers:* They are members of the laboratories and units of basic or applied research. They can create or acquire a business by exploiting a patent in the form of university spin-offs within the meaning of Pirnay (2001). Similarly, in our view, they can intraprise within the university, without leaving her, while conducting innovative research projects putting their reputation on the line (Paturel 2006, Jaziri and Paturel 2008a);

- *Professors:* These are players who can take in creating university spin-offs or intraprise in conducting research or creating new activities within the university (Faculty, Institute ... etc.). Recovery of existing businesses or entities is not for them to exclude.

5.2. The Acadepreneur Creates a New Activity (Type-1) or Overtakes an Existing One (Type-2)

In this situation, the acadepreneur is a member of the University engaged in a business of his employer legally dependent (change-mutation-geographical example more or less important depending on the location of the host university).

In fact, this activity must be under the administrative and financial university and, therefore, the acadepreneur not leave its parent organization. The acadepreneur, in this case, is in a situation of Intraprise or academic intrapreneurship (Type I and Type II). The activity can be exploited at the various types of projects that we return below:

- *Cultural, artistic or events' project*: this type of intrapreneurship is illustrated by organizing an art show, a publishing project. It can also be achieved through the realization of an event: conference, lecture series, show, exhibition, competition, creation of a student festival or theme days.
- *Technological or scientific project:* this type of intrapreneurship projects includes making the forefront of technology and science.
- *Social economy project*: the primary purpose of social economy projects is to improve working conditions and living conditions of members of the organization. These projects encourage the sharing of various types of resources to provide services or products to specific users.
- *Community project*: This type of intrapreneurship includes projects where human values have paramount importance on economic values. These projects are designed to support or management of a

community or a group of individuals (students, graduates, teachers, immigrants, foreigners, etc.). The provision of advice (legal, management, taxation, market research, etc.) By a consulting office or health services to "customers" who need, is one example of academic community projects.

- *Project of self-employment:* Intrapreneurship also affects students who offer their services to organizations as self-employed or professionals in the fields of knowledge. These are characterized by strong competition and require thorough preparation on the part of those who work for a project of making a career of self-employed or to support the development of a larger project.

- *Proposed change project or development in a particular organization within the university*: it is the development and project management by teachers as new services (eg, creation of a performance monitoring unit external to the university, creating a new laboratory or a research unit), the development of a new product (a new diploma), the integration of a new information system or the creation of a new training and research.

- *Project related to a grouping of students*: the proposed project to boost students (alumni associations of students following the same training, etc.) can be recognized and supported by the university teachers.

5.3. The Acadepreneur Gets into Business with a New (Type-3) or an Existing (Type-4) Activity

The acadepreneur is a member of the university that can create (Type III) or resume (Type IV) a legally independent organization of the university station. On leaving the university to create or acquire a business, the wearer does not leave the cap of acadepreneur but remains academic entrepreneur as he holds in the university. In fact, it is not the academic origin of the idea which is acadepreneur concept, but the origin of the person. In this case, we find the analysis made by Pirnay (2001), in his thesis focused on the development of scientific research through the creation of Spin-offs University. Indeed, Pirnay, Surlemont and Nlemvo (2000) defined a university spin-off as "*a new company created from a university in order to exploit for profit, knowledge resulting from academic activities.*" However, according to our analysis, university spin-offs refer to a single facet of Type III acadepreneurship, since the original idea is purely academic and is exploited as results of scientific research within the university. Consequently, we can consider, among others, as university spin-offs companies created or taken by a member of the University or actor (student, teacher, researcher, administrative staff, technicians and workers of Services, etc.) while operating a non-academic idea.

In this perspective, an acadepreneur can be any member of the university founder (Type III) or buyer (Type IV) as a legal organization is independent of it, using or not an original academic idea. Therefore, it is deemed acadepreneur because it comes from the university regardless the origin of his idea.

5.4. The Acadepreneur Must Create New Value or Capture an Existing One

To be considered acadepreneur, the faculty member must create a new value or obtain an existing according to Paturel (2011). It is understood that a new entity created training or research in a given university (intrapreneurship), the value is most often new if it corresponds to a previously unmet need, but may, in some cases, be a redistribution of existing value when it comes to a competing structure to those already formed in neighboring universities. The concern of the proximity of providing training for students may then be the main reason for this creation. In the case of a university which takes an existing structure, the term "acadepreneur" can be attributed only if the buyer is a sufficient reputation and brings a novelty in the list of courses offered or far or specialty not invested in the Laboratory now headed. We therefore cannot qualify as an academic entrepreneur or acadepreneur, a director of a university organization (institute, faculty, school, university work, etc.) which contains (by appointment, election and appointment, etc.) without actually add value to the new regional economic environment. If a member of the University beyond the scope of its establishment engages in business, the same type of reasoning can be conducted according to it creates ex nihilo he takes his business or an organization. In both practices of entrepreneurship, university can get the new value (case when operating in laboratory discoveries and having a solvent demand) or existing (but redistributed to the new entity or a new responsible of an ancient structure), and often undergoes a change of intensity.

5.5. Acadepreneur Is a Risk Taker

Researches of Jaziri & Paturel (2008a, 2008b, 2009, 2010, and 2011) have shown that there is no need to risk his financial capital to be an entrepreneur, but he must risk something important, such as reputation, his "public image," credibility, etc. Thus, if the establishment of a training institute so far non-existent in the region where the university suggests that there is no risk-taking by the intrapreneur within the university by compared to the conventional definition which considers the entrepreneur as one who undertakes his own money and taking the risk of losing all or part failure. Indeed, the risk borne by the official of the university is not the commitment of his personal fortune, but rather on its reputation or notoriety, with negative consequences for the rest of his career if he fails. This is especially the nature of the exchange risk, but the risk does exist and is a characteristic of the academic intrapreneurship. However, all other features of the classical entrepreneur exist for the entrepreneur of a new non-profit organization in this case.

Although, it will be understood that if the faculty member, regardless of its function, a company based outside the university, it is in the same position as any entrepreneur classic compared to financial risk. Only possibility to regain its original position characterizes in case of failure, but experience shows that the return is psychologically far from easy…

5.6. The Acadepreneur Undergoes Significant Changes

According to Jaziri and Paturel (2010, 2011) the acadepreneur may have to manage a change of greater or lesser intensity depending on whether the manager is simply a part or all of the following factors change for him. Thus, he will in a situation of great change if changes:

- His *status* by becoming entrepreneur instead of official (case of extrapreneurship) in the case of intrapreneurship, the faculty member is official, but will get some autonomy in the conduct of the project, autonomy granted by the University President and the texts provided in managing the National Education;
- His *business sector* by abandoning his intervention at the University to embark on a new business: "Thus, the engineer employed in a research organization that offers its behalf to implement results of his research in a new legal structure will undergo a change smaller than the same engineer who decides to mount a bar or tobacco shop in a village he knows more or less"(Paturel, 2005a: 6);
- His *function* by taking responsibility as manager (if the teacher takes a leadership training institute new or existing, without any experience in the field or member of the University who founded his company he will without competence);
- His *structure* of assignment (if the teacher or researcher who request a transfer to another university to take the direction of a Faculty or a research laboratory that will create or that already existed with in this latter case, the addition of a new value in a specialty has not so far);
- His *location* (commune, department, region, etc.). Problems with all organizational and cultural integration will arise. We do not handle individuals and a social network in the same way in the North of France and in its South.

Who Is an Acadepreneur? 187

In summary, based on the work of Jaziri and Paturel (2009, 2010), we can say that the notion of *change for the individual*, is a set of modifications of several kinds suffered by the acadepreneur, including:

- changing its status relative to its starting position;
- the transition to a more or less related to his original profession;
- The transition to a leader based organization unrelated to the function previously exercised;
- Integration of an organization more or less different from the left one;
- Possible geographical mobility.

In fact, the greater the change suffered by the individual, the more he is in an entrepreneurial situation. Indeed, if the individual legally change of status (elected or appointed as a director or dean) to launch a university activity, in this case, requiring distinct expertise of its initial business in another academic institution legally independent its original organization, and located in a remote area from where he currently resides with his family suffered more change is important and difficult to manage. However, the individual can remain employed at the same time "boss" in the organization he resumed, while remaining close to home and pursuing traditional activities not new to him. In this case, unlike the previous example, the change suffered by the individual is purely hierarchical, but is not negligible.

After describing the characteristics of the acadepreneur, it seems appropriate to better identify the essential concept and the concept of a separate adjoining the leader.

6. ACADEPRENEUR VERSUS MANAGER

According to D'Amboise (1989), while the manger is a simple technocrat who brings his expertise as an employee, without participation in the property. In fact, bearing the risk is the key factor of differentiation between entrepreneurs and executive directors (Jaziri and Paturel, 2008). A second distinction concerns the entrepreneur and the owner-manager. Gasse (2002) believes that the entrepreneur is someone who runs a business founded by himself, while the owner-manager is the one who assumes the management of a company that he would not have created. More specifically, the term owner-manager that we use here refers to the individual dimension, in the context of D'Amboise and Gasse (1980), "participates in a significant stake in the company and who takes an active part in decisions on the direction of the company and to the solution of everyday problems of the latter."

As the original founder of the company or organization does not always in the direction of his work, there is often a blurred vision about the entrepreneur-manager, who is also regarded as a true entrepreneur because that there is also emotionally and financially committed by it.

To clarify our conceptual framework, we use the following distinction between entrepreneur and leader. Thus, we consider:

- *Manager:* just a technocrat who brings his expertise as an employee, without capturing new or existing value (Jaziri, 20013; 2014);
- *Entrepreneur:* who (alone or in teams), "from an idea [operates] an opportunity within an organization driven or created from scratch in a recovery first, then later developed [...] undergoes significant change in his life, a process that leads to the creation of a new value or economic value of existing waste" (Paturel, 2007a).

We can very well go from manager to entrepreneur and vice versa depending on the time of life of the organization. Indeed, an acadepreneur or a university entrepreneur can be a simple leader technocrat who creates or obtains any new or existing value. However, he can become acadepreneur when he helps to create or resume academic activities (research laboratory, institute, department, etc.)., While obtaining new or existing value. Conversely, an acadepreneur can simply convert a leader when he loses his capacity for innovation and creativity and focuses on the daily technocratic management. In the same vein, Paturel (2005, 2007) explained that you cannot assign the term entrepreneur to a salaried officer of an organization which is simply entrusted with the management of a new entity (if management of a subsidiary of a group) he has no control and ownership. However, it considers that the preservation of employee status within an organization combined with the responsibility of controlling a particular project entrusted to the employee in question (intrapreneurship or acadepreneurship) is an entrepreneurial activity, mainly because of the change depending on the individual (op. cit.). Indeed, the principal or Dean elected or appointed at the head of a university after a creation ex nihilo or after a recovery towards the existing structure, is in a entrepreneurial situation.

CONCLUSION

At the end of this chapter we have sketched out conceptual framework of the neologism of acadepreneurship. In fact, there are many possible future ways of research, because the field of acadepreneurship seems to be fertile for conducting subsequent research in the academic sphere. But our reflection underlines the extent to which the acadepreneurship is simultaneously a matter of both individual and collective action. Some institutional arrangements, some common values or conventions seem more entrepreneurial than others. At the same time, whether the university is strongly oriented towards acadepreneurship or not, some individuals will reveal themselves as acadepreneurs and others will not.

Finally, last but not least, this contribution puts only one stone to the building that is being built little by little around and on the neologism of acadepreneurship, on which the debate is far from being closed.

REFERENCES

Aligaweesa, M.A.K. (1987), The Role of a University in National Development: A Case Study of Makarere University, *Journal of Educational Administration.* Volume : 25, pp. 294 - 307

190 *Raouf Jaziri*

Anu, L. (2007), Fostering intrapreneurship: the new competitive Edge. *Conference on Global Competition & Competitiveness of Indian Corporate*, 1st, 2nd, June 2007, Radisson Hotel New Delhi, India.

Barnett, R. (2000), *The University in an Age of Super-Complexity, Society For Research into Higher Education*. Open University Press.

Bramwell, A., Wolfe, D-A. (2008), Universities and regional economic development: The entrepreneurial University of Waterloo. *Research Policy*, 37, pp.1175–1187.

Brennan, M.C., Wall, A.P., McGowan, P. (2005), Academic entrepreneurship: Assessing preferences in nascent entrepreneurs, *Journal of Small Business and Enterprise Development*, Vol. 12 Iss: 3, pp. 307 - 322

Champagne, D., Carrier, C. (2004), Intrapreneurship Studies: Objects of Interest and Research Pathways. *Proceding du 7ème CIFEPME.* Montpellier.

Chrisman, J., Hynes, T., Fraser, S. (1995). Faculty Entrepreneurship and Economic development: The Case of the University of Calgary. *Journal of Business Venturing*, 10: 267-81.

Clark, B.R. (1983), *The Higher Education System: Academic Organization in Cross-National Perspective*. Berkeley, University of California Press.

Clark, B.R. (1987), *The Academic Life. Small Worlds, Different Worlds.* Carnegie Foundation, Princeton.

Clark, B.R. (1998), *Creating Entrepreneurial Universities: Organizational Ways of Transformation*, Oxford: Pergamon/Elsvier Science.

Clark, B.R. (2004), *Sustaining Change in Universities. Continuities in Case Studies and concepts*, Berkshire: Open University Press.

Clark, B.R. (2001), The Entrepreneurial University: New Foundations for Collegiality, Autonomy, and Achievement. *Higher Education Management.* Vol. 13, n° 2, pp: 9-24;

Clark, B.R. (2000a), *Collegial Entrepreneurialism in Proactive Universities: Lessons from Europe*, Change, Jan/Feb, pp: 10–19.

Clark, B.R. (2000b), Developing a Career in the Study of Higher Education, In *Higher Education: Handbook of Theory and Research*, edited by John C. Smart. Vol. 15. Flemington, NJ: Agathon Press, 2000. Pp. 1-36.

Clark, B.R. (2002), University Transformation: Primary Pathways to University Autonomy, and Achievement, in Steven Brint (ed), *The Future of the City of Intellect: The Changing American University*. Stanford, CA: Stanford University Press, 2002. Pp.322–342.

Clark, B.R. (2003), Sustaining Change in Universities: Continuities in Case Studies and Concepts. *Tertiary Education and Management*, 9 (2003): 99–116.

Clark, B.R. (2004), Delineating the Character of the Entrepreneurial University, *Higher Education Policy*, 17, 2004: 355–370.

Clark, B.R. (2005), Genetic Entrepreneurialism among American Universities, *Higher Education Forum*, 2, March 2005: 1-17.

Colyvas, J.A., Powell W.W. (2007), From vulnerable to venerated: the institutionalization of academic entrepreneurship in the life sciences. *Research in the Sociology of Organizations*, 25, 219–259.

Colyvas, J.A., Powell W.W. (2009), Measures, metrics, and myopia: the challenges and ramifications of sustaining academic entrepreneurship. In: Lidcap, G. (Ed.), *Advances in the Study of Entrepreneurship, Innovation and Economic Growth*, vol. 19. Emerald Group Publishing, Ltd., pp. 79–111.

Cooper, D. (2009), The University in National Development: the Role of Use-Inspired Research. *Case studies of research groups at universities of the Western Cape, South Africa*, Human Science Research Council Press (HSRC Press), Cape Town.

Dill, D. (1995), University-industry entrepreneurship: the organization and management of American university technology transfer units. *Higher Education*, 29: 369-384.

Emin, S. (2003), Public Researchers in Hard Science and Business Creation. Research Note 04-05, Publication of the Ministry of National Education, *Higher Education and Scientific Research.* http://idep:8000/dpd/reperes/default.htm.

Etzkowitz, H. (1989), Entrepreneurial science in the academy: A case of the transformations of norms. *Social problems*, 36(1):14-27.

Etzkowitz, H., (1998), The norms of entrepreneurial science: cognitive effects of the new university–industry linkages. *Research Policy*, 27, 823–833.

Etzkowitz, H. (2003), Research Groups as "Quasi-Firms": The Invention of the Entrepreneurial University, *Research Policy*, 32. (1): 109-121.

Etzkowitz, H., (2000), *The Second Academic Revolution: MIT and the Rise of Entrepreneurial Science.* Gordon and Breach, London.

Etzkowitz H., et al. (2000), The future of the university and the university of the future:evolution of ivory tower to entrepreneurial paradigm. *Research Policy*, 29 (2): 313- 330.

Etzkowitz, H., Asplund P., Nordmann N. (2000), The University and Regional Renewal:Emergence of an Entrepreneurial Paradigm in the US and Sweden, In Törnqvist, Gunnar and Sörlin, Sverker (eds.), *The Wealth of Knowledge.* Universities in the New Economy. City: Publisher.

Etzkowitz, H. (2002), *MIT and the Rise of Entrepreneurial Science.* New York: Routledge.

Etzkowitz, H. (2004), The evolution of the entrepreneurial university. *International Journal of Technology and Globalization*, I (1), 64-77.

Etzkowitz, H., Gulbrandsen, M., Levitt, J. (2000), *Venture capital government funding sources for technology entrepreneurs.* New York: Harcourt.

Etzkowitz, H., Loet L. (1999), Whose triple helix? *Science and Public Policy* 26(2):138-39.

Etzkowitz H., Webster A. (1998), *Capitalizing knowledge: New intersections of industry and academia*, Albany, NY: State University Press.

Etzkowitz H. et Klofsten M. (2006), The innovating region: toward a theory of knowledgebased regional development, *R&D Management*, 35 (3): 243-255.

Gasse, Y. et D'Amours A. (2000), *The Entrepreneur's profession.* Transcontinental Publishing, Canada.

Gasse, Y. (2000), *Canadian Entrepreneurs' researchers: Profile and Companies,* Working Paper, Center for Entrepreneurship and SMEs, Laval University, Canada.

George, G., Jain S., Maltarich, M. (2005), *Academics or Entrepreneurs? Entrepreneurial Identity and Invention Disclosure Behavior of University Scientists.* University of Wisconsin-Madison. Technology Transfer Society Conference, Kansas City

Gingras, Y. (2003), *Academic Enterprises, Proceedings of Social Science Research*, No. 148, June 2003.

Grimaldi, R. (2005), Are Universities Entrepreneurial?: A Review of AcademicEntrepreneurship: University Spin offs and Wealth Creation by Scott Shane. Edward Elgar UK. *Journal of Management Governance.* Vol: 9, Issue: 3-4, Publisher: Kluwer Academic Publishers, pp: 315-319

Haeussler, C., Colyvas J. (2011), Breaking the Ivory Tower: Academic Entrepreneurship in the Life Sciences in UK and Germany. *Research Policy*, 40, pp: 41–54.

Hatchuel, A. (2005), Towards an epistemology of collective action: management research as a responsive and actionable discipline. *European Management Review* (2005) 2, 36–47.

Hébert, P. (2001), *The New Warrior University*, Quebec, Nota Bene Publishing, Canada.

Henrekson, M., Rosenberg, N. (2000), *Incentives for Academic Entrepreneurship and Economic Performance: Sweden and the United States. Research program.* The Role of Universities for National Competitiveness and Regional Development coordinated by the Center for Business and Policy Studies (SNS) in Stockholm. March 8, 2000.

Jones-Evans, D. (1998), *Universities, technology transfer and spin-off activities – academic entrepreneurship in different European regions.* Final reports of the targeted socio-economic research project no 1042. University of Glamorgan, Business School.

Jacob, M., Lundqvist, M., Hellsmark, H., (2003), Entrepreneurial transformations in the Swedish University system: the case of Chalmers University of Technology, *Research Policy,*

Jaziri R., Parturel R. (2010b), academic entrepreneurship or acadépreneuriaship ? towards a reconfiguration of the entrepreneurial university model. *Proceedings of the 9th International Symposium on: Entrepreneurial Practices: Challenges of Innovation and Economic Growth in Algeria*, 30-31 May 2010. Hilton, Algiers.

Jaziri, R., (2014), *Acadepreneurship: Theory and Practice.* Editions Universitaires Européennes, 636 pages, Paris, ISBN : 978-6131562976.

Jaziri, R., (2013), The acadepreneurship: A new research theme in the field of entrepreneurship. Chapter 24 In *Entrepreneurship, sustainable SMEs and social networks. Economic and Social Movements Series*, coordinated by T. Levy-Tadjine and Zhan SU, L'Harmattan Edition, Paris ISBN 978-2-336-32575-0

Kirby, A.D. (2002), *Creating Entrepreneurial Universities: A Consideration*, Working Paper. School of Management, University of Surrey.

Kirby, A.D. (2011), Creating Entrepreneurial Universities in the UK: Applying Entrepreneurship Theory to Practice. *Actes du colloque international sur "L'université & l'entrepreneuriat"*, Université Badji Mokhtar d'Annaba, 21-23 novembre 2011, Algérie. [*Proceedings of the International Symposium on University & Entrepreneurship*]

Lacetera, N. (2005), *Multiple Missions and Academic Entrepreneurship.* Massachusetts Institute of Technology, December 17th, 2005.

Marginson S., Considine M. (2000), *The Enterprise University: Power, Governance and Reinvention in Australia*, Cambridge: Cambridge University Press.

Mc Gowan P., Van der Sijde P.C., Kirby D. (2008), The role of Universities in the entrepreneurship Industry: promoting the entrepreneurship agenda in HEI. *Industry & Higher Education*, 22 (1), 49 – 60.

Meira, S. et ali. (1999), The Entrepreneurial University: A Fine Answer to a Difficult Problem?, In *Higher Education in Europe*, vol. 24, no 1, pp.11-21.

Mendes, A., Kehoe C. (2007), *Academic entrepreneurship: possibilities and pitfalls.* Academy for entrepreneurial leadership. University of illinois, urbana-champaign, working papers and research notes. November 2007. WPRN 2007-001

Mosha, H. J. (1986), The role of African universities in national developments, *Higher education*, Vol 15, Numbers 1-2, Springer, pp. 113-134.

Newson, J., Bushbinder, H. (1988), *The University Means Business*, Universities, Corporations and Academic Work, Toronto, Garamond Press.

Paturel, R. (2005), Reflections for the construction of a Grid for the Entrepreneurial Practices Positioning, *Proceedings.of 4th Congress of the Academy of Entrepreneurship*, Paris.

Paturel, R. (2007), Magnitude and constraints of entrepreneurship. *International Review of Psychosociology*, N ° 31, autumn 2007.

Paturel, R. (2011), For a redesign of the paradigm of value creation. *Business Management Review*. Vol.1 (2), April-May-June 2011, pp: 14-23.

Philpott, K., Dooley, L., O'Reilly, C., Lupton G. (2011), The Entrepreneurial University:Examining the Underlaying Academic Tensions. *Technovation*, 31(1), 161-170.

Pirnay, F. (2001), *The economic valuation of university research results through the creation of new companies (university spin-offs) - Proposal of a procedural framework for spin-offs*, PhD thesis in Management Sciences, University of Law and Health, Lille 2, France.

Rasmussen, R. (2004), The university spin-off process. *NCSB 2004 Conference 13th Nordic Conference on Small Business Research*. May.

Röpke, J. (1998). *The Entrepreneurial University, Innovation, academic knowledge creation and regional development in a globalized economy*. Working Paper Department of Economics, Philipps- Universität Marburg, Germany: 15.

Subotzky, G. (1999), Alternatives to the entrepreneurial university: New modes of knowledge production in community service programs, *Higher Education*, 38: 401–440.

Saffu, K. (2003), *The role of 'acadepreneurs' in entrepreneurship education in Australian universities*, St Catharines, Brock University.

196   *Raouf Jaziri*

Shane, S. (2004a), Academic entrepreneurship: University spinoffs and wealth creation. In *New horizons in entrepreneurship*, ed. S. Venkataraman. Cheltenham, United Kingdom: Edward Elgar Publishing, Inc.

Shane, S. (2004b), Encouraging university entrepreneurship? The effect of the Bayh-Dole Act on university patenting in the United States. *Journal of Business Venturing*, 19, p.127–151

Schmitt, C., Bayad M. (2001), *Université et entrepreneuriat.* Université de Metz. http://asso.nordnet.fr/adreg/UE_METZ.pdf. [*University and entrepreneurship.* University of Metz]

Slaughter, S., Leslie, L.L. (1997), *Academic Capitalism Politics, Policies and the Entrepreneurial University.* The J. Hopkins University Press, Baltimore and London.

Stankiewicz, R. (1986), A*cademic Entrepreneurs: Developing University-Industry Relations*, Frances Pinter Publishers, London, 155p.

Van der Sijde, P., McGowan, P., Kirby, D. (2008), The entrepreneurial spirit in higher education and academic entrepreneurship. *Industry & Higher Education*, 22 (1), 3 – 8.

Van Vught, F. (1999), Innovative Universities. *Tertiary Education and Management*, 5(4): 347-354.

BIOGRAPHICAL SKETCH

Raouf Jaziri

Affiliation: College of Business, University of Jeddah, Saudi Arabia

Education: PhD, University of Brest, France

Research and Professional Experience: Assistant Professor

Professional Appointments: Director of Sectoral Center for Training in Services' Professions in Tunisia (Nominated by decree)

Publications from the Last 3 Years:

Articles

1. Jaziri, R., Alnahdi, S., Dhrifi, A. (2019), Public Health Effect of Financial Crisis and Governance: Evidence from Asian Countries, *International Journal of Scientific Study*, Vol 6 | Issue 9, pp.29-37.
2. Jaziri R., Touhami H. J. (2018), Predicting User Acceptance of an Entrepreneurship E-Training Platform: Evidence from Tunisia. *Eastern European Business and Economics Journal*, Vol. 4, No. 2, pp. 143-161, http://eebej.eu/Issues/.
3. Jaziri R., Khelifi R., Kharrouby A. (2018), Vers une instrumentalisation dynamique du modèle des 3 E : Une application à l'analyse des freins à la reprise d'entreprises en contexte tunisien, *Revue Internationale des Sciences de l'Organisation*, N°5-2018/1, pp. 79-113. https://www.cairn.info/revue-internationale-des-sciences-de-l-organisation-2018-1-p-81.htm. [Towards a dynamic instrumentalisation of the 3 E model: An application to the analysis of the brakes to the recovery of companies in Tunisian context, *International Review of the Sciences of the Organization*]
4. Jaziri, R., Shili, I., Mezriou, W. (2018), Facteurs d'insertion professionnelle des diplômés universitaires: Cas de la Tunisie de l'après révolution, *Revue Tunisienne d'Administration Publique*, n°5, 1er semestre 2018. http://www.ena.tn/wp-content/uploads/2018/06/rtap-n5-tables-matieres.pdf [Factors of professional integration of university graduates: Case of Tunisia after the revolution, *Tunisian Journal of Public Administration*]
5. Jaziri, R. (2018), "The perennity of family businesses after succession: The Tunisian case," *African Management Review*, Vol. 3(1), pp. 32-54.
6. Jaziri, R., El-Mahjoub, O., Boussaffa, A. (2018), Proposition of A Hybrid Methodology of Project Management, *American Journal of Engineering Research*, Volume-7, Issue-4, pp. 113-127.

7. Kmar, H., Jaziri, R., Abdellatif, T. (2017), Etude des relations entre l'entrepreneuriat social, la R. S. E et le développement durable. *Revue des Etudes Multidisciplinaires en Sciences Economiques et Sociales*, N° 6, Juillet – Décembre 2017, pp. 190-209. [Study of the relations between social entrepreneurship, the R. S. E and sustainable development. *Journal of Multidisciplinary Studies in Economics and Social Sciences*]

8. Jaziri, R. (2017), Quel modèle de gouvernance pour les universités tunisiennes, *Actes des troisièmes journées de réflexion sur la gouvernance des universités*, organisé par l'ATSG, 29 avril-1 Mai 2017. Hammamet, Tunisie. [What model of governance for Tunisian universities, *Proceedings of the third days of reflection on the governance of universities*]

9. Jaziri, R. (2016), Demystify the entrepreneur's enigma *International Journal of Innovation and Applied Studies,* Vol. 18 No. 4. Dec. 2016, pp. 1097-1122.

10. Jaziri, R., Garbaa, A. (2016), Les déterminants de la résistance au changement organisationnel: Validation empirique dans les universités tunisiennes. *Electronic Journal of Digital Entreprise*, eJDE - REM [Electronique], n. 40.1, 16p.

11. Jaziri, R., Bouzaien, A. (2016), *Evaluation des établissements universitaires: Expériences comparées et étude de cas*, Document de travail disponible: https://www.academia.edu/26071271/L_%C3%A9valuation_interne_des_%C3%A9tablissements_universitai res_Exp%C3%A9riences_compar%C3%A9es_et_%C3%A9tude_ de_cas [*Evaluation of Academic Institutions: Comparative Experiments and Case Study*]

Books

1. Jaziri, R., El-Mahjoub, O. (2018), *A new Blended Methodology of Project Management: A Combination Between PMBOK and PRINCE2*, LAP LAMBERT Academic Publishing, 688p, ISBN: 978-613-8-32996-1. https://www.morebooks.de/store/gb/book/a-

new-blended-methodology-of-project-management/isbn/978-613-8-32996-1.

2. Jaziri, R., (2017) "Entrepreneuriat Versus Management de Projet: Quel apport de la cartographie cognitive?," *Editions Universitaires Européennes*, 128 pages, Paris, ISBN: 978-6202265454. https://www.amazon.com/Entrepreneuriat-Versus-Management-Projet-cartographie/dp/6202265450/ref=sr_1_fkmr0_4?s= books&ie=UTF8&qid=1522152722&sr=1-4-fkmr0&keywords=%22raouf+jaziri%22 [Entrepreneurship Versus Project Management: What contribution of cognitive mapping ?, *European University Editions*]

In: The Power of Entrepreneurship
Editor: Daan Dirksen

ISBN: 978-1-53615-114-5
© 2019 Nova Science Publishers, Inc.

Chapter 6

THE ROLE OF VENTURE-SITTERS IN CREATING AND MANAGING KNOWLEDGE ECOSYSTEMS FOR HIGH-EXPECTATIONS START-UPS

Diego Matricano[*], *PhD*
Department of Management,
Università degli Studi della Campania "L. Vanvitelli",
Capua (CE), Italy

ABSTRACT

Aspiring entrepreneurs aiming to launch high-expectation start-ups – which are knowledge intensive ventures anticipating high growth rates – can be at a critical juncture. On the one hand, they need to get external knowledge and mix it with previously hold one in order to develop new knowledge. On the other hand, however, they can be not able to catch external knowledge in order to create new one since they can miss necessary capabilities and skills or instruments and tools.

---

[*] Corresponding Author Email: diego.matricano@unicampania.it.

202   *Diego Matricano*

In such a scenario, a major role is played by venture-sitters, i.e., a kind of knowledge promoters, transformers or gatekeepers who look after new high-expectation entrepreneurial ideas to ensure they are nurtured, developed and exploited through the launch of start-ups. Such experts can support the creation of voluntary and specific knowledge ecosystems and their management. This chapter offers five research propositions that are intended to form the basis for scholars carrying out further studies. Practitioners could also leverage on the insights provided in order to facilitate the creation and development of knowledge ecosystems for high-expectation start-ups.

Keywords: venture-sitter, knowledge management, knowledge ecosystem, high-expectation start-ups, entrepreneurship

INTRODUCTION

As emerging from some critical reviews (Hoang and Antoncic, 2003; Slotte-Kock and Coviello, 2010), the origins of the network approach to entrepreneurship can be dated back to 1985 when Granovetter proposed a seminal contribution entitled *"Economic Action and Social Structure: The Problem of Embeddedness"*. In Granovetter's contribution, the economic and sociological fields of research, which have always been considered as standing alone, are combined: economic action, which includes both managerial and entrepreneurial acting, is embedded in the relationships established and managed by individuals.

Networks, which supply both material and immaterial resources that are missing or scarce (Dubini, 2000), necessarily affect the economic choices of both established firms (Powell, 1990, 1996; Uzzi, 1997; Burt 1992, 2000) and start-ups (Birley, 1985; Aldrich and Zimmer, 1986; Johannisson, 1986, 1988; Starr and MacMillan, 1990). In particular, they can be relevant in reference to high-expectation start-ups, i.e., knowledge-intensive ventures anticipating high growth rates, a kind of start-ups that is attracting considerable academic attention (Davidsson and Henrekson, 2002; Delmar et al., 2003; Curley and Formica, 2008; Matricano, 2010).

It has been pointed out that aspiring entrepreneurs aiming to launch high-expectation start-ups are at a very critical juncture. On the one hand, they are about to enter hyper-competitive markets where competition is over intangible inputs and hence creation and exploitation of new knowledge lies at the basis of the most powerful competitive advantage (Carayannis and Formica, 2008; Matricano, 2010). In order to achieve and sustain their competitive advantage, it is necessary to obtain external knowledge held by partners involved in their networks – this underlies the concept of open innovation proposed by Chesbrough (2010, 2012) – and mix it with that previously held in order to create new knowledge. In this vein, intellectual capital – made up of human, structural and relational capital – seems to play a relevant role (Matricano, 2016). On the other hand, would-be entrepreneurs may be unable to capture new external knowledge and mix it with that previously held because they may lack the skills and tools able to capture, decode and use external knowledge.

In such a scenario, facilitation in capturing, decoding and using external knowledge is required (Thomas, 2013). Among the various practitioners who can perform this task, such as gatekeepers and knowledge transformers, a very important role is assigned to venture-sitters, i.e., experts who look after new high-expectation entrepreneurial ideas in order to ensure that they are nurtured, developed in the best way possible and exploited through the launch of start-ups (Matricano and Pietrobon, 2010; Iscaro et al., 2017). These experts, acting like knowledge promoters, transformers or gatekeepers, can support aspiring entrepreneurs in creating knowledge-based relationships and managing them.

In order to investigate the role venture-sitters can have in creating and managing knowledge-based relationships for high-expectation start-ups, this chapter proceeds as follows. In the following paragraph, the various definitions proposed in reference to knowledge transformers or gatekeepers are reviewed in order to clarify the concept of venture-sitter. Attention is then shifted to knowledge ecosystems, which are a specific kind of network. The differences between networks and business ecosystems are highlighted and then attention is focused on the characteristics of knowledge ecosystems, a sub-group of business ecosystems. In the next paragraph, the obstacles that can impede knowledge transfers in knowledge ecosystems (knowledge redundancy and stickiness) and the role that venture-sitters can assume (acting as translators/interpreters) to overcome such obstacles and favour knowledge exchanges are investigated. In the last paragraph of the chapter, some theoretical implications for future research and practice are discussed.

WHO ARE VENTURE-SITTERS?

In order to deal with all the difficulties (Thomas, 2013) that can arise when implementing and managing the new knowledge development process – consisting in capturing, decoding and using external knowledge, mixing it with that previously held in order to create new knowledge – aspiring entrepreneurs can leverage on: 1) the venture structure; 2) organizational technology; and 3) knowledge promoters.

As for the venture structure, would-be entrepreneurs should aim to implement a flexible structure (rather than a formalized one) that can be more easily adapted to emerging necessities (Schilling, 2000; Zenger and Hesterly, 1997; Sanchez and Mahoney, 1996). However, since any emerging necessities are unexpected, no stereotyped kind of structure can be hypothesized. As a consequence, the results may, or may not, be satisfactory.

As for organizational technology, such entrepreneurs can minimize limitations and barriers arising from not yet commonly shared knowledge or technology, although ambiguity, interference and the lack of equivalence (Holden and Von Kortzfleisch, 2004) can never be totally eliminated. Also in this case, positive results may, or may not, be achieved.

Eventually, aspiring entrepreneurs, who may lack the necessary competence (Curley and Formica, 2008), can decide to involve knowledge promoters, transformers or gatekeepers (Cranefield and Yoong, 2007). Because of their skills and competences (Hauschildt and Schewe, 2000; Gurtner and Dorner, 2009) knowledge promoters can overcome structural and technological constraints (cited above) and thus can support aspiring

The Role of Venture-Sitters in Creating and Managing Knowledge ... 205

entrepreneurs in capturing, decoding and using external knowledge in order to mix it with that previously held and create new knowledge.

According to the above analysis, structure and technology can never be ignored in the process of new knowledge development. These strategic factors can delay or accelerate the process, depending on how effectively they are deployed. The human factor, i.e., the presence or absence of an effective knowledge promoter, seems to play the most crucial role in the process of developing new knowledge.

On the assumption that the human factor is the key determinant for high-expectation start-ups, entrepreneurship scholars have been driven to investigate who knowledge promoters, transformers or gatekeepers are and what they really do. Up to now, however, there is no shared definition and so the debate about their features and characteristics is still *in fieri*.

One of the first scholars who underlined the importance of knowledge promoters was Likert (1961), for whom knowledge promoters were key individuals in *linking-pin positions*. In other words, they span two or more groups, units or teams and thus facilitate flows of communications, influence and resources.

In time, the concept of knowledge promoters assumed different meanings. At the beginning of the 2000s, the important role played by gatekeepers in R&D activities or in IT contexts was underlined. By knowledge promoters, for example, Harada (2003) intended all the key individuals who play a crucial role in R&D activities. Pawlowski and Robey (2004) highlighted the fact that boundary-spanning individuals can play multiple roles in IT contexts. They can act as filters and facilitators of knowledge exchanges.

Subsequently, in a general broadening of views, it was assumed that gatekeepers could establish information and communication networks and play a major role inside them or that they could act as a knowledge interface between two subjects, whoever they were (Cranefield and Yoong, 2007). According to the latter, knowledge promoters have two key roles: dealing with "*the upstream act of codification*" and "*the downstream act of interpretation*" (*ibidem*, p. 96). Their main task is to connect the organization with the external environment and to connect the different parts of the organization itself. This enforces the idea that knowledge promoters are individuals positioned where the action takes place. For this reason, they are "*seekers rather than knowers*" and "*cross-pollinators for new initiative processes*" (Andersson et al., 2009).

In recent years, in reference to *experimental labs* – i.e., virtual incubators that support the creation of high-expectation start-ups (Curley and Formica, 2008, 2010) – the concept of knowledge promoters/ transformers or gatekeepers has been recalled. These key individuals, renamed venture-sitters, represent a specific type of knowledge exchange facilitator (Matricano and Pietrobon, 2010; Iscaro et al., 2017). As argued in the original definition, "*venture-sitters are experts who, mirroring the approach of baby-sitters, aim to obtain the trust of other experts (the "relatives") and aspiring entrepreneurs (the "parents") while looking after new high-expectation entrepreneurial ideas (the "child") in order to ensure that they are nurtured, developed in the best way possible*" (Matricano and Pietrobon, 2010, p. 318). Venture-sitters are thus experts in the field of business who take care of high-expectation entrepreneurial ideas and try to make them grow in order to be exploited through the creation of high-expectation start-ups. In particular, venture-sitters promote involvement in personal networks in order to test high-expectation ideas (Iscaro et al., 2017). They are involved in searching for experts who can improve the would-be entrepreneur's ideas in order to create value. They drive individual action, providing knowledge created by experts, and are members of the personal network around the aspiring entrepreneurs.

In the following paragraphs, the role that venture-sitters can play in creating knowledge ecosystems (which are distanced from networks in the general sense) and managing them, dealing with obstacles that arise and assuming the role of translators and interpreters is investigated and clarified.

WHAT ARE THE AIMS OF VENTURE-SITTERS?

As already stated, venture-sitters are experts who take care of high-expectation entrepreneurial ideas and try to make them grow in order to be exploited through the creation of high-expectation start-ups (Matricano and Pietrobon, 2010; Iscaro et al., 2017). They are involved in searching for experts who can improve the would-be entrepreneur's ideas in order to create value. They drive individual action, providing knowledge created by experts, and become members of the personal network around the aspiring entrepreneurs.

At this stage, it is worth investigating the aims of venture-sitters. For this purpose, below the concepts of networks and business ecosystems are compared and then the main features of knowledge ecosystems, a sub-group of business ecosystems, are specified. This analysis shows the purpose of venture-sitters in aiming to create knowledge ecosystems to support high-expectation start-ups.

To start with, the differences between networks and business ecosystems are investigated. Of course, some entrepreneurship scholars have already attempted this (Peltoniemi, 2004; Lehto et al., 2013). Thus, it is possible to obtain an exhaustive list of differences occurring between them by recalling and combining the above-cited contributions (see Table 1).

Table 1. Differences occurring between networks and business ecosystems

	Network	Business ecosystem
Purpose	Efficiency – Service	Innovation – Novelty – Renewal
Value	Value is captured rather than created	Value is created rather than captured
Structure	Purposefully structured	Emergent structure
Boundaries	Well defined boundaries	Fluid boundaries
Governance	Agreed – Set – Defined	Inherent - Evolving
Strategy	Competition against other networks and collaboration within it	Coopetition against other ecosystems and within it
Evolution	Stagnation – Maintaining the *status quo*	Common - Constant flow – Self-renewal

Source: Adaptation by Peltoniemi (2004) and Lehto et al. (2013).

As emerges from Table 1, the differences between networks and business ecosystems are both copious and substantive. Ecosystems are focused on innovation and value creation. They have an emergent structure, with fluid boundaries, that evolves according to up-and-coming needs. The subjects involved adopt competition and cooperation strategies, i.e., coopetition (Jorde and Teece, 1989; Dagnino and Padula, 2002; Luo et al., 2006; Dagnino, 2007; Padula and Dagnino, 2007, Roy and Yami, 2009; Mina and Dagnino, 2013), both within them and against other ecosystems.

Because of the above characteristics, it should be easy to define a business ecosystem. Indeed, the concept has been analysed and discussed in several contributions (Moore, 1993, 1996, 1998; Kandiah and Gossain, 1998; Power and Jerjian, 2001; Iansiti and Levien, 2002, 2004; Peltoniemi, 2004, 2006; Peltoniemi and Vuori, 2004; Adner, 2006; Adner and Kapoor, 2010; Van der Borgh et al., 2012; Vargo and Lusch, 2010; Letho et al., 2013; Jansson et al., 2014) but it is still relatively new and as yet there is no shared definition.

The best way of proceeding in cases like this consists in recalling the main definitions and highlighting the main features. Moore (1998), for example, maintains that a business ecosystem is an *"extended system of mutually supportive organizations: communities of customers, suppliers, lead producers, and other stakeholders, financing, trade associations, standard bodies, labour unions, governmental and quasigovernmental institutions, and other interested parties. These communities come together in a partially intentional, highly self-organizing, and even somewhat accidental matter"* (*ibidem*, p. 168). The main aspects that clearly emerge are: interactions between the business ecosystems and decentralised decision-making and self-organization. Power and Jerjian (2001, p. 13), instead, define a business ecosystem as *"a physical community considered together with the non-living factors of its environment as a unit"*. Iansiti and Levien (2004) support the idea that business ecosystems are characterized by fragmentation, interconnectedness, cooperation and competition. According to the above definitions, it sounds clear that a business ecosystem is a set of several different subjects whose results – depending on value creation and ranging from success to failure passing through survival – are directly or indirectly related. Of course, if those involved in business ecosystems create value by knowledge exchanges, then we can refer to knowledge ecosystems. These are a sub-group of business ecosystems that, of course, show the same features (see Table 1). The only difference is that a knowledge ecosystem is *"a heterogeneous set of knowledge-intensive companies and other participants that depend on each other for their effectiveness and efficiency, and as such need to be located in close proximity"* (Van der Borgh et al., 2012, p. 151). This means that geographical distance does not matter for business ecosystems, but it really matters for knowledge ecosystems because of the effect of knowledge spillovers (Iansiti and Levien, 2004; Van der Borgh et al., 2012; Clarysse et al., 2014).

Starting from the above analysis, it is possible now to try to define the aim pursued by venture-sitters. Since they take care of high-expectation entrepreneurial ideas and try to exploit them through the creation of high-expectation start-ups, they are involved in searching for experts who – by providing knowledge – can improve the aspiring entrepreneurs' ideas in order to create value. Because of the above aim, venture-sitters are not interested in creating networks that are purposefully structured (with well-defined boundaries) in order to capture value (rather than create it) and preserve the *status quo*. Venture-sitters, instead, aim to create business ecosystems or, to be more precise, knowledge ecosystems because of high-expectation entrepreneurs' needs. The latter, in fact, look for external knowledge in order to improve their entrepreneurial ideas and launch them on the market. According to the above it is reasonable to hypothesize that:

> **P1:** In order to support the creation of high-expectation start-ups, venture-sitters are involved in the creation of knowledge ecosystems.

After hypothesizing that venture-sitters aim to create knowledge ecosystems able to support the creation of high-expectation start-ups, it is appropriate to specify what kind of knowledge ecosystems we are talking about. It is therefore suitable to start from two possible classifications of ecosystems proposed in the field of natural sciences and assume that ecosystems can be: forced or voluntary and generalized or specific.

In the field of natural sciences, forced ecosystems are top-down. They are imposed and, as such, may or may not perform satisfactorily. Voluntary

210   *Diego Matricano*

ecosystems, instead, are bottom-up, spontaneous and, generally speaking, more likely to achieve expected performances.

Natural ecosystems can also be classified as generalized or specific. Generalized ecosystems include many species of animals and plants. Specialized ecosystems, instead, include a limited amount of species of animals and plants.

With due diligence (which is always necessary in cases like this), the above-cited kinds of ecosystems can be transposed from natural sciences to entrepreneurial studies. Ecosystems, then, can be classified as forced or voluntary (in reference to their origins) and as generalized or specific (in reference to the pursued aim). In particular, forced ecosystems are implemented thanks to national or regional laws. Voluntary ecosystems, instead, are created because of entrepreneurial action. Generalized ecosystems aim to support the economic development of specific areas. They involve subjects from different industries in order to satisfy all the needs that can emerge from different industries. On the contrary, specific ecosystems aim to support the economic growth of a specific industry. They involve subjects from different industries in order to satisfy needs that can emerge in a specific industry.

Of course, knowledge ecosystems need to be classified according to their origins and their aim. For this reason, it is appropriate to consider the kinds of knowledge ecosystems resulting by matching the alternatives "forced" and "voluntary" with the alternatives "generalized" and "specific", as shown in Table 2.

After clarifying the differences between the four kinds of knowledge ecosystems, it is possible to exclude that venture-sitters can create forced ecosystems (neither generalized nor specific) since such ecosystems are created thanks to national or regional laws. Attention must then be focused on voluntary knowledge ecosystems that, according to previous definitions, are created bottom-up (it should be recalled that venture-sitters are members of the personal network around would-be entrepreneurs and so it is reasonable to assume that knowledge ecosystems are bottom-up). Voluntary knowledge ecosystems can be generalized and specific as well. In reference to high-expectation start-ups, which are based on the exploitation of a specific business idea, venture-sitters cannot be interested in creating generalized ecosystems that, by definition, aim to satisfy different needs emerging from different industries. By exclusion, it seems possible to maintain that venture-sitters, who aim to support the creation of high-expectation start-ups, are interested in the creation of voluntary and specific knowledge ecosystems. Thus it may be hypothesized that:

> **P2:** In order to support the creation of high-expectation start-ups, venture-sitters are involved in the creation of voluntary and specific knowledge ecosystems.

Table 2. A possible classification of knowledge ecosystems

	Forced	Voluntary
Generalized	They are implemented thanks to national or regional laws (top-down). They aim to support the economic development of specific areas and thus they involve subjects from different industries in order to satisfy needs that can emerge from different industries.	They are created because of specific and emerging needs (bottom-up). They aim to support the economic development of specific areas and thus they involve subjects from different industries in order to satisfy all the needs that can emerge from different industries.
Specific	They are implemented thanks to national or regional laws (top-down). They aim to support the economic growth of a specific industry and thus they involve subjects from different industries in order to satisfy needs that can emerge in that industry.	They are created because of specific and emerging needs (bottom-up). They aim to support the economic growth of a specific industry and thus they involve subjects from different industries in order to satisfy needs that can emerge in that industry.

Source: personal elaboration.

WHAT ARE THE MAIN OBSTACLES FACED BY VENTURE-SITTERS?

After assuming that venture-sitters are involved in creating and managing voluntary and specific knowledge ecosystems, it is time to conjecture and investigate what venture-sitters do in practice.

212　　　　　　　　　　　　　*Diego Matricano*

As for the creation of voluntary and specific knowledge ecosystems, venture-sitters are involved in identifying and selecting eligible subjects. Scholars seeking to study this process (Moore, 1993, 1996, 1998; Iansiti and Levien, 2002, 2004; Peltoniemi, 2004, 2006; Van der Borgh et al., 2012; Vargo and Lusch, 2010; Letho et al., 2013) have one major difficulty: the parameters that may be used to identify and select eligible subjects change according to the entrepreneurial idea to be nurtured. Venture-sitters, in fact, create voluntary and specific knowledge ecosystems in order to nurture specific entrepreneurial ideas. As a consequence, there is no shared rule that must be followed. Entrepreneurial ideas change time after time. Specific needs and related parameters change as well. Subjects involved in ecosystems change too. As a consequence, it seems that no generalization is allowed.

This is only partly true. Even if entrepreneurial ideas, needs, parameters and involved subjects change time after time, venture-sitters know that they can – at least – proceed by exclusion. This implies that venture-sitters – after identifying the subjects to be involved – know that they need to seek other subjects who can enrich the new knowledge development process by adding further – by further we mean new, different – knowledge. This means that they try to reduce knowledge redundancy (Nonaka, 1991; Nonaka and Takeuchi, 1995), i.e., the sharing of the same knowledge. According to the above, it is not possible to say what venture-sitters have to do and how they have to proceed, although we can say what they should not do and how they should not proceed (they should avoid redundancy). According to the above, it seems possible to hypothesize that:

> **P3:** In order to support the creation of high-expectation start-ups, venture-sitters try to reduce knowledge redundancy when creating voluntary and specific knowledge ecosystems.

Even if the creation of knowledge ecosystems is carried out properly – minimizing the risk of knowledge redundancy – this does not guarantee that the ecosystem is going to work as expected. In managing knowledge ecosystems, venture-sitters may face some obstacles that can impede the right functioning of the knowledge ecosystems themselves. In particular, two main obstacles can arise. The first concerns the amount of knowledge that parties involved in the knowledge ecosystem should share or hoard. The second, instead, deals with the ease of sharing the amount of knowledge with other parties involved.

As regards the first obstacle, for the parties involved in knowledge ecosystems it could be difficult to exercise an appropriate level of control over the diffusion of knowledge (Boisot and Li, 2006). On the one hand, the parties involved could be inclined to share all the knowledge they have in order to test high-expectation ideas and support the launch of high-expectations start-ups; on the other, parties may not be so inclined to do that and might prefer to hoard their knowledge. This choice might seem very tricky even if, on due reflection, it is not so. Knowledge ecosystems differ from networks. In the latter, as the actors involved are interested in capturing value rather than creating it, moral hazard may come into play (Arrow, 1968; Holmstrom, 1982). In knowledge ecosystems, instead, this problem seems to be minimized for two main reasons. First, the parties involved are not asked to share all the knowledge they have. They are asked to test and evaluate high-expectation entrepreneurial ideas in order to support – or discourage – their exploitation on the market through the launch of start-ups. This means that experts involved in knowledge ecosystems are expected to express a judgement and to explain and clarify their reasons. There is no need to share all the knowledge they hold. What matters here is the positive or negative judgement that is expressed. Second, the parties involved are experts who – because of their experience, skills and competences – aim to test high-expectation ideas in order to validate them and make them perform (create value). They are not interested in capturing value by stealing or copying new entrepreneurial ideas. They are experts in specific fields and, as such, they offer their consultancy services as they usually do. Thus, for experts committed to evaluating high-expectation ideas, the question about the amount of knowledge to be shared does not seem to constitute a real problem.

Au contraire, a real problem is how easy or difficult it is to share the amount of knowledge with other parties involved. Specifically, this problem is known as "knowledge stickiness" (Arrow, 1969; Teece, 1977; Von Hippel, 1994; Szulanski, 1996, 2000) and refers to all the barriers, impediments and obstacles that can delay or prevent knowledge exchange. Among the various contributions proposed about knowledge stickiness (Arrow, 1969; Von Hippel, 1994; Zander and Kogut, 1995), it is useful to recall that of Szulanski (1996) who argues that, over a typical transfer process made up of initiation, implementation, ramp-up and integration stages, there are four sets of factors causing the difficulty of knowledge transfer. These four sets of factors are related to the characteristics of transferred knowledge, of the source, the recipients and the context in which the transfer takes place (*ibidem*, p. 30). In particular, when talking about the characteristics of transferred knowledge the scholar refers to casual ambiguity; when dealing with the characteristics of the source there is a clear reference to lack of motivation and to perception of the source as not reliable; in reference to the characteristics of the recipients it is important to consider the lack of motivation, of absorptive capacity and of retentive capacity; finally, in reference to the characteristics of the context in which the transfer takes place, the scholar considers barren organizational contexts and arduous relationships (*ibidem*, p. 30 ss). As already stated, even if in the above contribution Szulanski (1996) analyses what happens within firms, the four sets of difficulties also seem to hold in reference to knowledge ecosystems. Because of the heterogeneity of parties involved in knowledge ecosystems, it seems reasonable to assume that each of them holds specific knowledge that others do not and therefore exchanges between sources and recipients of specific knowledge are not easy. Suffice it to consider that knowledge can be generated in different language systems and organizational cultures. This means that knowledge exchanges are subject to constraints affecting not just transfer, but transferability (Holden and Von Kortzfleisch, 2004). In reference to this, Szulanski (1996) underlines that incentive systems are inadequate to mitigate stickiness. The context, which is well identified in the case of firms but not in the case of knowledge ecosystems, makes knowledge exchanges even harder because of external factors that can intervene. Stickiness, then, causes a gap between what is known and what should be known. Since knowledge ecosystems are created,

The Role of Venture-Sitters in Creating and Managing Knowledge ... 215

venture-sitters should be interested in reducing stickiness, and the related gaps, in order to make knowledge exchanges easier. Thus, it may be hypothesized that:

> **P4:** In order to support the creation of high-expectation start-ups, venture-sitters try to reduce knowledge stickiness when managing voluntary and specific knowledge ecosystems.

According to the above, it seems fairly clear that knowledge stickiness can prevent knowledge ecosystems from working well and – above all – from achieving expected results. In this vein, it is important to clarify the role that venture-sitters can play. In other words, it is important to work out what venture-sitters really do in order to favour exchanges of already existing knowledge and create new knowledge.

In order to achieve the above goal, it seems appropriate to recall a contribution proposed by Cranefield and Yoong (2007), who argue that a typical process of knowledge transfer is made up of six stages:

1. Engaging;
2. Defining;
3. Seeking;
4. Articulating;
5. Integrating;
6. Disseminating.

During the first stage, it is important to determine the level and nature of engagement in the process of knowledge exchange; during the second, issues and problems are defined so that it is clear which knowledge must be sought over the third stage. When the required knowledge is found, it is possible to proceed with the fourth stage consisting in articulating it. Newly acquired or created knowledge is transformed into explicit knowledge that is integrated – during the fifth stage – with already existing knowledge. During the last phase, newly created knowledge – resulting from integration between that already held and newly acquired knowledge – is shared. By rebuilding the whole process through which new knowledge is created, Cranefield and Yoong (2007) aim to underline that key individuals involved in this process – they refer to gatekeepers or boundary spanners while we refer to venture-sitters – mainly act as translators and interpreters. During the whole process, these key individuals act in order to convert newly acquired knowledge and decode it so that potential recipients – who may, or may not, hold the same prior knowledge – can use it. The results achieved by Cranefield and Yoong (2007) are in line with previous studies in which scholars argue that key individuals involved in knowledge transfers mainly focus on the acts of transferring, translating and transforming knowledge (Carlile, 2004; Holden and Von Kortzfleisch, 2004). In order to avoid knowledge stickiness and favour knowledge exchanges, it seems reasonable to hypothesize that venture-sitters act as translators and interpreters. Thus we hypothesize that:

> **P5:** In order to support the creation of high-expectations start-ups, venture-sitters act as translators and interpreters in voluntary and specific knowledge ecosystems.

CONCLUSION

The present study attempted to determine the contribution that venture-sitters can lend to the creation and management of knowledge ecosystems for high-expectation start-ups. In particular, venture-sitters are expected to ensure the creation of knowledge ecosystems, which are voluntary and specific, and to manage their development by reducing knowledge redundancy and by assuming the role of translator/interpreter in order to overcome knowledge stickiness.

The main limitation that needs to be stressed is the only reference to what venture-sitters do in reference to creating and managing partnerships. Other aspects, which are usually considered when investigating entrepreneurship (like psychological traits and individual characteristics or environmental features), were ignored.

The Role of Venture-Sitters in Creating and Managing Knowledge ... 217

From a different perspective, the above limitation might represent strengths to leverage on. First of all, network theory helped to define the boundaries of the present research that, to our knowledge, is not so widespread among entrepreneurship scholars. How venture-sitters can promote and support the creation of high-expectation start-ups still needs theoretical and empirical research. If entrepreneurship scholars were to agree on this approach to venture-sitters' involvement in knowledge ecosystems, other perspectives (the psychological and the contextual ones cited above are a good example) might be included in order to enrich forthcoming analyses and research. Confidently, by proposing new contributions about this topic, academics could understand what venture-sitters are expected to do and, in turn, practitioners could really involve venture-sitters in order to support aspiring entrepreneurs in launching new high-expectation start-ups.

REFERENCES

Adner, R. & Kapoor, R. (2010). Value creation in innovation ecosystems: How the structure of technological interdependence affects firm performance in new technology generations. *Strategic Management Journal, 31*(3), 306-333.

Adner, R. (2006). Match your innovation strategy to your innovation ecosystem. *Harvard Business Review, 84*(4), 98-107.

Aldrich, H. E. & Zimmer, C. (1986). Entrepreneurship through social networks. In *Popoluation Perspective on Organizations*, edited by Aldrich H. E., Uppsala: Acta Universitatis Upaliensis.

Andersson, T., Curley, M. & Formica, P. (2009). *Knowledge-driven Entrepreneurship: The Key to Social and Economic Transformation*. New York: Springer.

Arrow, K. J. (1968). The economics of moral hazard: further comment. *The American Economic Review, 58*(3), 537-539.

218   *Diego Matricano*

Arrow, K. J. (1969). Classificatory notes on the production and transmission of technological knowledge. *The American Economic Review*, *59*(2), 29-35.

Birley, S. (1985). The role of networks in the entrepreneurial process. *Journal of Business Venturing*, *1*(1), 107-117.

Boisot, M. & Li, Y. (2006). Organizational versus market knowledge: From concrete embodiment to abstract representation. *Journal of Bioeconomics*, *8*(3), 219-251.

Burt, R. S. (1992). *Structural Holes: The Social Structure of Competition*. Cambridge: Harvard University Press.

Burt, R. S. (2000). Structural holes versus network closure as social capital. In *Social capital: Theory and Research* edited by Lin, N., Cook, C.S. and Burt, R.S., New York: Aldine de Gruyter.

Carayannis, E. G. & Formica, P. (2008). *Knowledge Matters: Technology, Innovation and Entrepreneurship in Innovation Networks and Knowledge Clusters*. Basingstoke: Palgrave Macmillan.

Carlile, P. R. (2004). Transferring, translating, and transforming: An integrative framework for managing knowledge across boundaries. *Organization Science*, *15*(5), 555-568.

Chesbrough, H. (2010). *Open Services Innovation: Rethinking Your Business to Grow and Compete in a New Era*. New York: John Wiley & Sons.

Chesbrough, H. (2012). Open innovation: Where we've been and where we're going. *Research-Technology Management*, *55*(4), 20-27.

Clarysse, B., Wright, M., Bruneel, J. & Mahajan, A. (2014). *Creating value ecosystems: crossing the chasm between knowledge and business ecosystems*. ERC Research Paper, N. 22.

Cranefield, J. & Yoong, P. (2007). The role of the translator/interpreter in knowledge transfer environments. *Knowledge and Process Management*, *14*(2), 95-103.

Curley, M. & Formica, P. (2008). Laboratory experiments as a tool in the empirical economic analysis of high-expectation entrepreneurship. *Industry and Higher Education*, *22*(6), 355-363.

The Role of Venture-Sitters in Creating and Managing Knowledge ... 219

Curley, M. & Formica, P. (2010). Accelerating venture creation and building on mutual strengths in experimental business labs. *Industry and Higher Education, 24*(1), 7-10.

Dagnino, G. B. (2007). Preface: Coopetition Strategy - Toward a New Kind of Inter-Firm Dynamics?, *International Studies of Management & Organization, 37*(2), 3-10.

Dagnino, G. B. & Padula, G. (2002). Coopetition strategy: A new kind of inter-firm dynamics for value creation. Paper presented at *"The European Academy of Management, Second Annual Conference – Innovative Research in Management"*, Stockholm, Sweden.

Davidsson, P. & Henrekson, M. (2002). Determinants of the prevalence of start-ups and high-growth firms. *Small Business Economics, 19*(2), 81-104.

Delmar, F., Davidsson, P. & Gartner, W. B. (2003). Arriving at the high-growth firm. *Journal of Business Venturing, 18*(2), 189-216.

Dubini, P. (2000). Il ruolo dei social network nello sviluppo delle aziende culturali. Il caso della New York Public Library. In *Imprenditore e Imprese*, edited by Lipparini, A. and Lorenzoni, G., Bologna: Il Mulino. [The role of social networks in the development of cultural companies. The case of the New York Public Library. In *Entrepreneur and Businesses*]

Granovetter, M. (1985). Economic Action and Social Structure: The Problem of Embeddedness. *The American Journal of Sociology, 91*(3), 481-510.

Gurtner, S. & Dorner, N. (2009). From roles to skills - key persons in the innovation process. *International Journal of Technology Marketing, 4*(2-3), 185-198.

Harada, T. (2003). Three steps in knowledge communication: the emergence of knowledge transformers. *Research Policy, 32*(10), 1737-1751.

Hauschildt, J. & Schewe, G. (2000). Gatekeeper and process promoter: key persons in agile and innovative organizations. *International Journal of Agile Management, 2*(2), 96-103.

Hoang, H. & Antoncic, B. (2003). Network-Based Research in Entrepreneurship: A Critical Review. *Journal of Business Venturing*, *18*(2), 165-187.

Holden, N. J. & Von Kortzfleisch, H. F. O. (2004). Why cross-cultural knowledge transfer is a form of translation in more ways than you think?, *Knowledge and Process Management*, *11*(2), 127-136.

Holmstrom, B. (1982). Moral hazard in teams. *The Bell Journal of Economics*, *13*(2), 324-340.

Iansiti, M. & Levien, R. (2002). *Keystones and Dominators: Framing the Operational Dynamics of Business Ecosystems*. Boston: Estados Unidos.

Iansiti, M. & Levien, R. (2004). *The Keystone Advantage: What the New Dynamics of Business Ecosystems Mean for Strategy, Innovation, and Sustainability*. Harvard: Harvard Business Press.

Iscaro, V., Castaldi, L., Sepe, E. & Turi, C. (2017). ExperimentaLab: a tool for the entrepreneurial università, *World Review of Entrepreneurship, Management and Sustainable Development*, *13*(5-6), 684-706.

Jansson, N., Ahokangas, P., Iivari, M., Perälä-Heape, M. & Salo, S. (2014). The competitive advantage of an ecosystemic business model: the case of OuluHealth. *Interdisciplinary Studies Journal*, *3*(4), 282-296.

Johannisson, B. (1986). Network strategies: management technology for entrepreneurship and change. *International Small Business Journal*, *5*(1), 19-30.

Johannisson, B. (1988). Business formation: a network approach. *Scandinavian Journal of Management*, *4*(3-4), 83-99.

Jorde, T. M. & Teece, D. J. (1989). Competition and cooperation: Striking the right balance. *California Management Review*, *31*(3), 25-37.

Kandiah, G. & Gossain, S. (1998). Reinventing value: the new business ecosystem. *Strategy & Leadership*, *26*(5), 28-33.

Lehto, I., Hermes, J., Ahokangas, P. & Myllykoski, J. (2013). *Collaboration in cloud businesses – value networks and ecosystems*. Paper presented at Department of Management and International Business, Oulu Business School.

Likert, R. (1961). *New Patterns of Management*. New York: McGraw-Hill.

The Role of Venture-Sitters in Creating and Managing Knowledge ... 221

Luo, X., Slotegraaf, R. J. & Pan, X. (2006). Cross-functional coopetition: The simultaneous role of cooperation and competition within firms. *Journal of Marketing*, *70*(2), 67-80.

Matricano, D. (2010). Achieving and sustaining new knowledge development in high-expectation start-ups. *Industry and Higher Education*, *24*(1), 47-53.

Matricano, D. (2016). The impact of intellectual capital on start-up expectations. *Journal of Intellectual Capital*, *17*(4), 654-674.

Matricano, D. & Pietrobon, A. (2010). Experimental labs for start-ups: the role of the venture-sitter. *Industry and Higher Education*, *24*(5), 318-322.

Mina, A. & Dagnino, G. B. (2013). Coopetition as an Emergent Construct: Identifying a Reification Process. *Academy of Management Proceedings*, *1*(1), 156-157.

Moore, J. F. (1993). Predators and prey: a new ecology of competition. *Harvard Business Review*, *71*(3), 75-83.

Moore, J. F. (1996). *The Death of Competition: Leadership and Strategy in the Age of Business Ecosystems*. New York: HarperCollins.

Moore, J. F. (1998). The rise of a new corporate form. *Washington Quarterly*, *21*(1), 167-181.

Nonaka, I. & Takeuchi, H. (1995). *The Knowledge Creating Company: How Japanese Companies Create the Dynamics of Innovation*. Oxford: Oxford University Press.

Nonaka, I. (1991). The knowledge creating company. *Harvard Business Review*, November–December, 162-171.

Padula, G. & Dagnino, G. B. (2007). Untangling the rise of coopetition: the intrusion of competition in a cooperative game structure. *International Studies of Management & Organization*, *37*(2), 32-52.

Pawlowski, S. D. & Robey, D. (2004). Bridging user organizations: knowledge brokering and the work of information technology professionals. *MIS Quarterly*, *28*(4), 645-672.

Peltoniemi, M. (2004). *Cluster, value network and business ecosystem: knowledge and innovation approach*. Paper presented at Organisations,

Innovation and Complexity: New Perspectives on the Knowledge Economy conference. Manchester, United Kingdom.

Peltoniemi, M. (2006). Preliminary theoretical framework for the study of business ecosystems. *Emergence: Complexity & Organization, 18*(1), 10-19.

Peltoniemi, M. & Vuori, E. (2004). *Business ecosystem as the new approach to complex adaptive business environments.* Paper presented at Frontiers of e-business research conference, Tampere, Finland.

Powell, W. W. (1990). Neither market nor hierarchy: network forms of organization. *Research in Organizational Behavior, 12*(1), 295-336.

Powell, W. W. (1996). Inter-organizational collaboration in the biotechnology industry. *Journal of Institutional and Theoretical Economics, 120*(1), 197-215.

Power, T. & Jerjian, G. (2001). *Ecosystem: Living the 12 Principles of Networked Business.* London: Pearson Education Ltd.

Roy, P. & Yami, S. (2009). Managing strategic innovation through coopetition. *International Journal of Entrepreneurship and Small Business, 8*(1), 61-73.

Sanchez, R. & Mahoney, J. T. (1996). Modularity, flexibility, and knowledge management in product and organization design. *Strategic Management Journal, 17*(S2), 63-76.

Schilling, M. A. (2000). Toward a general modular systems theory and its application to interfirm product modularity. *Academy of Management Review, 25*(2), 312-334.

Slotte-kock, S. & Coviello, N. (2010). Entrepreneurship research on network processes: a review and ways forward. *Entrepreneurship: Theory and Practice, 34*(1), 31-57.

Starr, J. A. & Macmillan, I. C. (1990). Resource cooptation via social contracting: resource acquisition strategies for new ventures. *Strategic Management Journal, 11*(4), 79-92.

Szulanski, G. (1996). Exploring internal stickiness: impediments to the transfer of best practice within the firm. *Strategic Management Journal, 17*(S2), 27-43.

Szulanski, G. (2000). The process of knowledge transfer: a diachronic analysis of stickiness. *Organizational Behaviour and Human Decision Processes*, *82*(1), 9-27.

Teece, D. J. (1977). Technology transfer by multinational firms: the resource cost of transferring technological know-how. *The Economic Journal*, *87*(346), 242-261.

Thomas, L. (2013). *Ecosystem Emergence: An Investigation of the Emergence Processes of Six Digital Service Ecosystems*, Doctoral Thesis. London: Imperial College Business School.

Uzzi, B. (1997). Social structure and competition in inter-firm networks: the paradox of embeddedness. *Administrative Science Quarterly*, *42*(1) 35-67.

Van der Borgh, M., Cloodt, M. & Romme, A. G. L. (2012). Value creation by knowledge-based ecosystems: evidence from a field study. *R&D Management*, *42*(2), 150-169.

Vargo, S. L. & Lusch, R. F. (2010). From repeat patronage to value co-creation in service ecosystems: a transcending conceptualization of relationship. *Journal of Business Market Management*, *4*(4), 169-179.

Von Hippel, E. (1994). Sticky information and the locus of problem solving: implications for innovation. *Management Science*, *40*(4), 429-439.

Zander, U. & Kogut, B. (1995). Knowledge and the speed of the transfer and imitation of organizational capabilities: An empirical test. *Organization Science*, *6*(1), 76-92.

Zenger, T. R. & Hesterly, W. S. (1997). The disaggregation of corporations: Selective intervention, high-powered incentives, and molecular units. *Organization Science*, *8*(3), 209-222.

In: The Power of Entrepreneurship
Editor: Daan Dirksen

ISBN: 978-1-53615-114-5
© 2019 Nova Science Publishers, Inc.

Chapter 7

AN EPISTEMOLOGICAL CRITICISM OF SOCIAL ENTREPRENEURSHIP: IS SOCIAL ENTREPRENEURSHIP A SOUND AND SCIENTIFIC FIELD OF RESEARCH?

Amir Forouharfar[*]
Department of Public Administration, Management and Economics
Faculty, University of Sistan and Baluchestan, Zahedan, Iran

"No man's knowledge here can go beyond his experience"
John Locke

ABSTRACT

The paper was shaped around the pivotal question: Is SE a sound and scientific field of research? The question has given a critical tone to the paper and has also helped to bring out some of the controversial debates in the realm of SE. The paper was organized under five main discussions to be able to provide a scientific answer to the research question: (1) is "social

---

[*] Corresponding Author Email: amir.forouharfar@gmail.com.

entrepreneurship" an oxymoron?, (2) the characteristics of SE knowledge, (3) sources of social entrepreneurship knowledge, (4) SE knowledge: structure and limitations and (5) contributing epistemology-making concepts for SE. Based on the sections, the study relied on the relevant philosophical schools of thought in *Epistemology* (e.g., *Empiricism, Rationalism, Skepticism, Internalism* vs. *Externalism, Essentialism, Social Constructivism, Social Epistemology, etc.*) to discuss these controversies around SE and proposes some solutions by reviewing SE literature. Also, to determine the governing linguistic discourse in the realm of SE, which was necessary for our discussion, *Corpus of Contemporary American English (COCA)* for the first time in SE studies was used. Further, through the study, SE buzzwords which constitute SE terminology were derived and introduced to help us narrowing down and converging the thoughts in this field and demarking the epistemological boundaries of SE. The originality of the paper on one hand lies in its pioneering discussions on SE epistemology and on the other hand in paving the way for a construction of sound epistemology for SE; therefore in many cases after preparing the philosophical ground for the discussions, it went beyond the prevalent SE literature through meta-analysis to discuss the cases which were raised. The results of the study verified previously claimed embryonic pre-paradigmatic phase in SE which was far from a sound and scientific knowledge, although the scholarly endeavors are the harbingers of such a possibility in the future which calls for further mature academic discussion and development of SE knowledge by the SE academia.

Keywords: social entrepreneurship (SE), epistemology of social entrepreneurship, social entrepreneurship knowledge, social entrepreneurship and philosophy

1. INTRODUCTION

SE as a discipline and university subject still "lacks an established epistemology" (Nicholls 2010, 611).We know SE better in practice (through what the social entrepreneurs and social entrepreneurship organizations (SEOs) do) than the knowledge in theory. As the nascent, suppressed or ill-fulfilled social needs of the communities and undeserved of the societies are emerging day in day out, the necessity and lack of sound and sold epistemology for SE become more evident.SE must theoretically erect a well epistemologically justified structure to be able to pass its current condition as "a field of action in a pre-paradigmatic state" (Nicholls 2010, 611). Such a condition shapes the philosophy behind writing the paper to contribute to the establishment of SE epistemology. Social entrepreneurs and practitioners all around the world are constantly busy with alleviating the miseries and needs of human being, provide societies free from any prejudice, race and nationality with a better life and communal wellbeing; therefore they do not have enough time (even if they have theoretical knowledge of SE) to be able to push the scientific realm of SE forward. This is a responsibility that have to be shouldered by academia. On the other hand, philosophy and philosophizing had always been the undergirding support for social sciences. But why should we apply epistemology for making the head and tail of SE creature? Since it deals with the concepts of perception, knowledge and its justification. It helps us to know what we know in a discipline. Also it could help us to classify, sort and form the backbone of our knowledge of SE; to be able to demarcate scientific from unscientific[1]; in a sense empowers us to set a justifiable ground to say if SE a sound and scientific knowledge or vice versa.

To be disciplined in the presentation of epistemologically supported justifications based on SE literature we had to organize the research process based on a thought flowchart (Figure 1). In other words, through the paper first we discussed the collocating application of the adjective "social" with the noun "entrepreneurship." By the discussion we intended to clarify whether we could have an entrepreneurship which is social or not. We used comprehensive secondary data taken from *Corpus of Contemporary American English (COCA)* for the first time in entrepreneurial studies, accompanied with secondary data of a *Bibliometrics* study in SE. In this section of the paper the tone for SE criticism is a type of *Discourse Analysis* which is called *Critical Linguistic Analysis*. Then we discussed the characteristics of SE as human knowledge (i.e., epistemology of SE). Through this section of the paper we fell on the concept of epistemological justification in relation to SE. We wanted to clarify what kind of justification

---

[1]"As Popper represents it, the central problem in the philosophy of science is that of *demarcation*, i.e., of distinguishing between science and what he terms 'non-science'…" (Thornton, 2017, on-line *Stanford Encyclopedia of Philosophy*).

(*Internalism* vs. *Externalism*) was suitable for SE knowledge to determine the relevant epistemological school(s) of thought (*Skepticism, Rationalism* and *Empiricism*) to SE in order to classify SE knowledge (*Episteme* vs. *Techne, Intuitive, Logical* or *Empirical* knowledge) in the next step.[2]Later we discussed the structure and limitations of SE knowledge by the application of its own terminology and the *Representationism* concept. Finally, in our discussions, we referred to the following philosophical discussions to shed more light on the research question to be able to determine if SE a sound and scientific knowledge: SE *Essentialism*, SE social context, SE *Reflexivity*, SE and *Scientism*, SE *Contextualism*, SE theory making, SE and *Social Constructivism* and at the end SE and *Social Epistemology*.

2. LITERATURE REVIEW

SE as a human knowledge encounters numerous problems which are the barriers towards the formation of a sound epistemology for this academic discipline. One of the main problems is the inadequacies of theorizing in this field (Mair and Marti 2006; Dees and Anderson 2006a; Nyssens 2006; Nicholls 2009), in other words it is under-theorized (Dacin et al. 2010). Such a situation presented SE as an immature discipline which "lacks the deep, rich, explanatory or prescriptive theories expected in a more mature academic field" (Dees and Anderson 2006b, 39). The other barrier is the current situation of SE which is still "in the stage of conceptualization" (Sekliuckiene and Kisielius 2015, 1015). Moreover, lack of theories and lack of a well-formed conceptualization has gone hand in hand and has made a "proliferation of definition" for SE (Bacq and Janssen, 2011: 373) that begot not only a shaky thought foundation among the academia but also neutralized any endeavor for the formation of scientific paradigm.

---

[2] Successful classification of SE knowledge contributes considerably to the choice of true scientific approach in SE studies, in other words researchers will be able to choose the relevant research approaches based on the type of SE knowledge.

An Epistemological Criticism of Social Entrepreneurship 229

Therefore, SE suffers from a widespread "lack of unifying paradigm" (Bacq and Janssen 2011, 373). Still there is a struggle to define SE (Cuvier et al. 2011) but the struggle has been ended to different shades of meaning for SE (Dees 1998c) with the blame has been partly laid on the multiple sectors (e.g., public, private, for-profit and not-for-profit) that potentially SE took place in them (Christie and Honig 2006; Weerawardena and Mort 2006). Deep down, the disciplines such as non-profit organizations and entrepreneurship which were mother to SE, "largely lack theoretical consensus themselves" (Mair 2010, 2). SE growth in practice has been so speedy which has left SE in theory behind. Newbert (2014, 239) believes that the aforementioned speedy growth of SE has made a "fragmented body of literature" which has ended to no "well-established theories" and a weak "unified body of empirical research." Pondering over the current situation of SE, which was reflected above, pose the research question: Is social entrepreneurship a sound and scientific knowledge?

3. METHODOLOGY

All the data shaped the paper was secondary, in other words for the following critical discussions:

- Whether "Social" and "Entrepreneurship" words are oxymoron[3] or not
- Characteristics of SE knowledge
- SE knowledge structure and limitations

We used the following secondary data, respectively:

---

[3] Oxymoron is defined as "a combination of contradictory or incongruous words" (Merriam-Webster's Collegiate Dictionary, 2002: 832).

- Corpus of Contemporary American English (COCA) and Bibliometrics' secondary data
- SE literature review
- SE terminology

The data collection from *Corpus of Contemporary American English (COCA)* was directly from its on-line website[4]. The author applied the search customization facilities of the website to define and sort the data based on the collocation and frequency of the words "social" and "entrepreneurship" together and the potential words that are usually used with them, i.e., the data are derived directly out of approximately 520 million words of text by the help of search customization facilities of the website. Moreover, the SE *Bibliometrics'* data was also secondary which was collected from one of the authentic studies[5].Therefore, the data collection approach was judgmental, i.e., the data are collected based on their relevancy to contribute the author in his discussions on "social entrepreneurship" phrase, characteristics of SE knowledge and its limitations and boundaries (Table 1).

Table 1. Summary of paper's methodology

Research Philosophy	Contributing to the establishment of SE epistemology
Research paradigm	Epistemological thought
Research goal	Reviewing possible epistemological thought relevant to SE critically in order to help SE to form an epistemology
Research approach	Criticism through meta-analysis
Research data	Secondary Data

Source: Author's own work.

To answer the research question the author had to have a comprehensive view towards SE epistemology which is reflected in Figure 1.

---

[4] http://corpus.byu.edu/coca/.
[5] A *Bibliometric* study by Rey-Martí, Ribeiro-Soriano and Palacios-Marqués in 2015, entitled, *"A Bibliometric Analysis of Social Entrepreneurship"* that has used the *Web of Science* database.

An Epistemological Criticism of Social Entrepreneurship

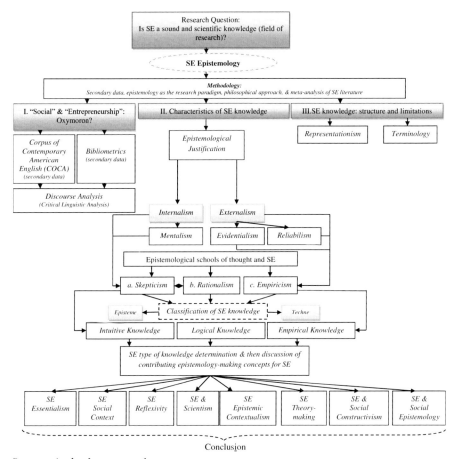

Source: Author's own work.

Figure 1. Methodological flowchart of paper's conclusion drawing.

4. RESULTS AND DISCUSSION

SE authors (Table 2) have usually accompanied the characteristics of commercial entrepreneurship with the adjective "social" and reused them for SE (i.e., SE is usually redefined the characteristics of commercial entrepreneurship but with social perspectives for itself, which metaphorically implies SE is a shadow to commercial entrepreneurship, in other words the social shadow of entrepreneurship which was shown in

232 *Amir Forouharfar*

Figure 2). Therefore, it is recommendable that those who want to study SE have some familiarities with other social knowledge like sociology or social economy.

Table 2. Frequently-mentioned characteristics of SE

SE characteristics	Literature
Making Social Value	Nicholls 2006; Dees 1998b; Gartener 1990; Hibbert, Hogg and Quinn 2002; Austin, Stevenson, and Wei-Skiller 2006; Boschee 1998; Alvord et al. 2004; Mort, Weerawardena, and Carnegie 2002; Sarasvathy and Wicks, 2003; Peredo and McLean 2006, Anderson and Dees 2002; Townsend and Hart 2008; Matin 2004
Innovation	Schumpeter 1951; Drucker 1985; Herbert and Link 1989; Nijkamp 2003; Martín, Picazo, and Teresa 2008; CovinandSlevin 1991; Lumpkin and Dess 1996; Morris and Kuratko 2002; Kuratko et al. 2005; Zakić et al. 2008; Miller and Friesen 1982; Covin and Miles 1999; Burgelman 1984; Kanter 1985; Alterowitz, 1988; Naman and Slevin 1993; Zahra and Covin 1995; Rwigema and Venter 2004; Slater and Narver 2000; Smart and Conant 1994; Lumpkin and Dess 1996; Ussahawanitchakit 2007; Mohd Osman et al. 2011; Salarzehi and Forouharfar 2011
Seeking Opportunity	Shane et al. 2003; Christiansen 1997; Ferreira 2002; Timmons and Spinelli 2003; Rwigema and Venter 2004; Kuratko and Hodgetts 1995; Simon 1996; Ireland et al. 2003; Miles and Snow 1978; Stevenson, Roberts, and Grousbeck 1989; Berthon, McHulbert, and Pitt 2004; Amabile 1997; Gilad 1984; Timmons 1978; Ward 2004; Whiting 1988
Making Social Change	Nicholls and Cho 2006; Skoll Foundation 2008; Prabhu 1999; Hoffman et al. 2010; Choi and Gray 2008; Cohen and Winn 2007; Waddock and Post 1991; Stryjan 2006; Picot 2012
Making Social Welfare	Bugg-Levine, Kogut, and Kulatilaka 2012; Scheuerle et al. 2013; Alvord et al. 2004; Battilana et al. 2012; Haigh and Hoffman 2012; Weisbrod 1977
Having Social Results	Dees 1998a, 1998b; Thake and Zadek 1997; Emerson and Twersky 1986

Source: Rowshan and Forouharfar 2014.

Source: Author's own work.

Figure 2. Shadow metaphor for SE.

4.1. Is "Social Entrepreneurship" an Oxymoron?

Initially, we should determine whether "social entrepreneurship" phrase is oxymoronic or not. Here we intend to elaborate the combination of two words a noun, "entrepreneurship" and an adjective "social." We want to see how relevant and possible is to apply the phrase "social entrepreneurship." Almarri (2014, 26) believes, "The word 'social entrepreneurship' already presents a definitional dilemma, as the world 'social' typically relates to non-economic ventures, whereas the word 'enterprise' highlights the financial side of such ventures." Additionally, Santos (2012) disagrees with the collocation of the word "social" with "entrepreneurship" since the connotation of the word social in SE practices includes some activities and excludes some others, such as giving money to the low-income people is social but the same to the high-income people is not social. On the other hand some scholars such as Seelos and Mair (2005, 243-244) believe the annexed adjective "social" is because of the services and products that social entrepreneurs develop to "cater directly to basic human needs that remain unsatisfied by current economic or social institutions." Even according to Phan et al. (2014, 20) "some authors use the terminology [social entrepreneurship] at lower intensity as a social intend, some conceptualize the phenomenon in terms of strong social objectives."

4.1.1. Discourse Analysis and SE

Discourse Analysis can help us to determine whether "social entrepreneurship" is an oxymoronic phrase or not (Figure 3).

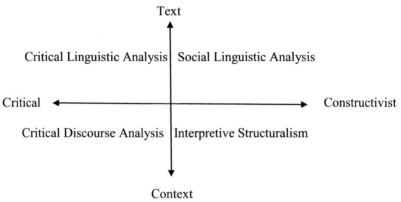

Source: Philips and Hardy 2002.

Figure 3. Various approaches to discourse analysis.

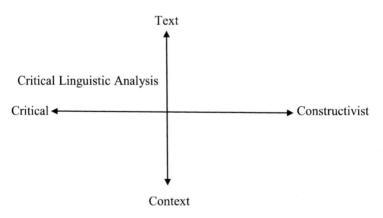

Figure 4. Selected approach to discourse analysis for the analysis of the prevailing SE discourse in this section.

Seymour (2012) believes discourse analysis is "well-suited" method of analysis to SE that aims to study the formation of new and emerging social

An Epistemological Criticism of Social Entrepreneurship 235

phenomena by the investigation and analysis of text bodies. Therefore, for the analysis of the existence or nonexistence of the oxymoron in SE phrase, *Critical Linguistic Analysis* approach, because of its relevance to the intention of the author in this section, has been selected (Figure 4).

Two authentic corpora for corpus-based discourse analysis of SE are present: *Corpus of Contemporary American English (COCA)* [6]and *British National Corpus (BNC)*[7]. In this section of the paper the *Corpus of Contemporary American English (COCA)* was applied. This gaves us this unique opportunity to investigate the contextual usage of the word "social entrepreneurship" among approximately 520 million words of text. I did not go into the details or use very sophisticated and technical approaches, because I did not want to deviate from the intension of this research, in other words the abovementioned corpora are used to help us in unfolding the contextual usage (discourse) and in the next stage to help us to have a better view towards the epistemological understanding of SE as knowledge. By study of the collocations, I intend to focus on the recurring patterns in respect to SE language. I want to see in the analysis of SE language which is used by the media, academia, public, etc. what words SE is collocated with and how often (frequency of word usage). I focus on the collocated SE language and the context which the language is used and have tried to see the big picture and not to fall into detailed linguistic discussions because it needs a separate research.

The *COCA* is divided its samples evenly among the five genre: academic20%, fiction20%, popular magazines 20%, newspaper 20%and spoken20%.[8]Therefore, *COCA's* data help us in understanding SE application in each genre evenly.

Table 3, showed what words "social entrepreneurship" (4 words before and 4 words after) has collocated with them. Moreover, the contexts and repeated names for the first four frequently collocated words with "social entrepreneurship" (Social (29) corporate (6) Richards (3) foundation (3)) were also presented in the table. The frequency of the words "social" as

---

[6] It has more than 520 million words of text.
[7] It has a 100 million sample of spoken and written English.
[8] http://corpus.byu.edu/coca/compare-bnc.asp.

236 *Amir Forouharfar*

adjective (not the "social" in the compound noun "social entrepreneurship"), beside "corporate" show the linguistic context for SE.

Table 3. Corpus of Contemporary American English (COCA) data for SE collocations and contexts

SE Collocations[9]	Social (29), corporate (6), Richards (3), foundation (3), innovative (2), exploring (2), dedicated (2), responsibility (2), finding (2), design (2), ways (2), having (2), school (2), promulgating (1), closed-loop (1), early stage (1), Drayton (1), disciple (1), philanthropic (1), deutche (1), academies (1), entails (1), pioneering (1), promotes (1), integrate (1), strictly (1), grants (1), introduced (1), consultant (1), aimed (1), defend (1), founded (1), element (1), interaction (1), i.e.(1), examples (1), defined (1), offering (1), core (1), push (1), scale (1), provides (1), term(1), starting (1), perfect(1), global (1), organization (1), activities (1), bank (1), career (1), learned (1), calls (1), happen (1), include (1), seemed (1), bill (1), local (1), business (1), doing (1), important (1), course (1), kind (1), country (1), things (1)
SE Contexts[10]	Corporate social entrepreneurship, Corporate social responsibility, corporate philanthropy, social investing
Repeated Proper Nouns[11]	Drayton, Dees, Richards Foundation, Bill Draper, Robin Richards

Source: Derived by the author from *COCA* website.

The prevailing nature of SE based on the corpus is a phenomenon which is "social" and strongly related to "corporate" matters (with most frequent phrases: corporate social entrepreneurship, corporate social responsibility, corporate philanthropy, social investing), at least in American SE discourse. Moreover, the interesting issue is the frequency of the adjective "innovative" which is placed after the two above-mentioned words. It could be interpreted that the nature of SE; in respect to scientific fields, is more oriented towards sociology ("social") and management ("corporate") than entrepreneurship

---

[9] Numbers in parenthesis show the frequency.
[10] For the first four frequently collocated words (Social (29) corporate (6) Richards (3) foundation (3)) with "social entrepreneyrship."
[11] For the first four frequently collocated words (Social (29) corporate (6) Richards (3) foundation (3)) with "social entrepreneyrship."

("innovative") and economy (Figure 5). Furthermore, the repetitions of the names: Drayton, Dees, Richards Foundation, Bill Draper, Robin Richards, could show the importance of them in discourse-makings.

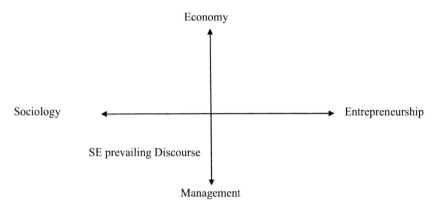

Source: Author's own work.

Figure 5. SE prevailing discourse among academia, popular magazines, newspapers and spoken genres.

According to Table 4, which shows derived data from *Corpus of Contemporary American English (COCA)*, the phrase "social entrepreneurship" more frequently was used between the years 2005-2009 with the frequency of 0.18 per million. It reveals that the SE discourse has been more prevalent through these years. The frequency of the phrase, per million, is 0.09 (academic), 0.08 (magazine), 0.08 (newspaper), and 0.01 (spoken) with no frequency in fiction. It shows that the phrase is more frequently is applied in the written texts and among the academia.

On the other hand, SE discourses could be seen from different perspectives. For example following Nicholls (2010, 612) there are three dominant *legitimating discourses* in the realm of SE: "narrative logics based on hero entrepreneur examples; ideal type organizational models based on business; and logics based on communitarian values and social justice." Based on Philips and Hardy (2002) framework presented in Figure 3, the adopted approach by Nicholls (2010) was *Interpretive Structuralism*, which tries to discover the prevailing structures, and is different from the approach which is taken by us, *Critical Linguistic Analysis*.

238
Amir Forouharfar

Table 4. Corpus of Contemporary American English (COCA) data for SE

Genre/Year	size (million)	Freq. per million	Freq.%
Spoken	109.4	0.01	1%
Fiction	104.9	0.00	0%
Magazine	110.1	0.08	9%
News Paper	106.0	0.08	9%
Academic	103.4	0.09*	9%
1990-1994	104.0	0.00	0%
1995-1999	103.4	0.00	0%
2000-2004	102.9	0.02	2%
2005-2009	102.0	0.18*	18%
2010-2015	121.6	0.07	8%

Source: Derived by the author exactly from *COCA* website.

Considering the frequent collocation of the adjective "social"[12] with the phrase "social entrepreneurship" in the corpus, shows that at least linguistically the phrase "social entrepreneurship" is not an oxymoron and it could be accepted as a well-suited name for this knowledge and university major among the academia and media.

4.1.2. Bibliometrics and SE

If we narrow done the discourse on SE to the academic field a bibliometric study by Rey-Martí; Ribeiro-Soriano and Palacios-Marqués (2015) entitled, *A Bibliometric Analysis of Social Entrepreneurship* that has used the *Web of Science* database for, a sample of 2922 academic reviews and materials on SE. The results of the research were interesting for the analysis of discourse makers in academic realm on SE. It revealed that the first ten rankings of research languages on SE were as the following:

English (2728), Spanish (37), Slovack (30), Czech (17), Chinese (17), German (14), Croatian (12), Portuguese (10), Russian (6) French (6). Moreover, areas of knowledge that SE research has been carried out in them are presented in the following: (1) Business Economics (1851); (2) Public

---

[12] Note: "social" as an adjective is frequently situated (in the technical term, collocated) within the four words before or after the phrase "social entrepreneurship," and is not the "social" in the "social entrepreneurship" phrase.

Administration (347); (3) Social Sciences/Other Topics (231); (4) Education/Educational Research (189); (5) Sociology (171); (6)Environmental Sciences Ecology (145); (7)Engineering (129); (8) Psychology (104); (9)Geography (90); (10) Computer Science (87); (11) Operations Research/Management Science (86). Additionally, the ten journals which have published the most researches on SE according to the mentioned research were as the following: (1) *Journal Of Business Venturing* (83); (2) *Entrepreneurship And Regional Development* (80); (3) *Entrepreneurship Theory And Practice* (57); (4) *Journal Of Business Ethics* (56); (5) *International Small Business Journal* (53); (6) *Small Business Economics* (53); (7) *Research Policy* (33); (8) *International Entrepreneurship and Management Journal* (31); (9) *Organization Studies* (28); (10) *Organization Science* (21).

Table 5. Prolific researchers of SE

Ranking	Author	No. of Publications	Total Citations	H-Index	C/P
1	Anderson A.R.	12	539	10	44.92
2	Mair J.	10	421	6	42.1
3	Shepherd D.A.	9	206	6	22.89
4	Nijkamp P.	9	44	3	4.89
5	Ireland R.D.	9	572	8	63.56
6	Honig B.	9	811	8	90.11
7	Zahra S.A.	8	411	5	51.38
8	Wright M.	8	235	6	29.38
9	Urbano D.	8	79	3	9.88
10	Tracey P.	8	213	5	26.62
11	Jack S.	8	177	5	22.12
12	Dodd S.D.	8	210	5	26.25
13	De Clercq D.	8	137	7	17.12
14	Welter F.	7	275	7	39.29
15	Webb J.W.	7	264	6	37.71
16	Haugh H.	7	84	4	12

Source: Rey-Martí; Ribeiro-Soriano and Palacios-Marqués 2015.

Table 5, shows 16 frequently mentioned researchers in SE. The most prolific author until 2015 is Anderson A.R. with 12 publications, and the most cited researcher is Honig B. with 811 citations and 90.11citation per publication.

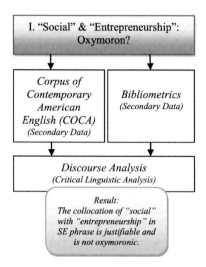

Source: Author's own work.

Figure 6. The flow chart of discussion for "social" and "entrepreneurship" potential oxymoronic relationship.

Therefore it could be concluded that the discourse makers in the academic arena were mostly used English language in areas of knowledge such as Business Economics, Public Administration, educational researches and Sociology, which are "social" sciences which inherently verifies and strongly justifies the annexation of the adjective "social" to "entrepreneurship" in "social entrepreneurship" phrase. Moreover, some of the prolific researchers in SE who are cutting-edge and expanding the discourses and boundaries of SE are: Anderson A.R., Mair J., Shepherd D.A., Nijkamp P., Ireland R.D., Honig B., Zahra S.A., Wright M., Urbano D., Tracey P., Jack S., Dodd S.D., De Clercq D., Welter F., Webb J.W., and Haugh H. Moreover, some of the top and prominent academic journals which are expanding SE knowledge and theory are *Journal of Business Venturing*; *Entrepreneurship and Regional Development*; *Entrepreneurship Theory and Practice*; *Journal of Business Ethics*; *International Small Business Journal*; and *Small Business Economics*. These researchers and journals are truly the forerunners of SE.

An Epistemological Criticism of Social Entrepreneurship 241

The results of COCA and *Bibliometrics* for SE revealed that the collocation of "social" with "entrepreneurship" in SE phrase was first justifiable and second was not oxymoronic. Figure 6 has summarized the discussions in this section of the paper.

4.2. Characteristics of SE Knowledge

Three concepts (*Truth, Belief* and *Justification*) [13]form the nature of each knowledge jointly.SE as a human knowledge is not an exception but this paper did not discuss the concepts of *Truth* and *Belief* in SE because they are philosophically too abstract features to discuss in a paper like this, moreover they did not contribute the author to reach the paper's goal which is reviewing critically possible epistemological thought relevant to SE in order to contribute to SE to form an epistemology. Concerning the third concept or *Justification*, it was a feature which was mostly used in the paper. Each philosophical thought which was raised in the paper was a justification for or against answering the research question whether SE is a sound and scientific knowledge or not. Therefore, above all we should determine what kind of epistemological justification is philosophically pertaining to SE criticism.

4.2.1. Epistemological Justification for SE as Knowledge

Epistemologists either take *Internalism* or *Externalism* for epistemic justification, accordingly the justification for beliefs, facts and reasons for SE principally could be internal or external.

---

[13] Knowledge is "justified true belief: *S* [subject] knows that *p* [proposition] if and only if *p* is true and *S* is justified in believing that *p*. According to this analysis, the three conditions - truth, belief, and justification - are individually necessary and jointly sufficient for knowledge" (Steup, 2016, on-line *Stanford Encyclopedia of Philosophy*).

242   *Amir Forouharfar*

4.2.1.1. Internalism

Internalism[14] claims that the justification of the belief is internal to the believer or subject, in other words internalists justify their beliefs based on their perceptions and mental images. Reviewing SE literature, there were examples of internalist justifications in plenty. For example numerous definitions for SE (e.g., Alvord et al. 2004, Austin et al. 2006a, Brouard et al. 2008, Dees 1998b, Fowler 2000, Harding 2004, Hibbert et al. 2005, Lasprogata and Cotton 2003, Mair and Marti 2006, Martin and Osberg 2007, Mort et al. 2002, Peredo and McLean 2006, Perrini and Vurro 2006, Roberts and Woods 2005, Seelos and Mair 2005) or specifying different and sometimes contrary sectors for the occurrence of SE (e.g., not-for-profit, for-profit and governmental sectors in Austin et al. (2006a), not-for-profit sector in Lasprogata and Cotton (2003) or for-profit and not-for-profit in Yunus (2008)) all are convincing that *Internalism* is the governing perspective in SE literature. Such a perplexity and dissonance in the fundamental concepts of SE is an implication of a type of epistemological *Internalism* which is called *Mentalism*. *Mentalism* which is defined as different "mental state[s] of the epistemic agent[s]" (Pappas 2014)[15] is the main criticism to the current SE literature which took us nowhere but to more confusion and lack of setting a solid and scientifically justifiable foundation for SE.

4.2.1.2. Externalism

By contrast, *Externalism* does not accept that "a person either does or can have a form of *access* to the basis for knowledge or justified belief" (Pappas 2014, on-line *Stanford Encyclopedia of Philosophy*) by internal mentality or thought and there is no need to apply internal reasons and facts to justify what he believes (Bonjour 2008, 365). Therefore, subjective perception (i.e., what we understand as a human being) comes from the

---

[14] There are three forms of *Internalism*: (1) the *access* form which claims the believer could have access to the basis for knowledge; (2) *Mentalism* form which claims, "that what ultimately justifies any belief is some mental state of the epistemic agent holding that belief." And (3) *deontological* form, "whose main idea is that the concept of epistemic justification is to be analyzed in terms of fulfilling one's intellectual duties or responsibilities " (Pappas 2014, on-line *Stanford Encyclopedia of Philosophy*).

[15] On-line *Stanford Encyclopedia of Philosophy*.

outside (hence, external) of the subject (Sosa et al. 2008). As we move towards more externalist justifications in SE literature we could overcome the prevailing ambiguity and confusion and we could discuss and set SE on more tangible grounds (Figure 7).

Additionally, other justifications for SE could be discussed as following:

Source: Author's own work.

Figure 7. The principal role of externalist or internalist justification in SE epistemology formation.

4.2.1.3. Evidentialism

"According to *Evidentialism*, what makes a belief justified ... is the possession of evidence. The basic idea is that a belief is justified to the degree it fits *S*'s evidence" (Steup 2016)[16] and moreover, according to Chignell (2016) "Many Evidentialists (Locke, Hume, and Clifford, for example) add the condition that the amount of evidence in one's possession must be proportioned to one's degree of belief, and that one should only *firmly* believe on the basis of "sufficient" evidence."[17]

In discussing Evidentialism for SE, we have three different types of *Evidentialism* (*Prudential Evidentialism*, *Moral Evidentialism* and *Epistemic Evidentialism*) what we intend is the *Epistemic Evidentialism*, in other words the *Evidentialism* which emphasizes on "sufficient" evidence on the side of the subject, hence the subjects are the theorists in the realm of SE. The other two types of *Evidentialism* that are not intended and usually

---

[16] On-line *Stanford Encyclopedia of Philosophy*.
[17] On-line *Stanford Encyclopedia of Philosophy*.

244   *Amir Forouharfar*

are used for ethical discussions of evidence emphasize on "counterexamples"[18] and "morally good or bad evidences"[19], respectively.

Evidence will lead to belief, and justified true belief makes our knowledge, but this philosophical knowledge is not equivalent with to be scientific. Here, to discuss the sufficient evidence could lead us to truly justify the belief that there could be a realm of knowledge known as SE. SE mostly collects it evidence from real world, in other words first there had been many successful examples which are founded to directly or indirectly solve a social problem or serve the people innovatively not with primarily with financial intentions but with the philanthropist ones. Therefore all researches on SEOs (social entrepreneurship organizations) large or small can provide sufficient evidence for the justification of belief in a knowledge known as SE. Moreover, it could be discussed that SE collects its *evidence* by different methodologies, from qualitative and statistical approaches (Seymour, 2012) to quantitative ones, that Hoogendoorn, Pennings and Thurik (2010: 71) believe are mostly reflected in "conceptual papers." They believe: "research in the past two decades has been primarily dedicated to establishing a conceptual foundation, which has resulted in a considerable stream of conceptual papers."

4.2.1.4. Reliabilism

This view is a form of Externalism and emphasizes on "S's belief" to have "a high objective probability of truth and therefore, if true, is not true merely because of luck. One prominent idea is that this is accomplished if, and only if, a belief originates in reliable cognitive processes or faculties. This view is known as *Reliabilism*" (Steup 2016)[20]. The touchstone to these "reliable cognitive processes" according to Goldman (2008) is the ability to produce true beliefs.

---

[18] Such as, "Wouldn't it be better for the grief-stricken widower to believe that his wife is enjoying life in heaven, or for the devoted spouse to fight off the belief that her husband is unfaithful, even though she regularly finds lipstick on his collar?"(Chignell 2016).

[19] Such as, "'You simply shouldn't believe that about your friend!'-expressed in a context where the friend's disloyalty is not conclusively supported by the evidence." (Chignell 2016).

[20] on-line *Stanford Encyclopedia of Philosophy*

An Epistemological Criticism of Social Entrepreneurship   245

The objectivity that *Reliabilism* is searching for is very hard to find in SE, since SE is a social knowledge and always there is an extreme possibility of bias in social sciences.[21] In comparison to empirical sciences, it is very hard to distinguish the border between subjective justification or the objective one, in other words sometimes it is very hard or impossible for a human who is a construct of a complicated and in some cases complex social culture and context to detach himself and then evaluate the social issue objectively or by a "reliable cognitive processes." Therefore, by *Reliabilism* glasses SE could not be proved to be "reliable" since it is very hard to prove that it produces "true beliefs" even if they exist.

4.2.2. The Nature of SE

Basically, in Epistemology we have three forms of knowledge: (1) Propositional Knowledge (Knowledge-That), (2) Knowledge of Acquaintance and (3) Knowledge-How. According to Fantl (2016) the definitions of the abovementioned knowledge are: "There's the kind of knowledge you have when it is truly said of you that you know how to do something—say, ride a bicycle [Knowledge-How]. There's the kind of knowledge you have when it is truly said of you that you know a person— say, your best friend [Knowledge of Acquaintance]. And there's the kind of knowledge you have when it is truly said of you that you know that some fact is true—say, that the Red Sox won the 2004 World Series [Propositional Knowledge or Knowledge-That]."SE must be in the realm of the first or the last knowledge. The old Greek philosophers had two concepts of *Episteme* and *Techne* which according to Fantl (2016) are roughly synonymous to knowledge-that and knowledge-how, or theoretical knowledge and practical knowledge, respectively. Here, we can discuss if SE belongs to the realm of

---

[21] For more information see:

Shelley E. Taylor. 1982. "The Availability Bias in Social Perception and Interaction." In *Judgment under Uncertainty: Heuristics and Biases*, edited by Daniel Kahneman, Paul Slovic, and Amos Tversky: 190-200. UK: Cambridge University Press.

Gordon, Edmund W., Fayneese Miller, and David Rollock. "Coping with Communicentric Bias in Knowledge Production in the Social Sciences." *Educational Researcher* 19(3): 14-19.

Episteme (knowledge-that or theoretical knowledge) or *Techne* (Knowledge-how or practical knowledge).

SE belongs to the both realms. In theory like most of the social sciences is knowledge-that or episteme and in practice by the SE practitioners in socially entrepreneurial organizations and institutes could be considered as knowledge-how or *Techne*. Moreover the *Techne* orientation of SE knowledge had been more progressive in comparison to the theory making and theoretical side, which could be because of the preexistence of socially entrepreneurial practices before the formation of such an academic study known as SE. Such an unsatisfactory situation in theorizing, according to Newbert (2014, 239) is due to "its rapid growth" that " has resulted in a rather fragmented body of literature that lacks both a set of well-established theories and a robust, unified body of empirical research" but indirectly and through entrepreneurship, the economic theories could build its knowledge-that. In this sense it could be said knowledge-that partially builds the theoretical foundations of SE deep down. On the other hand, the knowledge of how to start up social entrepreneurial enterprises for example approaches the realm of knowledge-how, which could be formed by the study of the successful cases in SE. Moreover, there are not any hard and fast rules to distinguish the border of the two mentioned knowledge and sometimes some aspects of the field could embrace knowledge-that and some other aspects knowledge-how.

4.3. Sources of Social Entrepreneurship Knowledge

4.3.1. Empericism[22] and SE

The term "empirical" is derived from the Greek "empeiria" and it indicates a school of thought which claims that knowledge merely originates and comes from sensory experience (Psillos and Curd 2010). Epistemologically, here "empirical evidence" has a pivotal role in the formation of ideas against the innate ideas (Baird 2008). To answer how

---

[22] Greek empeiria, "experience."

An Epistemological Criticism of Social Entrepreneurship 247

much empirical approaches have impacts on SE, here we can rely on bibliometric studies. *Bibliometrics* which is a quantitative method for the production of metrics in scientific literature (Rauter 2006; Ball and Tunger 2005; Garfield 1998; Harsanyi 1993; White and McCain 1989; Solla Price 1981; Solla Price 1976; Garfield 1973; Pritchard 1969; Solla Price 1963; Lotka 1926) and usually presents the big picture has been applied in SE too. A bibliometric study by Sassmannshausen and Volkmann (2013) entitled *"A Bibliometric Based Review on Social Entrepreneurship and its Establishment as a Field of Research"* revealed that most of frequently-cited articles in SE lacked empirical section with mostly qualitative approaches application. Such a condition for SE researches had been also claimed by Granados et al. (2011). Sassmannshausen and Volkmann (2013,17) concluded that, "(Single) case studies and exemplary cases or (single) narratives as well as good practice reports are the most often used forms of empirical research." Short, Moss and Lumpkin (2009, 161) have reflected the research in SE as "conceptual articles outnumber empirical studies, and empirical efforts often lack formal hypotheses and rigorous methods. These findings suggest that social entrepreneurship research remains in an embryonic state."

Therefore it could be inferred that SE literature and accordingly researches are not; at least up to the present, dominantly empirical-evidence oriented, as Hoogendoorn, Pennings and Thurik (2010) believe that the papers on SE is dominantly conceptual and to evolve SE we have to pay more attention to empirical articles.

4.3.2. Rationalism[23] and SE

Encyclopedia Britannica in defining Rationalism asserts that *reason* has seen "as the chief source and test of knowledge." Even reason has been used as tool for justification (lacey 1996), since "the criterion of the truth is not sensory but intellectual and deductive" (Bourke 1962). *Rationalism* in granting reason as the source of knowledge is in contrast to *Empiricism* that places experience in place of rationalist's reasoning. *René Descartes* as the

---

[23] Latin *ratio,*"reason."

248 *Amir Forouharfar*

outstanding figure in this school of thought believed, "by means of reason alone, certain universal, self-evident truths could be discovered, from which the remaining content of philosophy and the sciences could be deductively derived. He assumed that these self-evident truths were innate, not derived from sense experience" (West 2009, Microsoft Student). It is very hard to claim purely rationalistic approach as a suitable procedure for SE source knowledge. Relying excessively on Rationalism can spoil SE by making it merely a philosophical debate and keeps it far from the realities and practices which could be understood mostly empirically.

4.3.3. Skepticism[24] and SE

Skepticism is the "doctrine that denies the possibility of attaining knowledge of reality as it is in itself, apart from human perception," and in nature is epistemological since, "it is based on views about the scope and validity of human knowledge" (Microsoft Student 2009). Looking skeptically at the epistemology of SE, and in reference to *Friedrich Nietzsche* who "denied the possibility of complete objectivity, and thus of objective knowledge, in any field (Microsoft Student 2009) we can claim that usually there is possibility of subjectivity in SE literature. Although social knowledge (hence, SE), in comparison to the experimental knowledge, has a propensity towards subjectivity because of its nature, we should be careful to take some defendable measures to lead it towards objective reasoning. The lived experiences of the subjects in social sciences (hence, SE scholars) have a potential probability to be reflected in their conclusion. Therefore, to build up on *Friedrich Nietzsche's* skepticism SE literature at least at the theoretical level could be dominantly the reflection of the authors' (subjects) mind not the true objective reality, or to take *Immanuel Kant* who "denied the possibility of knowing things in themselves or of achieving metaphysical knowledge," (Ibid.) we can claim SE is the *reflection* of reality, not the reality itself. To be subjective and reflection of reality are the claims that are usually raised for the social sciences, and hence SE, since they have abstract nature. Wide spectrum of definitions for SE and

---

[24] Greek *skeptesthai,* "to examine."

An Epistemological Criticism of Social Entrepreneurship 249

lack of consensus on any one of them (Haugh 2005; Choi and Majumdar 2014) that in a wider scope could also consist of entrepreneurship itself and its lack of universal definition (Anderson and Starnawska 2008) reflect a deep subjectivity in SE. To overcome subjectivity, social sciences and hence SE have usually tried to quantify social phenomena, in other words the social scholars in numerous examples in the history of social sciences development were applied mathematical and numerical approaches to contribute them in discussing social issues objectively. Hartmann and Sprenger (2011) believe:

> "In fact, the use of mathematical and statistical methods is now ubiquitous: Almost all social sciences rely on statistical methods to analyze data and to form hypotheses, and almost all of them use (to a greater or lesser extend) a range of mathematical methods to help us understand the social world." (p. 594)

Impartially, such reliance on mathematics and statistics (mathematization) have had its own advantages for social sciences and hence SE (e.g., objectivity and precision, Hartmann and Sprenger 2011) but we should be alerted that it could be a double-edged sword, that is too much obsession with mathematical or statistical application in the realm of social sciences, and hence SE, could yield a passive and deformed reality, because the nature of the social phenomena is fundamentally different from the nature of the issues mathematics, statistics and calculations are dealing with them. To apply quantitative methodologies, we have to accept *Reductionism* and reduce the social phenomenon, by neglecting its multidimensional features, to some researcher-made constructs, which are not usually the social entity or feature itself but the quantified perception of the researcher about what the previous entity could be in numbers. We should be guarded against such oversimplification in SE by applying qualitative methodologies wherever it is possible and relevant.

According to the above-mentioned schools of thought we can generally classify knowledge to one of the following classifications:

4.3.4. Intuitive Knowledge

Encyclopedia Britannica defines intuition as "the power of obtaining knowledge that cannot be acquired either by inference or observation, by reason or experience."[25]Therefore, it is "a form of knowledge or of cognition independent of experience or reason" (Microsoft Student 2009) A more philosophical definition is offered by Pust (2016)[26]who defines *intuitions* as, "mental states or events in which a proposition *seems true in the manner of these propositions*:

[I1] If non-not-*p*, then *p*.
[I2] Torturing a cat for fun is wrong.
[I3] It is impossible for a square to have five sides.
[I4] A person would survive having their brain transplanted into a new body."

In the epistemological sense of the word, intuition can also be rational.

Different philosophers have given different connotations to intuition. Therefore in discussing intuition it is better to mention the name of the philosopher. For example, "in *Spinoza's* philosophy, intuition is the highest form of knowledge, surpassing both empirical knowledge derived from the senses and "scientific" knowledge derived from reasoning on the basis of experience. Intuitive knowledge gives an individual the comprehension of an orderly and united universe and permits the mind to be a part of the Infinite Being" or *Kant* mentions intuition as "a portion of perception" that came into being by the mind; moreover, *Bergson* opposed *instinct* to *intelligence*, and believed intuition is the instinct in the purest form, to him *intelligence* deals with the material world and cannot get to the nature of thought or life, on the other hand, intuition as "instinct that has become disinterested, self-conscious, capable of reflecting upon its object and of enlarging it indefinitely " makes the absolute comprehensible (Microsoft Student, 2009). Another connotation to this concept is *Rational Intuition*, which is the intuition of an epistemological rationalist, comes out of a belief that belief in propositions is not justifiable by mere memory, sense

---

[25] https://www.britannica.com/topic/intuition.
[26] on-line *Stanford Encyclopedia of Philosophy*.

An Epistemological Criticism of Social Entrepreneurship 251

experience or introspection (Bealer 1998; Bonjour 1998).Since the concept of intuition is deeply abstract, any struggle to offer a precise definition of what intuitive knowledge is could be hard. According to Bertrand Russell (1912):

> "Our immediate knowledge of *truths* may be called *intuitive* knowledge, and the truths so known may be called *self-evident* truths. Among such truths are included those which merely state what is given in sense, and also certain abstract logical and arithmetical principles, and (though with less certainty) some ethical propositions. Our *derivative* knowledge of truths consists of everything that we can deduce from self-evident truths by the use of self-evident principles of deduction." (p. 171)

Creativity as a mental concept, and innovation as a practical one, and two principal concepts in any entrepreneurship could emerge from intuition, or for example, *Entrepreneurial Timing* could be classified as this type of knowledge since it relies heavily on the intuitive understanding of the entrepreneurial strategist and its timing intuition for strategy formulation and implementation (Forouharfar, Yaghoubi and Motamedifar 2014). SE, also benefits from intuitive entrepreneurial timing concept, since first, it is a type of entrepreneurship and second timing could have a pivotal role in its success.

4.3.5. Logical Knowledge

In this classification of knowledge *Reason* plays a pivotal role. *Rationalism* is the source of this knowledge which is discussed before.

4.3.6. Empirical Knowledge

This classification of knowledge is exactly opposite to *Intuitive Knowledge*, since it put the emphasis on the scientific method and believe the hypotheses must be tested experimentally. According to Shelley (2006) Empiricism which is mostly used by natural scientists believe that "knowledge is based on experience" and consider continued revision and falsification processes for knowledge. Therefore, *Karl Popper's Falsificationism* as a distinguishing factor between scientific and unscientific knowledge is weighty.

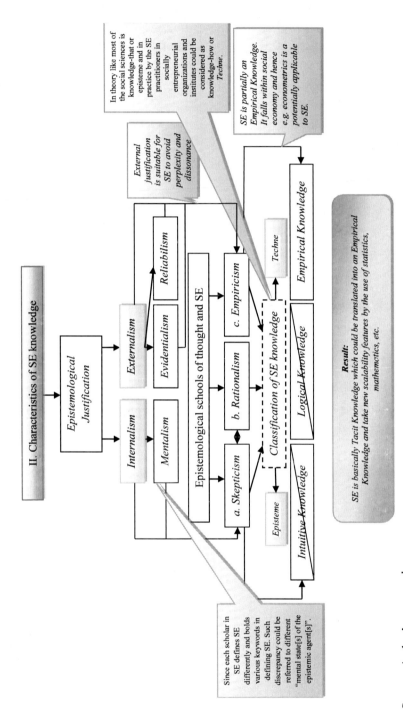

Source: Author's own work.

Figure 8. The flow chart of characteristics of SE knowledge.

An Epistemological Criticism of Social Entrepreneurship   253

Sensory experience has seen as the source of knowledge. Through *Logical Empiricism (logical positivism)* the emphasis on sensory experience took a vigorous form. The outcome was *Verificationism*, a view which asserts only the statements that are empirically verifiable are cognitively meaningful; in other words, statements or philosophical propositions must be either true (verifiable) or false (falsifiable) otherwise they are meaningless and nonscientific.

4.3.7. SE Knowledge Classification

By considering the above-mentioned classifications of knowledge, and the fact that there are other different types of knowledge such as explicit, tacit, embrained and embodied (Sheldon and Daniele 2017). SE could be classified as tacit knowledge. Such knowledge needs more empirical studies to bring out its undercover aspects. *Explicate knowledge* could be easily transformed into words or numbers, SE because of its pre-paradigmatic phase cannot be classified in this realm. *Tacit knowledge* is hard to pour into words and is highly dependent on the individualistic traits of the person, in other words it is dependent on the values, experiences and belief system of the person who carries it (Nonaka and Takeuchi 1995). Since SE relies on an innovative enterprise of the social entrepreneurs which is especially in the successful cases originates from the tacit knowledge of the individual social entrepreneur and its superb statement of the local problem and its effective remedy or solution it is highly tacit too. Each context and local problem could be unique. Such a situation pushes SE to be as many as the social problems and local realities unique and innovative situations which are highly tacit and partially could be originated from the intuition of the social entrepreneur. For example, SE takes advantage of market-based strategies to cope with social issues in special contexts and also apply local knowledge and market knowledge as two leverages for social innovation (Sheldon and Daniele 2017). On the other hand the possibility of applying statistics and mathematics in SE reveals that it could be an empirical knowledge too, i.e., the unique and fundamental experiences of SE practitioners (tacit knowledge) could be translated into numerical, statistical and mathematical approaches which basically shows SE could be an

254 *Amir Forouharfar*

empirical knowledge. Figure 8 has summarized the discussions in this section of the paper.

4.4. SE Knowledge: Structure and Limitations

Mire and Marti (2006, 36) believe SE is "poorly defined" and "its boundaries to other fields of study are still fuzzy." Different scholars specified various boundaries and limitation to the realm of SE. Some views were extended the domain of SE and some others limited the realm of SE. The result of such discrepancies in a single phenomenon which is called SE is eye-catching. The domain of SE as a knowledge was not specified, that is SE was not placed unanimously in a specific and firm realm which inherently prevented any formation of sound epistemology for SE. Therefore, the boundary to SE is blurred. A few scholars limited SE to traditional not-for-profit sector (Singh 2016), while Irwin (2007) puts social enterprises between charitable organizations and for-profit organizations. Such a placement by Irwin (2007) implies that SE is potentially a hybrid phenomenon. On the other hand, some authors related the realm of SE to the public organizations (Waddock and Post 1991) which implicitly extends the domain of SE to public administration knowledge (i.e., SE is a public issue and it should be administered by the governments and through bureaucracies). Furthermore, for Dees (1998b) SE even could embrace for-profit businesses if it was concentrated on a social mission. It did not end here, SE not only stretched to include *Community-Based Enterprises (CBE)* (Peredo and Chrisman 2006) but also took a more extreme inclusion as *Corporate Social Responsibility (CSR)* in other words an organization would be counted as an SEO by pursuing a social responsibility which in some cases could be disguises which were worn by some businesses to restore their lost publicity and reputation or to justify some of their antisocial measures. Therefore some organizations introduced *Cause Marketing*. Although it benefits society, underneath there is a profit maximization intension. Later the phenomenon took a more extensive meaning in *Corporate Social Entrepreneurship (CSE)* which granted corporations as

An Epistemological Criticism of Social Entrepreneurship 255

social entrepreneurs (e.g., John 2007; Austin et al. 2006a, b; Prahalad 2004). Finally some researchers (e.g., Neck et al. 2008; Mair and Noboa 2003; Johnson 2000; Nicholls 2006) added to the domain perplexity and extended the boundary of SE to all three sectors: Private, public and not-for profit/ the Third[27]. Lack of consensus on the domain of SE reveals deep ambiguity in the functions, expectations and constructs in this phenomenon. Therefore, finally SE is ended up in a boundless domain which shaped it as a ubiquitous discipline that takes the definitions and intentions of the authors. Human thought can effectively imagine and theorize those concepts which take limits otherwise the limitless concepts fall in pluralities and force the subject to define the concept based on his subjective perceptions which could by far from reality.

4.4.1. SE and Representation

One of the concepts which could lead us in the formation of scientific limits for any knowledge is the concept of *Representation*. According to Santos (2001, 254) for example *Representation* means "archaeology, involved in the study of objects and behaviors in very distant time, astronomy, involved in the study of objects very distant in space, cartography, concerned with representation of space through maps, and photography, concerned with representation as reproduction." We should set the limits of SE based on the concepts it is formed on their basis (e.g., economics, management, entrepreneurship, etc.). Applying *Representationism* to SE means as a human knowledge what SE wants to represent, in other words what SE is concerned with and what it stands for. If SE scholars succeed in determining the concepts that SE represents then they will be successful in defining SE universally and unanimously. For determining the key concepts that SE represents it should study its frequently-dependent issues and concepts which were used for its analysis and explanation. The key concepts should be searched within what SE

---

[27] Third Sector: "a term used to describe the range of organizations that are neither public sector nor private sector. It includes voluntary and community organizations (both registered charities and other organizations such as associations, self-help groups and community groups), social enterprises, mutuals and co-operatives."(*National Audit Office* Website)

mostly relies on for solving or relieving the social problems of the community, the country or the world. Furthermore, genuine representation of SE could set the true boundaries of SE knowledge. Such genuine *Representation* should be based on relevant selection of concepts in each of the constituting disciplines of SE (i.e., we should determine which economic, managerial, entrepreneurial or sociological concepts are relevant to the realm of SE and what true justifications could we present for their inclusion inside SE as some knowledge with social intentions. The problem that arises here is what epistemological approach should be selected for the inclusion of truly justifiable epistemic concepts in SE? The answer to the approach selection is still unsolved since in a big picture there is not a hard and fast rule for the selection of approaches in social sciences and usually the approaches were chosen by the researchers' scientific and tacit acumen. Consequently, some scholars have relied on empirical or pragmatic (*Positivistic*) approaches; for example they have applied *Mathematicism*, [28] or sometimes *Physicism*, [29] to the realm of social sciences to contribute them in determining what their social subject under study could truly represent. In contrary to the first scholars, some have relied on *Antipositivistic* approaches and they have tried to apply phenomenology, constructionism, discourse analysis, etc. as their approaches for epistemic selections (hence, inclusion of representing features in their social sciences). Up to now there had been sporadic researches to discuss the representing features of SE[30]. Our mental perspective leads us which tool to apply, but finally there could be this hope that at the end the selected concepts by the use of different schools of thought be divergent and represent as much as possible the true concepts that encircle the realm of SE.

---

[28] "The effort to employ the formal structure and rigorous method of mathematics as a model for the conduct of philosophy" (Encyclopedia Britannica, 1998) or according to *on-line Collins English Dictionary*, "The belief that everything can be explained in mathematical terms."

[29] "The belief in the physical and material world as opposed to the spiritual world in matters of philosophy and religion" (*on-line Collins English Dictionary*).

[30] For example see: Certo, S. Trevis, and Toyah Miller. "Social entrepreneurship: Key issues and concepts." *Business horizons* 51, no. 4 (2008): 267-271. And Martin, Roger L., and Sally Osberg. *Social entrepreneurship: The case for definition*. Vol. 5, no. 2. Stanford: Stanford social innovation review, 2007.

4.4.2. SE Terminology

The other concept which is noteworthy in shedding light on the scope of SE is the extent of SE terminology. As a knowledge broadens its realm by research the necessity for the coinage of new terms come in to existence, in other words the quantity and number of newly-coined terms could show the researchers the speed and acceleration of knowledge production in that scientific field, and on the other hand, the total number of terms in a discipline could show how deep that knowledge has gone. Usually bulky dictionaries of terminology in well-established sciences imply the collective endeavor of the experts through a long time in that field. Each term stands for a thought.

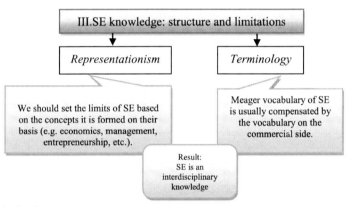

Source: Author's own work.

Figure 9. The flow chart of SE knowledge: structure and limitations.

By browsing on the Internet, media and among the articles on SE we can make a list for SE terminology (Table 6). Paying attention to the number and extension of SE terminology we could figure out how often the necessity arose to pour new ideas in newer words and phrases. If a field of knowledge entrapped in stagnation the former terms will be sufficient, but as it is on the track to scientific development and evolution, it calls for a more solid and vast terminology to help the maneuvering of thought in that field; in other words we would need new terms to discuss new phenomena in that knowledge. Unfortunately, we cannot see a vast terminology for SE. Meager

258 *Amir Forouharfar*

vocabulary of SE is usually compensated by the vocabulary on the commercial side; although, some endeavors which are the fruits of new thoughts has led to new terms (e.g., Zahra et al. (2009) typology of social entrepreneurs to *Social Bricoleurs*, *Social Constructionists*, and *Social Engineers*, or Rowshan and Forouharfar (2014) *Customized Social Entrepreneurship*). Such frugal terminology could be another sign for the pre-paradigmatic phase that SE is situated in.

Table 6. Buzzwords of Social Entrepreneurship

Social Entrepreneurship Terminology	Explanation
Venture Philanthropy	A word, coined by *John D. Rockefeller III* in 1969, and it "provides a blend of performance-based development finance and professional services to social purpose organizations (SPOs) – helping them expand their social impact" (John 2007, 5).
Social Return On Investment (SROI)	"A method for measuring and communicating a broad concept of value that incorporates social, environmental and economic impacts" (Social Impact Scotland Website).[31]
Social Intrapreneurship	"Inspir[ing] people in large organizations such as companies or administrations to recognize their innovative power and to realize their ideas within their organization in an entrepreneurial" to lead to a social change within the organization (BMW Foundation Website).[32]
Social Intrapreneur	"people within a large corporation who take direct initiative for innovations that address social or environmental challenges while also creating commercial value for the company" (Forbes Website).[33]
Social Innovation	"A social innovation is a novel solution to a social problem that is more effective, efficient, sustainable, or just than current solutions." (Graduate School of Business Stanford Website).[34]
Social Impact	"The effect an organization's actions have on the well-being of the community."[35]

---

[31] http://www.socialimpactscotland.org.uk/understanding-social-impact/methods-and-tools/sroi/what-is-sroi/.

[32] http://www.bmw-stiftung.de/en/what-we-do/social-intrapreneurship/.

[33] https://www.forbes.com/sites/ashoka/2014/02/24/the-innovative-beat-of-corporate-social-intrapreneurs/#2e146217e33c.

[34] https://www.gsb.stanford.edu/faculty-research/centers-initiatives/csi/defining-social-innovation.

[35] kwhs.wharton.upenn.edu/term/social-impact/.

An Epistemological Criticism of Social Entrepreneurship   259

Social Entrepreneurship Terminology	Explanation
Social Enterprise	"Social enterprise applies an entrepreneurial approach to addressing social issues and creating positive community change," or it is "a revenue-generating business with primarily social objectives whose surpluses are reinvested for that purpose in the business or in the community, rather than being driven by the need to deliver profit to shareholders and owners." (BC Center for Social Enterprise Website).[36]
Social Entrepreneur	"A person who establishes an enterprise with the aim of solving social problems or effecting social change."[37]
Social Capital	"The web of cooperative relationships between citizens that facilitate resolution of collective action problems" (Brehm and Rahn 1997, 999).
Social Investing or Socially Responsible Investing (SRI)	"Also known as sustainable, socially conscious, "green" or ethical investing, is any investment strategy which seeks to consider both financial return and social good to bring about a social change."[38]
Shared Value	"Shared value is created when companies recognize that there are tremendous opportunities for innovation and growth in treating social problems as business objectives" (FSG Website).[39]
Blended Value	A word coined by *Jed Emerson* to include both social and financial goals (Bornstein and Davis 2010).
Impact Investing	"Investments made into companies, organizations, and funds with the intention to generate social and environmental impact alongside a financial return" (Global Impact Investment Network Website).[40]
Effective Altruism	"A philosophy and social movement that applies evidence and reason to determine the most effective ways to benefit others."[41]
Corporate Social Responsibility (CSR)	It "is a corporation's initiatives to assess and take responsibility for the company's effects on environmental and social wellbeing." (Investopedia Website).[42]
Collective Impact	"The commitment of a group of actors from different sectors to a common agenda for solving a specific social problem, using a structured form of collaboration."[43] Or "it is an innovative and structured approach to making collaboration work across

---

[36] http://www.centreforsocialenterprise.com/what-is-social-enterprise/.

[37] https://www.google.com/webhp?sourceid=chrome-instant&ion=1&espv=2&ie=UTF-8#q=Social+Entrepreneur.

[38] https://en.wikipedia.org/wiki/Socially_responsible_investing.

[39] http://www.fsg.org/ideas-in-action/shared-value.

[40] https://thegiin.org/impact-investing/ and https://web.archive.org/web/20160902224437/ https://thegiin.org/assets/documents/pub/Introducing_the_Impact_Investing_Benchmark. pdf.

[41] https://en.wikipedia.org/wiki/Effective_altruism.

[42] http://www.investopedia.com/terms/c/corp-social-responsibility.asp.

[43] https://en.wikipedia.org/wiki/Collective_impact.

Amir Forouharfar

Table 6. (Continued)

Social Entrepreneurship Terminology	Explanation
Collective Impact	government, business, philanthropy, non-profit organizations and citizens to achieve significant and lasting social change" (Collaboration for Impact Website).[44]
Benefit Corporation (B Corp)	"A type of for-profit corporate entity, authorized by 30 U.S. states and the District of Columbia that includes positive impact on society, workers, the community and the environment in addition to profit as its legally defined goals."[45]
Triple Bottom Line (TBL)	It "is an accounting framework that incorporates three dimensions of performance: social, environmental and financial" (Indiana Business Review Website).[46]
Change maker	"A term coined by the social entrepreneurship organization, *Ashoka,* meaning one who desires change in the world and, by gathering knowledge and resources, makes that change happen " (Creative Tracks Website).[47]
Social Firm or Affirmative Business	They are "businesses created to employ people with disabilities and to provide a needed product or service" (Warner and Mandiberg 2006, 1488).[48]
Cause-Related Marketing	It is a "joint funding and promotional strategy in which a firm's sales are linked (and a percentage of the sales revenue is donated) to charity or other public cause" (Business Dictionary Website).[49]
Community-Benefit Clauses	They are "contractual clauses that can be used to build a variety of economic, social or environmental conditions into the delivery of public contracts. By specifying contractual requirements that seek to deliver wider social benefits, CBCs allow organizations to contribute to the achievement of outcomes that will benefit their communities" (Irish Social Enterprise Network Website). [50]
Community Interest Company (CIC)	"A type of company introduced by the UK government in 2005 under the *Companies* (Audit, Investigations and Community Enterprise) *Act 2004*, designed for social enterprises that want to use their profits and assets for the public good."[51]

Source: Author's own work.

---

[44] http://www.collaborationforimpact.com/collective-impact/.
[45] https://en.wikipedia.org/wiki/Benefit_corporation.
[46] http://www.ibrc.indiana.edu/ibr/2011/spring/article2.html.
[47] http://www.creativetracks.org/response/101412/-changemakers-.
[48] https://www.ncbi.nlm.nih.gov/pubmed/17035570.
[49] http://www.businessdictionary.com/definition/cause-related-marketing.html.
[50] http://www.socent.ie/community-benefit-clauses/.
[51] https://en.wikipedia.org/wiki/Community_interest_company.

An Epistemological Criticism of Social Entrepreneurship   261

SE *Representationism* and terminology revealed that SE is an interdisciplinary knowledge. Figure 9 has summarized the discussions in this section of the paper.

4.5. Contributing Epistemology-Making Concepts for SE

4.5.1. Essentialism and SE

Essentialism is a perspective which believes any entity has a set of traits and attributes that make its essence and therefore they are essential to its function and identity (*Cartwright* 1968). *Merriam-Webster's Collegiate Dictionary* defines it as, "a philosophical theory ascribing ultimate reality to *essence* embodied in a thing perceptible to the senses." Although there had been opposes to essentialism such as in *Wittgenstein's* attempt in clarifying the essence of language or *Popper* who sees essentialism's "ultimate reality" claim that accordingly everything could be explained as, "stultifying to the pursuit of ever better explanations" in science (Shand 1993); epistemologically, taking essentialists" view could help us first, to accept that some traits are existing in reality for SE knowledge and then to try to determine the pivotal and main attributes which form SE. Determining the essence-forming attributes of SE is a giant leap in providing a firm basis for its understanding and research that could be beneficial in setting its true boundaries as well. To get to the *Form* and *Idea* or the *essence* behind SE is not a task which a single research could shoulder but it needs the collective endeavor on the side of the SE scholars. Up to now such essentialist orientation in SE studies has not been taken that could be inherently and at least very fruitful in overcoming lack of consensus over SE definitions and attributions. Because of such lack of consensus, that is mentioned previously, whatever we claim over the general attributes of SE could be easy rejected by the scholars, therefore we feel one of the main criticisms to SE is its inability up to now to solve this principal stage in progress of science.

4.5.2. Social Constructivism and SE

Social constructivism is looking at knowledge sociologically, in other words it is the sociological theory of knowledge which believes knowledge constructed via social interactions (McKinley 2015).Being in connection to society and other individuals help us to gain some knowledge of the issue that is also applicable for the discussion of SE. Taking this school of thought we have to accept the prerequisite that, "the natural world has a small or non-existent role in the construction of scientific knowledge," (Wright 2005) that is a claim against positivistic and empirical view to the object under study, hence SE. The epistemological *Truth* in social constructivism is relative, this means that there is not an independent and detached concept as *Truth* but it forms through the social connections and interactions. Robert Rocco Cottone's "Bracketed Absolute Truth," or "consensuality" discusses the truth which in one community is granted as absolute but in other communities the same truth is granted as a relative concept which is in connection with other truths (Cottone 2012).

Accordingly, Truth is a social phenomenon and could be as diverse as the diversity of different communities which construct it.SE in a sense is the construct of the society that works and defines within. The media, prevailing discourse, and even the dominant religion of the community or in a larger scale, the country form the SE concept and defines it as close as possible to the cognitive world and social norms of that society/community. For example if the community is dominantly Christian, SE among the commons will be defined as a Christian concept of *Tithe*, *Offertory*, etc. and if the religion substituted with Islam, it would be defined through some religious concepts as *Vagf, Enfagh, Enfal*, etc. and here comes the concept of SE as a religious social construct.

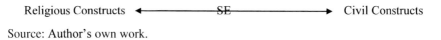

Source: Author's own work.

Figure 10. Construct-making spectrum for SE knowledge in respect to social constructivism.

An Epistemological Criticism of Social Entrepreneurship   263

In discussing such a social construct, it should not be neglected that religion is only one of such affecting variables and there could be some other determining and construct-making factors or variables too. In communities that religion has a dominance on the social interactions, SE constructs which are usually poured through religious terms is more near to the left extreme of the spectrum (e.g., defining such Attributions as philanthropy, alms-giving, social donations, within SE is the product of such religious construct-making to SE) and in communities with dominant civil concerns among the majority of the members of the community it has orientation towards the right of the spectrum and SE will be defined through civil and social terminology (Figure 10). Such constructs could be the fruit of the prevailing social discourses which is very close to how *Foucault* looks at discourse as:

> "Ways of constituting knowledge, together with the social practices, forms of subjectivity and power relations which inhere in such knowledge and relations between them. Discourses are more than ways of thinking and producing meaning. They constitute the 'nature' of the body, unconscious and conscious mind and emotional life of the subjects they seek to govern" (Weedon 1987, 108).

The media has a principal role in the promulgation and publication of such prevailing social and construct-making discourses or according to Happer and Philo (2013) in *The Role of the Media in the Construction of Public Belief and Social Change*, which verifies the way that the media, "shape public debate in terms of setting agendas and focusing public interest on particular subjects" also the media is able to shape "specific ways of understanding" (Briant, Philo, and Watson 2011; Philo and Berry 2004, 2011; Philo 1996). Therefore the way SE knowledge is defined and practiced in the West is different from the same concept in the East and especially Islamic countries or as Almarri (2014, 1) states, "The Islamic context encompasses both institutional entrepreneurship and Islamic philanthropy, and sees them as essential and often also inseparable parts of it - perhaps even more so than in a Western context." Moreover, most of the SE research has been done in the Western context (Lés and Kolin 2009; Kerlin 2006, 2010; Noya 2009; Nyssens 2009; Hoogendoorn, Pennings and Thurik 2010;

264 *Amir Forouharfar*

Travaglini 2009) which inevitably attributed western constructs to SE.It should not be neglected that in respect to research approaches, the western SE is also different in Europe and America (Almarri 2014). In all it could be concluded that social interactions, discourses and norms forms SE concept in each community and hence it is a society-bound knowledge.

4.5.3. Social Epistemology and SE

Social Constructivism drive us towards *Social Epistemology* as an epistemology, "positioned within a particular social and historical context" and sees "scientific facts as social constructions" which conveys this claim that, "scientific theories are laden with social, cultural, and historical presuppositions and biases" and in a sever format of it asserts that, "truth and reality are themselves socially constructed" (Steup 2016)[52]. Looking at SE, through *Social Epistemology* glasses we can claim that social context, which inherently the sum of political, economic, traditional, religious, and cultural norms, is the entity that really forms the concept which we call SE and it does not have an actual independent form and reality out of the social context realm and the ambiguities that SE is dealing with comes from the mentality which believes SE is a single concept which could have a single definition and attributions. Therefore we have to accept a "plurality" in what SE could refer to and extend such a plurality to its definition and nature - or as Trexler (2008, 1) puts it a "simple term with a complex range of meanings"- because SE is the offspring of its society; in other words, the social construct of its society. The society has formed SE and for better understanding of this phenomenon should understand the societies which are constructed it.

4.5.4. The Social Context and SE

SE is the product of the interplay between human mind and the social setting and milieu as the context to this social phenomenon. Therefore, it would be beneficial to use the concept of *Sociology of Knowledge*[53]to explain such an interplay which leads to the nature of a so-called knowledge

---

[52] On-line *Stanford Encyclopedia of Philosophy.*
[53] "Wissenssoziologie" a term coined by *Max Scheler.*

An Epistemological Criticism of Social Entrepreneurship 265

which we call SE. To take the proposition of *Marx*, "that man's consciousness is determined by his social being," (Berger and Luckmann 1966, 5) the root nature of the SE should be seen in how human being defines his social being. How we define an entity as a social phenomenon which could be itself the product of man's social consciousness. If we could determine where SE as knowledge stands in relation to society then maybe we could succeed in illuminating the concept. It is very hard since the social world is understood in different ways. Here, we deal with a cognitive understanding of man in relation to social realm, in other words, individualistic knowledge in social setting. If this cognitive understanding interpreted as Durkheim "logical thought" then according to his argumentation in *The Elementary Forms of Religious Thought*, "certain aspects of logical thought common to all humans did exist, but that they were products of collective life and that they were not universal *a priori* truths since the content of the categories differed from society to society"[54]. Then, the concept of SE could be different from a society to society and hence we do not have a unified concept which consequently has not yet reached a unified definition. Mair (2010, 4) elaborating on this changing concept of SE, adds "if the opportunity space" is defined according to "local social, economic, and political arrangements" then SE "manifests itself differently in different contexts," or as Dees (1998b, 1) describes, it "means different things to different people." Therefore, according to Short, Moss and Lumpkin (2009, 162) "lack of a unified definition" makes it hard to establish "the legitimacy of a field or construct," although Nicholls (2010) has tried to do so in his article *The Legitimacy of Social Entrepreneurship: Reflexive Isomorphism in a Pre-Paradigmatic Field*. Through the article he discussed SE actors whose activities and discourses drive SE towards a paradigm by *Reflexive Isomorphism*, which is "a type of isomorphic pressure privileges agency over structure by suggesting that dominant organizations can shape the legitimacy of an emergent field to reflect their own institutional logics and norms," (p.614) in other words, the acting entities, in a closed-loop by self-referencing make their own self-reproduction an shape SE paradigm

---

[54] Cited from Wikipedia, taken from Émile Durkheim. 1912. "Les Formes Élémentaires De La Vie Religieuse." Le Système Totémique En Australie: 14-17 and 19-22.

(Table 7). Legitimacy as "a generalized perception or assumption that the actions of an entity are socially desirable, proper or appropriate within some socially constructed system of norms, value, beliefs and definitions" (Suchman 1995, 574) and is the purpose behind an organization or institution's isomorphism with the expectations of main stakeholders in the environment (Di Maggio and Powell 1983; Meyer and Rowan 1977; Tolbert and Zucker 1983). SE still is struggling for such legitimacy.

Table 7. Reflexive isomorphism in SE

Paradigm-Building Actor	Internal Logic	Logic of Reflexive Isomorphism	Legitimating Discourse
Government	Deliver public goods	Maximize efficiency, responsiveness, sustainability	Business model ideal type
Foundations	Mobilize resources to bring about change	Maximize return on investment	Hero entrepreneur
Fellowship organizations	Build social capital	Maximize leverage effects	Hero entrepreneur
Pure network organizations	Build community voice	Maximize engagement and empowerment	Social justice

Source: Nicholls 2010, 624.

Nicholls (2010, 626) by proposing a solution for overcoming such insufficiency of legitimacy for SE believes, "from a Kuhnian perspective, the paradigm of SE can only establish its legitimacy by means of further academic work focused on rigorous theory building and careful empirical testing," and Dart (2004) proposes that social enterprises are seeking to acquire their legitimacy through "moral legitimacy" as a "legitimacy that is normative and based on an evaluation of whether an activity of a focal organization is the proper one (relative to external norms) rather than whether it specifically benefits those who are making the evaluation." Moreover, he continues that the social enterprises moral legitimacy fluctuates in accordance to the SE practitioners and their ideas. On the other hand, Zainon et al. (2014) believe social enterprises take their legitimacy and sustainability in generating simultaneously social and economic values. Uniformity of SE organizations or isomorphism among SE organizations could be discussed at least at three other cases too. (1) Coercive isomorphism; (2) Mimetic isomorphism; and (3) Normative isomorphism. Nicholls (2010, 616) defines the abovementioned isomorphisms as *"Coercive Isomorphism* captured the process by which powerful external actors, such as the state or resource providers, forced organizations toward uniformity. *Mimetic Isomorphism* encouraged organizations to imitate other models to counter the risks of organizational uncertainty in underdeveloped fields. In terms of *Normative Isomorphism*, the influence of professional bodies and standards was shown to exert influence." Undeveloped theories and absence of epistemological *evidence* in any knowledge make a legitimacy crisis for it.SE is within such a struggle for legitimacy. Even in reality the active organizations in the field of SE from heterogeneous sectors (public, private, and the third) taking different organizational structures from not-for profit, for-profit to hybrid (Bosma and Levie 2010, 45). Therefore in reality it is very hard to find isomorphism among the SEOs. In real world, what is apprehensive is the enforcement of *Coercive Isomorphism* from the side of the governments or financial institutes only within the public sector, although successful cases like microfinancing in SE encouraged some of the credit institutes to imitate the successful role models (e.g., *Grameen Bank*), *Mimetic Isomorphism* is hard to find in other SE fields. Moreover, relying on isomorphism could not solve the legitimacy crisis among SEOs. Moreover; as it was mentioned, SE is at the *Pre-Paradigm Phase*, the first phase out of the five-step Kuhnian *Scientific Revolution*[55]. To elaborate on such a claim we should consider the mentioned Pre-paradigm phase characteristics by Kuhn as there is no consensus on any particular theory (Kuhn 1962). Bird (2013) in on-line *Stanford Encyclopedia of Philosophy* explains this phase as:

---

[55] 1. Pre-Paradigm Phase, 2. Normal Science Phase, 3. Crisis Period, 4. Paradigm Shift, 5. Post-Revolution Phase.

Kuhn describes an immature science, in what he sometimes calls its 'pre-paradigm' period, as lacking consensus. Competing schools of thought possess differing procedures, theories, even metaphysical presuppositions. Consequently there is little opportunity for collective progress. Even localized progress by a particular school is made difficult, since much intellectual energy is put into arguing over the fundamentals with other schools instead of developing a research tradition.[56]

Whereas, it should not be neglected that Kuhn in the preface to *The Structure of Scientific Revolutions* asserts that the development of paradigm concept was to distinguish natural sciences from the social ones, and he inherently did not believe in the application of this concept in the realm of social sciences as Dogan (2001) asserted because of the polysemious concepts in social sciences there could be no paradigms in social sciences. Maybe the *Mathematicism* and *Physicism* had been a response to get rid of this polysemy.

Moreover, Lack of research tradition which could be originated from what Zahra et al. (2009) know as dissonance in understanding of SE and Lepoutre et al. (2011, 694) mention as "one of the major barriers to the advancement of scholarly research on the subject" beside, lack of unified definition or lack of consensus on SE definition (Littlewood and Holt 2015; Braunerhjelm and Hamilton 2012) verify the Kuhnin pre-paradigm phase. Some researchers directly points out SE still has pre-paradigmatic nature (Newbert 2014; Nicholls 2010), or as Martin (2004, 9) claims it "is currently at a stage prior to the establishment of a dominant paradigm." We lack clear conceptions and models for the understanding of this phenomenon (Karlberg and Ryberg 2007). Even some researchers believe that the research in this field is at the "embryonic state" (Short, Moss, and Lumpkin 2009, 161) and generally, "as a distinct field of academic inquiry, it is still in its infancy" (Dees and Anderson 2006a, 144).

---

[56]https://plato.stanford.edu/archives/fall2013/entries/thomas-kuhn/.

4.5.5. Epistemic Contextualism and SE

On the other hand, SE is deeply involved in *Epistemic Contextualism* as a, "view that what is expressed by a knowledge attribution — a claim to the effect that S 'knows' that p — depends partly on something in the context of 'the attributor', and hence the view is often called 'attributor contextualism' " (Rysiew 2016[57]) therefore the concepts of "knowing," "reasoning" and "being true" are dependent on the context-dependent and consequently and potentially could be different. This is exactly what Dees (1998b, 1) attributes to SE, as a concept "means different things to different people." *Contextualism* in epistemology discusses the word *knows* as a context-sensitive issue which makes various propositions because of various contexts of application (Stanley 2005).Lack of consensus on SE definition which is discussed before is also the reflection of such *Contextualism*, which DeRose (2000, 91) concludes:

> Thus, the contextualist will allow that one speaker can truthfully say "S knows that P," while another speaker, in a different context, where higher standards are in place, can truthfully say "S doesn't know that P," though both speakers are talking about the same S and the same P at the same time.

4.5.6. Scientism and SE

Here, we could pose this question that how much SE corresponds with scientific prerequisites?

Relying too much on *Scientism* with its excessive emphasis on empirical sciences and *Logical Positivism*; especially, in social sciences is misleading. *Jürgen Habermas* explains, in *On the Logic of the Social Sciences* (1967), that "the positivist thesis of unified science, which assimilates all the sciences to a natural-scientific model, fails because of the intimate relationship between the social sciences and history, and the fact that they are based on a situation specific understanding of meaning that can be

---

[57] https://plato.stanford.edu/entries/contextualism-epistemology/.

270 *Amir Forouharfar*

explicated only hermeneutically ... access to a symbolically pre-structured reality cannot be gained by observation **alone**" (Outhwaite 1988, 22). Moreover, *Scientism* with its tendency to reduce science as far as to be measurable is, "the view that the characteristic inductive methods of the natural sciences are the only source of genuine factual knowledge and, in particular, that they alone can yield true knowledge about man and society"(Bullock and Trombley 1999, 775). According to *Keith Ward* Scientism is a "self-refuting" concept, since the truth of Scientism's claims such as "no statements are true unless they can be proven scientifically (or logically)" or "no statements are true unless they can be shown empirically to be true" cannot themselves be verified scientifically, empirically, or logically (Ward 2006[58]; Alston 2003). So, inherently it faces a paradoxical essence and is not applicable to social sciences and hence SE. The conceptual frameworks and context of natural sciences are different from the uncertainty, ambiguity and unpredictability which we encounter usually in social sciences and hence the application of the natural sciences methodology and mentality to social sciences is a fatal flaw.

4.5.7. Theory-Makings and SE

The other problem with SE research is abundance of case studies in top management especially in the past (McKenny et al. 2012) and still according to Short, Ketchen, and Bergh (2014) in their book *Social Entrepreneurship and Research Methods* case study is the dominant analytic technique for SE studies or according to Lepoutre et al. (2011, 4)[59] " a predominant focus on case studies and success stories of 'leading social entrepreneurs'" that is also mentioned by other scholars in the field (Sharir and Lerner 2006; Van Slyke and Newman 2006). Case study reflects the case not the world (Stake 2000)

---

[58]https://ipfs.io/ipfs/QmXoypizjW3WknFiJnKLwHCnL72vedxjQkDDP1mXWo6uco/wiki/Scientism.html.

[59] https://edisciplinas.usp.br/pluginfile.php/2327154/mod_resource/content/5/Artigo6-%20GEM-WorkingPaper11-07.pdf.

moreover it studies the complexity of a single subject (Stake 1995). Lack of enough researches in SE to establish theories in this field is evident.

Theories explicitly and implicitly interact with each other, usually the best theories complete the previously proposed ones, even in some cases the newly-proposed ones only have added new perspectives, variables, constituents, etc. but proposed in such a way which could modify and explain the social situations more comprehensively. Such a concept could be called *Ecology of Theories*. In this concept each theory has some other related theories which make its environment, hence ecology. Such theoretical environment has variable, constituent, concept, giving and taking with each member of the environment and in such a case help each other to improve and develop, but usually one or some of them will get the supremacy to the other theories in the interpretation of the cases or situations, phenomena and problems.

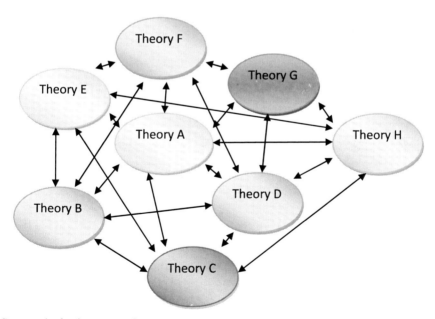

Source: Author's own work.

Figure 11. A group of interrelated theories in a field of science which makes an ecological environment.

Such a situation could also takes place for the theories in SE, but it as a prerequisite for such a complementary, regulatory and moderating situation is to have sufficient theories in the realm of SE. Theories like chemical substances have interactions with each other. This concept could be also seen from the evolutionary concept in *Darwinism*. In other words, such ecology has some new theories as its products, these theories have rivalry and each one of them which could explain the scientific environment and atmosphere will remain up to the time that another theory could be matched better with the scientific milieu. In such a case the old theory(ies) will be obsolete and lose the rivalry, and the new ones will be chosen and selected by the scientific ecology. Such a situation has a *modifying effect* on the theories. To discuss it metaphorically the theories do what a sculptor does with a piece of marble. In other words, the relevant and surrounding, and hence interacting theories in the *Ecology of Theories* are functioning as "the shoulders of giants" which the best and final theory stands upon (Figure 11).

4.5.8. Reflexivity and SE

The other concept which could be discussed applied properly for the discussion on SE is *Reflexivity* as a concept in social sciences which have been used by different social philosophers in various fields of social knowledge from anthropology to economics (e.g., *William Thomas, Karl Popper, Ernest Nagel, Anthony Giddens, Pierre Bourdieu, and Michel Foucault*) and each one has attributed some features to it in explaining his thoughts. Hence, it could be applied for SE too. To take *Reflexivity* in the social theory sense, it is the application of the same theories and concepts in a science for the practitioners of that science or field of knowledge itself; in other words, the theories and concepts in a field of knowledge will be applied for or against that knowledge which has been a mother to them. In this sense the scientific field wears its own glasses which use for the understanding of the surrounding phenomena, but now for better understanding of itself. It should not be neglected that this is only one application under the concept of reflexivity and each field of knowledge and philosophers has given his own connotation to it.

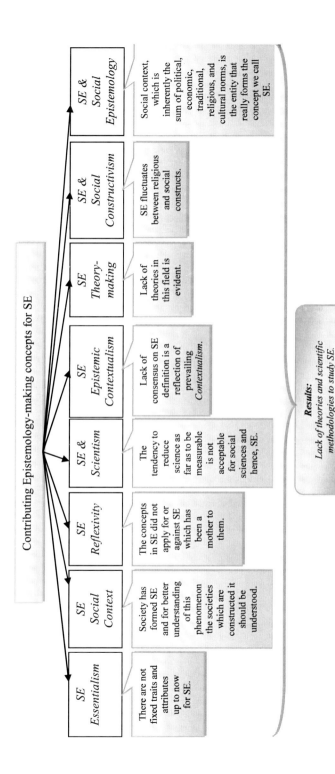

Source: Author's own work.

Figure 12. Complementary philosophical discussions' flow chart.

274 *Amir Forouharfar*

According to Bourdieu (1992, 236), "a scientific practice that fails to question itself does not, properly speaking, know what it does," or Schirato and Webb (2010, 551) believe, "reflexivity is best understood as a collective, rather than an individual, process, and it is largely specific to those fields that have institutionalized, through the mechanisms of training and dialogue, a disposition for subjects to turn those mechanisms 'against themselves'." By a simple literature review in SE we figure out that the discourse-makers and scholars of SE have not started and applied such a reflexivity touchstone for SE. To enhance the epistemological understanding of SE, the field should sometimes look inwardly and experiment what constitutes its nature as a field of knowledge. Lack of such inward-looking orientation in SE studies should be compensated by the scholars of the field. Making its scientific foundation more compelling, SE could also benefit from its relevant fields of study such as social economy, sociology, entrepreneurship and management. Each discipline could expand the perspective and panorama in SE as knowledge.

Figure 12 has summarized the paper discussions on contributing epistemology-making concepts for SE.

CONCLUSION

Day in day out, philanthropists and benevolent organizations that are really the citizens and humane organizations of the world, free from any national or racial prejudices, do their best to heal the pains of humanity. Seeing such a situation, SE scholars and researchers got a stamina to do their best in conceptualization of SE, a scientific endeavor which set SE as an academic discipline and definitely in the future will show its sweet fruits for humanity and human society.

The results of section (1) which was discussing is "social entrepreneurship" an oxymoron? Were the frequency of the words "social" as adjective in *COCA*'s database (not the "social" in the compound noun "social entrepreneurship"), beside "corporate" showed the linguistic context for SE, in other words, the dominant nature of SE based on the corpus was a phenomenon which was "social" and strongly related to "corporate" matters. Moreover, the SE *Bibliometrics'* results revealed the discourse makers in the academic arena were mostly used English language in areas of knowledge such as Business Economics, Public Administration, educational researches and Sociology, which were "social" sciences which inherently verified and strongly justified the annexation of the adjective "social" to "entrepreneurship" in "social entrepreneurship" phrase. Therefore, the collocation of "social" with "entrepreneurship in SE phrase was justifiable. Later in the second section on the characteristics of SE knowledge, the paper reveled that internalist justification for SE was not suitable, since it would fall in *Mentalism*, in other words each scholar would try to explain SE based on his mental images which were fundamentally could be different from country to country or their social perception and mental cognition of the phenomenon. Therefore, to avoid the current perplexity in SE and move towards epistemology formation in one hand and paradigm formation on the other, SE justification should be relied on externalist justifications and empirical evidence in order to make unanimity among the SE scholars. The third section on sources of social entrepreneurship knowledge, discussed that innovative social enterprises of the social entrepreneurs originated from the tacit knowledge of the individual social entrepreneur and its superb statement of the local problem and its effective remedy or solution. SE knowledge was fundamentally tacit since each social problem was rising from unique causes which were bound to the complicated social structure of the community that social entrepreneur resided in. Such a situation pushed SE to be as many as the social problems. On the other hand the possibility of applying statistics and mathematics in SE reveals that it could be an empirical knowledge too, i.e., the unique and fundamental experiences of SE practitioners (tacit knowledge) could be translated into numerical, statistical and mathematical approaches which basically showed SE could be an empirical knowledge too. Furthermore, the discussions on the fourth section (SE knowledge: structure and limitations) formed by the application of *Representationism* concept and SE terminology. According to *Representationism* concept it was discussed that there is not a universal consensus among the SE scholars on the characteristics or fundamental features which represent SE. Such a situation has led to inability in demarcating SE boundaries and numerous definitions of SE. Moreover in the same section the buzz words of SE were derived from SE literature, on-line websites and media. The results showed there was not a vast terminology for SE and meager vocabulary of SE was usually compensated by the vocabulary on the commercial side, in other words the commercial entrepreneurship vocabularies has usually redefined with social shades of meanings or adjectives for SE. Finally the fifth section on contributing epistemology-making concepts for SE reveled that there were not fixed traits and attributes up to now for SE (*SE Essentialism*); moreover society has formed SE and for better understanding of this phenomenon the societies which were constructed it should be understood (*SE Social Context*). Also, the concepts in SE did not apply for or against SE itself which has been a mother to them so far (*SE Reflexivity*). Later we discussed that the tendency to reduce science as far as to be measurable was not acceptable for social sciences and hence, SE (*SE & Scientism*). Furthermore, lack of consensus on SE definition was a reflection of prevailing *Contextualism* (*SE Epistemic Contextualism*) and lack of theories in this field was evident as well (*SE Theory-making*).Finally, it was not only revealed that in some societies SE fluctuated between religious and social constructs (*SE & Social Constructivism*), but also social context, which was inherently the sum of political, economic, traditional, religious, and cultural norms, was the entity that really formed the concept we call SE (*SE & Social Epistemology*). Holistically we can conclude that lack of unifying paradigm, definition, research methodology, epistemology and boundary beside meager terminology of SE lead us to verify that SE is a pre-paradigmatic knowledge which is not still sound and scientific and deeply suffers from lack of a well-established epistemology (Figure 13). Therefore, SE embryonic formation calls for philosophical theorizing to base a solid foundation for this pre-paradigmatic human knowledge. Since SE is at this stage, its researchers and scholars have to act interdisciplinary and benefit from other relevant knowledge with more progressive paradigmatic stage such as economy, sociology and management until it could present enough unanimous theories that harbinger a scientific paradigm for it.

An Epistemological Criticism of Social Entrepreneurship

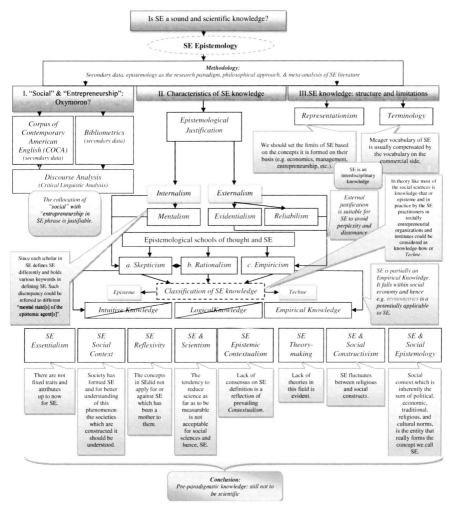

Source: Author's own work.

Figure 13. Thought flow chart through the paper to reach to the paper's conclusion.

Besides, to establish an epistemology for SE we should initially start with a unanimous definition of SE. At the end the results of this paper verifies Nicholls (2010, 611) who emphasizes, "following Kuhn, the current status of SE can be conceptualized as a field that has yet to achieve a paradigmatic consensus and that lacks a 'normal science' or clear epistemology."

Figure 13 has summarized the comprehensive thought flow chart through the paper to reach to the paper's conclusion.

REFERENCES

Almarri, J. 2014. *Social Entrepreneurship in Practice: The Multifaceted Nature of Social Entrepreneurship and the Role of the State within an Islamic Context*. Dissertation. University of Oulu Graduate School, Oulu Business School. Finland: Department of Management and International Business.

Alston, W. P. 2003. "Religious Language and Verificationism." In *The Rationality of Theism*, Paul K. Moser, edited by Paul Copan, 26–34. New York: Routledge.

Alterowitz, R. 1988. *New Corporate Ventures*. New York: John Wiley and Sons.

Alvord, S. H., L. D. Brown, and C. W. Letts. 2004. "Social Entrepreneurship and Societal Transformation: An Exploratory Study." *Journal of Applied Behavioral Science* 40(3): 260–282.

Amabile, T. M. 1997. "Entrepreneurial Creativity through Motivational Synergy." *Journal of Creative Behavior* 31(1):18–26.

Anderson, B. B., and J. G. Dees. 2002. "Developing Viable Earned Income Strategies." In *Strategic Tools for Social Entrepreneurs: Enhancing the Performance of Your Enterprising Nonprofit*, edited by J. G. Dees, J. Emerson, and P. Economy. New York: John Wiley and Sons.

Anderson, A. R., and M. Starnawska. "Research Practices in Entrepreneurship: Problems of Definition, Description and Meaning." *The International Journal of Entrepreneurship and Innovation* 9(4): 221-230.

Ashmore, M. 1991. *Reflexive Epistemology: The Philosophical Legacy of Otto Neurath*. Reviewed by Danilo Zolo, and David McKie. *Isis* 82(4): 787-788. The University of Chicago Press on behalf of The History of Science Society. Available at http://www.jstor.org/stable/233405

An Epistemological Criticism of Social Entrepreneurship 279

Austin, J., H. Stevenson, and J. Wei-Skillern. 2006a. "Social and Commercial Entrepreneurship: Same, Different, or Both?" *Entrepreneurship Theory and Practice* 30(1):1–22.

Austin, J. E., H. B. Leonard, E. Reficco, and J. Wei-Skillern. 2006b. "Social Entrepreneurship: It Is for Corporations, Too." In *Social Entrepreneurship: New Models of Sustainable Change*, edited by Alex Nicholls, 169–180. New York: Oxford University Press.

Ball, R., and D. Tunger. 2005. "Bibliometrische Analysen: Daten, Fakten und Methoden-Grundwissen Bibliometrie für Wissenschaftler." Wissenschaftsmanager, Forschungseinrichtungen und Hochschulen, *Schriften des Forschungszentrums Jülich*, Vol. 12. [*Bibliometric Analyzes: Data, Facts, and Methodological Basics Bibliometrics for Scientists*. Science Managers, Research Institutes, and Universities, Schriften der Forschungszentrum Jülich]

Bacq, S. and F. Janssen. 2011. "The Multiple Faces of Social Entrepreneurship: A Review of Definitional Issues Based on Geographical and Thematic Criteria." *Entrepreneurship and Regional Development* 23(5-6): 373-403. Available at http://www.tandfonline.com/doi/abs/10.1080/08985626.2011.577242.

Baird, F. E. 2008. *From Plato to Derrida*. Upper Saddle River, New Jersey: Pearson Prentice Hall.

Battilana, J., M. Lee, J. Walker, and C. Dorsey. 2012. "In Search of the Hybrid Ideal." *Stanford Social Innovation Review* summer: 51–56.

Bealer, G. 1998. "Intuition and the Autonomy of Philosophy." In *Rethinking Intuition,* edited by Michael DePaul and William Ramsey, 201–240. Lanham: Rowman and Littlefield.

Berger P. L., and T. Luckmann. 1966. *The Social Construction of Reality: A Treatise in the Sociology of Knowledge*. USA: Penguin Books.

Berthon, P., J. McHulbert, and L. Pitt. 2004. "Innovation or Customer Orientation? An Empirical Investigation." *European Journal of Marketing* 38(9/10): 1065–1090.

Bird, A. 2013. "Thomas Kuhn." In *The Stanford Encyclopedia of Philosophy*, edited by Edward N. Zalta. Available at https://plato.stanford.edu/archives/fall2013/entries/thomas-kuhn/.

Bonjour, L. 1998. *In Defense of Pure Reason*. Cambridge: Cambridge University Press.

Bonjour, L. 2008. "Externalist Theories of Empirical Knowledge." In *Epistemology*, edited by Ernest Sosa, Jaegwon Kim, Jeremy Fantl, and Matthew McGrath: 365. Malden: Blackwell.

Bosma, N., and J. Levie. 2010. *Global Entrepreneurship Monitor 2009: Executive Report*. Available at https://dspace.library.uu.nl/handle/1874/209570.

Bornstein, D. and S. Davis. 2010. *Social entrepreneurship: What Everyone Needs to Know*. Oxford University Press: New York.

Bourdieu, P., and L. J. D. Wacquant. 1992. *An Invitation to Reflexive Sociology*. Chicago: University of Chicago Press.

Bourke, V. J. 1962. "Rationalism." In *Dictionary of Philosophy*, edited by D. D. Runes: 263 Littlefield, Totowa, New Jersey: Adams and Company.

Braunerhjelm, P., and U. S. Hamilton. 2012. "Social Entrepreneurship: A Survey of Current Research." *Swedish Entrepreneurship Forum*: Working Paper No. 2012: 09. Available at http://entreprenors kapsforum.se/wp-content/uploads/2013/03/WP_09. pdf.

Brouard, F., Hebb, T., and Madill, J. 2008. *Development of a Social Enterprise Typology in a Canadian Context*. Available at https://carleton.ca/3ci/wpcontent/uploads/SETypologyPaper2.pdf.

Brehm, J., and W. Rahn. 1997. "Individual-Level Evidence for the Causes and Consequences of Social Capital." *American Journal of Political Science* 41: 999 – 1023.

Briant, E., G. Philo, and N. Watson. 2011. *Bad News for Disabled People: How the Newspapers Report Disability*. Available at http://eprints. gla.ac.uk/57499/1/57499.pdf.

Bugg-Levine, A., B. Kogut, and N. Kulatilaka. 2012. "Unbundling Societal Benefits and Financial Returns Can Dramatically Increase Investment." *Harvard Business Review*: 120–122.

Burgelman, R. A. 1984. "Designs for Corporate Entrepreneurship." *California Management Review* 26: 154 –166.

Cartwright, R. L. 1968. "Some Remarks on Essentialism." *The Journal of Philosophy* 65(20): 615–626. doi:10.2307/2024315.

Chignell, A. 2016. "The Ethics of Belief." In *The Stanford Encyclopedia of Philosophy,* Edited by Edward N. Zalta. Available at https://plato.stanford.edu/archives/win2016/entries/ethics-belief/.

Choi, D., and E. Gray. 2008. "The Venture Development Processes of 'Sustainable' Entrepreneurs." *Management Research News* 8(31): 558–569.

Choi, N., & S. Majumdar. 2014. "Social Entrepreneurship as an Essentially Contested Concept: Opening a New Avenue for Systematic Future Research." *Journal of Business Venturing* 29(3): 363-376.

Christie, M., and B. Honig. 2006. "Social entrepreneurship: New Research findings." *Journal of World Business* 41(1): 1–5.

Christiansen, C. 1997. *The Innovators Dilemma.* Cambridge: Harvard Business School Press.

Cohen, B., and M. Winn. 2007. "Market Imperfections, Opportunity and Sustainable Entrepreneurship." *Journal of Business Venturing* 22 (1):29–49.

Collins English Dictionary. "Mathematicism." Available at https://www.collinsdictionary.com/dictionary/english/mathematicism.

Collins English Dictionary. "Physicism." Available at https://www.collinsdictionary.com/dictionary/english/physicism.

Corpus of Contemporary American English (COCA). Available at http://corpus.byu.edu/coca/.

Cottone, R. R. 2012. *Paradigms of Counseling and Psychotherapy.* Available at www.smashwords.com/books/view/165398.

Covin, J. G., and D. P. Slevin. 1991. "A Conceptual Model of Entrepreneurship as Firm Behaviour." *Entrepreneurship Theory and Practice* 16(1): 7–25.

Covin, J.G., and M.P. Miles. 1999. "Corporate Entrepreneurship and the Pursuit of Competitive Advantage." *Entrepreneurship Theory Practice* 23(3): 47–64.

Cukier, W., S. Trenholm, D. Carl, and G. Gekas. 2011. "Social Entrepreneurship: A Content Analysis." *Journal of Strategic Innovation and Sustainability* 7(1): 99–119.

Dacin, T. M., P.A. Dacin, and P. Tracey. 2011. "Social Entrepreneurship: A Critique and Future Directions." *Organization Science* 22(5): 1203-1213. doi: 10.1287/orsc.1100.0620.

Dart, R. 2004. "The Legitimacy of Social Enterprise." *Nonprofit Management and Leadership* 14(4): 411- 424.

Dees, J. G. 1998a. "Enterprising Nonprofits: What Do You Do When Traditional Sources of Funding Fall Short?" *Harvard Business Review* January/February: 55-67.

Dees, J. G. 1998b. *The Meaning of Social Entrepreneurship.* Comments and Suggestions Contributed from the Social Entrepreneurship Funders Working Group, October 31.

Dees, J. G. 1998c. *The Meaning of Social Entrepreneurship.* Revised 2001. Available at https://entrepreneurship.duke.edu/news-item/the-meaning-of-social-entrepreneurship/.

Dees, J. G., and B. B. Anderson. 2006a. "Rhetoric, Reality, and Research: Building a Solid Foundation for the Practice of Social Entrepreneurship." In *Social Entrepreneurship: New Models of Sustainable Social Change*, edited by Alex Nicholls: 144–168. New York: Oxford University Press.

Dees, J. G., and B. B. Anderson. 2006b. "Framing a theory of social entrepreneurship: Building on two schools of practice and thought." *Research on social entrepreneurship: Understanding and contributing to an emerging field* 1, no. 3 39-66.

DeRose, K. 2000. "Now you know it, now you don't." In *The Proceedings of the Twentieth World Congress of Philosophy* 5: 91-106.

Di Maggio, P., and W. W. Powell. 1983. "The Iron Cage Revisited: Institutional Isomorphism and Collective Rationality in Organizational Fields." *American Sociological Review* 48: 147–160.

Dogan, M. 2001. "Paradigms in the Social Sciences." In *International Encyclopedia of the Social and Behavioral Sciences*, edited by Neil J.,

Smelser, and Paul B. Baltes Vol. 16: 11023– 11027. Amsterdam: Elsevier.

Drucker, P. F. 1985. *Innovation and Entrepreneurship*. New York: Harper and Row Publishers.

Emerson, J., and F. Twersky. 1996. *New Social Entrepreneurs: The Success, Challenge and Lessons of Non-Profit Enterprise Creation*. San Francisco: Roberts Foundation, Homeless Economic Development Fund.

Encyclopedia Britannica. Intuition. Available at https://www.britannica.com/topic/intuition.

Encyclopedia Britannica. Mathematicism. Available at https://www.britannica.com/topic/mathematicism.

Fantl, J. 2016. "Knowledge How." In *The Stanford Encyclopedia of Philosophy*, edited by Edward N. Zalta. Available at https://plato.stanford.edu/archives/spr2016/entries/knowledge-how/.

Ferreira, J. 2002. "Corporate entrepreneurship: A strategic and structural perspective." In *Proceedings of the 47th World Conference of the International Council for Small Business, June, San Juan, Puerto Rico, Argentina*.

Forouharfar, A., N. M. Yaghoubi, and M. Motamedifar. 2014. "Entrepreneurial Timing Theory: Time Entrepreneurship and Time Strategy." *Asian Journal of Research in Business Economics and Management* (4)11: 1–27.

Fowler, A. 2000. "NGDOs as a Moment in History: Beyond Aid to Social Entrepreneurship or Civic Innovation?" *Third World Quarterly, 21*(4), 637–654.

Garfield, E. 1973. "Uncitedness III - The Importance of not Being Cited." *Current Contents* 8: 5-6.

Garfield, E. 1998. "Der impact faktor und seine richtige anwendung." *Der Anaesthesist* 47(6): 439-441. [The impact factor and its proper application. *The anesthesiologist*]

Gilad, B. 1984. "Entrepreneurship: The Issue of Creativity in the Market Place." *Journal of Creative Behavior* 18(3): 151–161.

Goldman, A. I. 2008. "What is Justified Belief?" In *Epistemology*, edited by Ernest Sosa, Jaegwon Kim, Jeremy Fantl, and Matthew McGrath: 333–347. Malden: Blackwell.

Granados, M. L., V. Hlupic, E. Coakes, and S. Mohamed. 2011. "Social Enterprise and Social Entrepreneurship Research and Theory: A Bibliometric Analysis from 1991 to 2010." *Social Enterprise Journal* 7(3): 198–218.

Haigh, N., and A. Hoffman. 2012. "Hybrid Organizations: The Next Chapter of Sustainable Business." *Organizational Dynamics* 41:126–134.

Happer, C., and G. Philo. 2013. "The Role of the Media in the Construction of Public Belief and Social Change." *Journal of Social and Political Psychology* 1(1). doi:10.5964/jspp.vlil.96

Harding, R. 2004. "Social Enterprise: The New Economic Engine?" *Business Strategy Review* 15(4): 39-43.

Harsanyi, M. A. 1993. "Multiple Authors, Multiple Problems - Bibliometrics and the Study of Scholarly Collaboration: A Literature Review." *Library and Information Science Research* 15(4): 325–354.

Hartmann, S., and J. Sprenger. 2011. "Mathematics and Statistics in the Social Sciences." In *The SAGE Handbook of the Philosophy of Social Sciences*, edited by Ian Jarvie and Jesus Zamora-Bonilla: 594-612. London: SAGE.

Haugh, H. 2005. "A Research Agenda for Social Entrepreneurship." *Social Enterprise Journal* 1(1): 1-12.

Hérbert, R. F., and A. N. Link 1989. "In Search of the Meaning of Entrepreneurship." *Small Business Economics* 1(1):39–49.

Hibbert, S. A., G. Hogg, and T. Quinn. 2002. "Consumer Response to Social Entrepreneurship: The Case of the Big Issue in Scotland." *International Journal of Non-profit and Voluntary Sector Marketing* 7(3): 288–301.

Hibbert, S. A., G. Hogg, and Quinn, T. 2005. "Social Entrepreneurship: Understanding Consumer Motives for Buying the Big Issue." *Journal of Consumer Behaviour* 4(3): 159- 172.

Hoffman, A. J., K. K. Badiane, and N. Haigh. 2010. "Hybrid Organizations as Agents of Positive Social Change: Bridging the For-Profit and Non-Profit Divide." In *Using a Positive Lens to Explore Social Change and*

Organizations: Building a Theoretical and Research Foundation, Edited by Karen Golden-Biddle and Jane Dutton: 131-153. New York: Routledge.

Hoogendoorn, B., E. Pennings, and A. R. Thurik. 2010. "What Do We Know about Social Entrepreneurship: An Analysis of Empirical Research." *International Review of Entrepreneurship* 8(2): 71–112.

Irwin, D. 2007. *The Future for Social Entrepreneurship and Social Enterprise.* England: Cobweb Information Ltd.

John, D. 2007. "Social Entrepreneurship in Eye Health: A Sustainable and Equitable Model." In *Developmental Aspects of Entrepreneurship*, edited by S. Bhargava: 195–210. New Delhi: SAGE.

John, R. 2007. *Beyond the Cheque: How Venture Philanthropists Add Value.* Skoll Center for Social Entrepreneurship. Available at http://eureka. sbs.ox.ac.uk/732/.

Johnson, S. 2000. *Literature Review on Social Entrepreneurship.* Canada, Alberta: Canadian Centre for Social Entrepreneurship.

Kanter, R. M. 1985. "Supporting Innovation and Venture Development in Established Companies." *Journal of Business Venturing* 1(1): 47–60.

Karlberg, F., and Ryberg, S. 2007. *An Explorative Journey in Understanding Social Entrepreneurship.* Master Thesis. Department of Business and Administration, Lund University. Available at https://lup.lub.lu.se/ student-papers/search/publication/1349585.

Kerlin, J. A. 2006. "Social Enterprise in the United States and Europe: Understanding and Learning from the Differences." *International Journal of Voluntary and Nonprofit Organizations* 17(3): 246–262.

Kerlin, J. A. 2010. "A Comparative Analysis of the Global Emergence of Social Enterprise." *International Journal of Voluntary and Non-profit Organizations* 21(2): 162–179.

Kuhn, T. S. 1962. *The Structure of Scientific Revolutions.* U.S.A.: University of Chicago Press.

Kuratko, D. F., J. S. Hornsby, and J. W. Bishop. 2005. "Managers' Corporate Entrepreneurial Actions and Job Satisfaction." *International Entrepreneurship and Management Journal* 1(3): 275–291.

Kuratko, D. F., and R. M. Hodgetts. 1995. *Entrepreneurship: A Contemporary Approach.* Orlando: Dryden Press.

Lacey, A. R. 1996. *A Dictionary of Philosophy.* London: Routledge.

Lepoutre, J., R. Justo, S. Terjesen, and N. Bosma. 2011. "Designing a Global Standardized Methodology for Measuring Social Entrepreneurship Activity: The Global Entrepreneurship Monitor Social Entrepreneurship Study." *Small Business Economics* 40(3): 693-714.

Lés, E., and M. Kolin. 2009. "East-Central Europe." In *Social Enterprise: A Global Comparison,* edited by Janelle A. Kerlin: 35–63. Lebanon, NH: Tufts University Press.

Lasprogata, G. A., and Cotton, M.N. 2003. "Contemplating Enterprise: The Business and Legal Challenges of Social Entrepreneurship." *American Business Law Journal* 41(1): 67.

Littlewood, D., and D. Holt. 2015. "Social Entrepreneurship in South Africa: Exploring the Influence of Environment." *Business and Society* Oct.30: 1 –37. Available at https://doi.org/10.1177/0007650315613293.

Lotka, A.J. 1926. "The Frequency Distribution of Scientific Productivity." *Journal of the Washington Academy of Science* 16(12): 317–323.

Lumpkin, G. T., and G. G. Dess. 1996. "Clarifying the Entrepreneurial Orientation Construct and linking it to Performance." *The Academy of Management Review* 21(1): 135-172.

Mair, J. 2010. "Social Entrepreneurship: Taking Stock and Looking Ahead." In *Handbook of Research on Social Entrepreneurship,* edited by Alain Fayolle and Harry Matlay: 15-28. Cheltenham: Edward Elgar.

Mair, J., and I. Marti. 2006. "Social entrepreneurship Research: A Source of Explanation, Prediction and Delight." *Journal of World Business* 41(1):36–44.

Mair, J., and E. Noboa. 2003. *The Emergence of Social Enterprises and Their Place in the New Organizational Landscape.* Working Paper, WP No. 523, IESE Business School, University of Navarra. Available at http://www.iese.edu/research/pdfs/DI-0523-E.pdf.

Martin, M. 2004. "Surveying Social Entrepreneurship: Toward an Empirical Analysis of the Performance Revolution in the Social Sector." *View Points*: 12-38.

Martín, M. Á. G., M. T. M. Picazo, and M. Teresa. 2008. "Emprendedores y objetivos de política económica." *Información Comercial Española, ICE: Revista de economía* 841: 29-40. [Entrepreneurs and economic policy objectives. *Spanish Commercial Information, ICE: Economics Magazine*]

McKenny, A. F., J. C. Short, and G. T. Payne. 2012. "The Challenges for Researchers." In *Handbook of Research Methods on Social Entrepreneurship*, edited by Richard Seymour: 231–249. UK: Edward Elgar.

McKinley, J. 2015. "Critical Argument and Writer Identity: Social Constructivism as a Theoretical Framework for EFL Academic Writing." *Critical Inquiry in Language Studies* 12(3): 184–207. doi:10.1080/15427587.2015.1060558.

Merriam-Webster's Collegiate Dictionary. 2002. U.S.A.: Springfield, Massachusetts.

Miles, R. E., and C. C. Snow. 1978. "Organizations New Concepts for New Forms." *California Management Review* 28(3): 62–73.

Miller, D., and P.H. Friesen. 1982. "Innovation in Conservative and Entrepreneurial Firms: Two Models of Strategic Momentum." *Strategic Management Journal* 3(1):1–25.

Microsoft Student. 2009. *Intuition.* [DVD]. Redmond, WA: Microsoft Corporation.

Microsoft Student. 2009. *Skepticism.* [DVD]. Redmond, WA: Microsoft Corporation.

Microsoft Student. 2009. *Rationalism.* [DVD]. Redmond, WA: Microsoft Corporation.

Martin, R. L. and S. Osberg. 2007. "Social entrepreneurship: The case for definition." *Stanford Social Innovation Review* 5(2):28-39.

Meyer, J., and B. Rowan, 1977. "Institutional Organizations: Formal Structure as Myth and Ceremony." *American Journal of Sociology* 83(2): 340–363.

Mohd Osman, M. H., M. A. Rashid, F. S. Ahmad and G. Hussain. 2011. "Entrepreneurial Orientation: An Overview of Theory and Insinuations for Women Owned SMBs to Model Business Performance in

Developing Countries." *Interdisciplinary Journal of Contemporary Research in Business* 3(3): 329-340.

Morris, M. H., and D. F. Kuratko. 2002. *Corporate Entrepreneurship.* Mason, OH: South-Western College Publishers.

Mort, G., J. Weerawardena, and Carnegie, K. 2002. "Social Entrepreneurship: Towards Conceptualization." *International Journal of Non-profit and Voluntary Sector Marketing* 8(1): 76-88.

Naman, J. L., and D. P. Slevin. 1993. "Entrepreneurship and the Concept of Fit: A Model and Empirical Tests." *Strategic Management Journal* 14(2):137–154.

National Audit Office. Available at https://www.nao.org.uk/successful-commissioning/introduction/what-are-civil-society-organisations-and-their-benefits-for-commissioners/.

Neck, H., C. Brush, and E. Allen. 2008. "The Landscape of Social Entrepreneurship." *Business Horizons* 52(1):13–19.

Newbert, S. L. 2014. "Editorial: Building Theory in Social Entrepreneurship." *Journal of Social Entrepreneurship* 5(3):239–242.

Neurath, O. 1944. *Foundations of the Social Sciences.* Chicago: University of Chicago Press.

Nijkamp, P. 2003. "Entrepreneurship in a Modern Network Economy." *Regional Studies* 37(4) 395-405.

Nicholls, A., and A. Cho. 2006. "Social Entrepreneurship: The Structuration of a Field." In *Social Entrepreneurship: New Models of Sustainable Social Change,* edited by Alex Nicholls: 99–118. New York: Oxford University Press.

Nicholls, A. 2006. *Social Entrepreneurship: New Models of Sustainable Change.* New York: Oxford University Press.

Nicholls, A. 2009. "Learning to Walk: Social Entrepreneurship – A Research Review." *Innovations* (Special Issue on Social Entrepreneurship): 209–222.

Nicholls, A. 2010. "The Legitimacy of Social Entrepreneurship: Reflexive Isomorphism in a Pre- paradigmatic Field." *Entrepreneurship Theory and Practice* 34(4): 611–633.

Nonaka, I. and Takeuchi, H. 1995. *"The Knowledge-Creating Company:*

How Japanese Companies Create the Dynamics of Innovation." Oxford: Oxford University Press.

Noya, A. 2009. "Executive Summary." In *The Changing Boundaries of Social Enterprises*, edited by Antonella Noya. Paris: OECD.

Nyssens, M. 2006. "Social Enterprise: At the Cross-roads of Market, Public Policies and Civil Society." In *Social Enterprise: At the Cross-roads of Market, Public Policies and Civil Society,* edited by Marthe Nyssens: 313- 329. London: Routledge.

Nyssens, M. 2009. "Western Europe." In *Social Enterprise: A Global Comparison,* edited by Janelle A. Kerlin: 12–34. Lebanon, NH: Tufts University Press.

Outhwaite, W. 1988. *Habermas: Key Contemporary Thinkers.* Cambridge: Polity Press.

Pappas, G. 2014. "Internalist vs. Externalist Conceptions of Epistemic Justification." In *The Stanford Encyclopedia of Philosophy*, edited by Edward N. Zalta. Available at https://plato.stanford.edu/archives/fall2014/entries/justep-intext/.

Perrini, F., and C. Vurro. 2006. "Social Entrepreneurship: Innovation and Social Change across Theory and Practice." In *Social Entrepreneurship,* edited by Johanna Mair, Jeffrey Robinson and Kai Hockerts: 57–85.UK: Palgrave Macmillan.

Phan, P. H., J. Kickul, S. Bacq, and M. Nordqvist. 2014. *"Theory and Empirical Research in Social Entrepreneurship.*" UK: Edward Elgar Publishing Ltd. doi: 10.4337/9781782546832.

Phillips, N., and C. Hardy. 2002. "Discourse Analysis: Investigating Processes of social construction." *Qualitative Research Methods Series*, Vol. 50. U.S.A.: SAGE.

Prahalad, C. K. 2004. "*Fortune at the Bottom of the Pyramid: Eradicating Poverty through Profits.*" New Delhi, India: Wharton School Publishing.

Peredo, A. M., and M. McLean. 2006. "Social Entrepreneurship: A Critical Review of the Concept." *Journal of World Business* 41(1): 56-65.

Peredo, A. M., and J. J. Chrisman. 2006. "Toward a Theory of Community-Based Enterprise." *Academy Management Review*, 31(2):309–328.

290   *Amir Forouharfar*

Philo, G. 1996. *Media and Mental Distress*. London, UK: Longman.

Philo, G., and M. Berry. 2004. *Bad News from Israel*. London, UK: Pluto.

Philo, G., and M. Berry. 2011. *More Bad News from Israel*. London, UK: Pluto.

Picot, S. 2012. *Jugend in der Zivilgesellschaft: Freiwilliges Engagement Jugendlicher im Wandel*. Gütersloh, Germany: Verlag Bertelsmann Stiftung. [*Youth in Civil Society: Voluntary Engagement of Young People in Transition*. Gütersloh, Germany: Publisher Bertelsmann Stiftung.]

Psillos, S. and Curd, M. 2010. *The Routledge Companion to Philosophy of Science*. London: Routledge.

Pust, J. 2016. "Intuition." In *The Stanford Encyclopedia of Philosophy*, edited by Edward N. Zalta. Available at https://plato.stanford.edu/archives/spr2016/entries/intuition/.

Prabhu, G. N. 1999. "Social Entrepreneurship Leadership." *Career Development International* 4(3): 140–145.

Rauter, J. 2006. *Zitationsanalyse und Intertextualität: Intertextuelle Zitationsanalyse und zitatenanalystische Intertextualität*. Hamburg: Kovac. [*Citation Analysis and Intertextuality: Intertextual Citation Analysis and Citation Analyst Intertextuality*.]

Rey-Martí, A., D. Ribeiro-Soriano, and D. Palacios-Marqués. 2015. "A Bibliometric Analysis of Social Entrepreneurship." *Journal of Business Research* 69(5): 1651–1655.

Pritchard, A. 1969. "Statistical Bibliography or Bibliometrics?" *Journal of Documentation* 25(4): 348–349.

Rowshan, S. A., and Forouharfar, A. 2014. "Customized Social Entrepreneurship Theory and Customized Social Entrepreneurship Strategy as a Theory Conceptualization and Practice towards Sustainable Development in Iran." *Asian Journal of Research in Social Sciences and Humanities* 4(8):367–385.

Roberts, D., and C. Woods. 2005. "Changing the World on a Shoestring: The Concept of Social Entrepreneurship." *Business Review* 7(1): 45–51.

Russell, B. 1912. *Problems of Philosophy*. London: Williams and Norgate.

Rwigema, H., and R. Venter. 2004. *Advanced Entrepreneurship*. Cape Town, SA: Oxford University Press.

Rysiew, P. 2016. "Epistemic Contextualism." In *The Stanford Encyclopedia of Philosophy*, edited by Edward N. Zalta. Available at https://plato.stanford.edu/archives/win2016/entries/contextualism-epistemology/.

Salarzehi, H. and A. Forouharfar. 2011. "Understanding Barriers to Intrapreneurship in Work and Social Affairs Governmental Organization (A Case Study in Iran)." *Interdisciplinary Journal of Contemporary Research in Business* 2(12): 490–503.

Santos, B. S. 2001. "Toward an Epistemology of Blindness: Why the New Forms of 'Ceremonial Adequacy' Neither Regulate nor Emancipate." *European Journal of Social Theory* 4(3):251–279.

Santos, F. M. 2012. "A Positive Theory of Social Entrepreneurship." *Journal of Business Ethics* 111(3): 335–351.

Sarasvathy, S. D., and A. C. Wicks. 2003. "Value Creation through Entrepreneurship: Reconciling the Two Meanings of the Good Life." Under revision at *Academy of Management Review*.

Sassmannshausen, S. P. and C. Volkmann. 2013. "A Bibliometric Based Review on Social Entrepreneurship and its Establishment as a Field of Research." *Schumpeter Discussion Papers* 2013-003. Germany: University of Wuppertal.

Scheuerle, T., B. Schmitz, R. Schües, and S. Richter. 2013. "Mapping Social Entrepreneurship in Germany: A Quantitative Analysis." *International Journal of Social Entrepreneurship and Innovation* 3(6): 484-511.

Schumpeter, J. A. 1951. *Essays: On Entrepreneurs, Innovations, Business Cycles, and the Evolution of Capitalism*. Cambridge: Addison-Wesley.

Seelos, C., and J. Mair, 2005. "Social Entrepreneurship: Creating New Business Models to Serve the Poor." *Business Horizons* 48(3): 241-246.

Sekliuckiene, J., and Kisielius, E. 2015. "Development of Social Entrepreneurship Initiatives: A Theoretical Framework." *20th International Scientific Conference Economics and Management - 2015 (ICEM-2015), Procedia - Social and Behavioral Sciences*, 213:1015-1019.

Seymour, R. G. 2012. *Handbook of Research Methods on Social Entrepreneurship*. UK: Edward Elgar Publishing Ltd.

Sharir, M., and M. Lerner. 2006. "Gauging the Success of Social Ventures Initiated by Individual Social Entrepreneurs." *Journal of World Business* 41(1): 6–20.

Steup, M. 2016. "Epistemology." In *The Stanford Encyclopedia of Philosophy*, edited by Edward N. Zalta. Available at https://plato.stanford.edu/archives/fall2016/entries/epistemology/.

Shand, J. 1993. *Philosophy and Philosophers: An Introduction to Western Philosophy*. London: UCL Press.

Sheldon, P. J., and Daniele, R. 2017. *Social Entrepreneurship and Tourism: Philosophy and Practice*. Springer International Publishing, doi: 10.1007/978-3-319-46518-0.

Shelley, M. 2006. "Empiricism." In *Encyclopedia of Educational Leadership and Administration*, edited by Fenwick W. English: 338–339. Thousand Oaks, CA: SAGE.

Short, J. C., T.W. Moss, and G. T. Lumpkin. 2009. "Research in Social Entrepreneurship: Past Contributions and Future Opportunities." *Strategic Entrepreneurship Journal* 3(2):161-194.

Short, J., D. J. Ketchen, and Bergh D. D. 2014. "Social Entrepreneurship and Research Methods." *Research Methodology in Strategy and Management*, Vol. 9, Emerald Group Publishing.

Simon, H. A. 1996. *The Architecture of Complexity, the Sciences of the Artificial*. Cambridge, MA: MIT Press.

Singh, A. 2016. *The Process of Social Value Creation: A Multiple-Case Study on Social Entrepreneurship in India*. India: Springer.

Schirato, T., and Webb, J. 2010. "Bourdieu's Concept of Reflexivity as Metaliteracy." *Cultural Studies* 17(3-4): 539-553.

Slater, S. F., and Narver, J. C. 2000. "Intelligence Generation and Superior Customer Value." *Journal of the Academy of Marketing Science* 28(1): 120–127.

Solla Price, D. J. 1963. *Little Science, Big Science*. London: Columbia University Press.

Solla Price, D. J. 1981. "Multiple Authorship." *Science* 212(4498): 986-986.

An Epistemological Criticism of Social Entrepreneurship 293

Solla Price, D. J. 1976. "A General Theory of Bibliometric and Other Cumulative Advantage Processes." *Journal of the Association for Information Science and Technology* 27(5): 292– 306.

Sosa, E., J. Kim, J. Fantl and M. McGrath. 2008. "Introduction to Part V. Epistemology." In *Epistemology,* edited by Ernest Sosa, Jaegwon Kim, Jeremy Fantl, and Matthew McGrath: 305-309. Malden: Blackwell.

Smart, D. T., and J. S. Conant. 1994. "Entrepreneurial Orientation, Distinctive Marketing Competencies and Organizational Performance." *Journal of Applied Business Research* 10(3): 18–28.

Stanley, J. 2005. *Knowledge and Practical Interests.* Oxford: Oxford University Press.

Stevenson, H. H., M. J. Roberts, and H. L. Grousbeck. 1989. *New Business Ventures and the Entrepreneur.* IL. Irwin: Homewood.

Stryjan, Y. 2006. "The Practice of Social Entrepreneurship: Notes toward a Resource Perspective." In *Entrepreneurship as Social Change: A Third Movements in Entrepreneurship Book,* edited by Chris Steyaert and Daniel Hjorth: 35-55. Cheltenham: Edward Elgar Publishing.

Suchman, M.1995. "Managing Legitimacy: Strategic and Institutional Approaches." *Academy of Management Review* 20(3): 571–610.

Thake, S., and S. Zadek. 1997. *Practical People, Noble Causes: How to Support Community- based Social Entrepreneurs.* London: New Economics Foundation.

Thornton, S. 2017. "Karl Popper." In *The Stanford Encyclopedia of Philosophy, edited by* Edward N. Zalta. Available at https://plato. stanford.edu/cgi-bin/encyclopedia/archinfo.cgi?entry= popper.

Timmons, J. A. 1978. "Characteristics and Role Demands of Entrepreneurship." *American Journal of Small Business* 3(1): 5–17.

Timmons, J. A., and S. Spinelli. 2003. *New Venture Creation: Entrepreneurship for the 21st Century.* Boston: McGraw-Hill.

Tolbert, P. S., and L. G. Zucker. 1983. "Institutional Sources of Change in the Formal Structure of Organizations: The Diffusion of Civil Service Reform, 1880–1935." *Administrative Science Quarterly* 28(1): 22–39.

Townsend, D. M., and T. A. Hart. 2008. "Perceived Institutional Ambiguity and the Choice of Organizational Form in Social Entrepreneurial Ventures." *Entrepreneurship Theory and Practice* 32(4): 685-700.

Travaglini, C. 2009. "Social enterprise in Europe: Governance models." In *2nd International Conference on Social Enterprise*, Trento, Italy.

Trexler, J. 2008. "Social Entrepreneurship as an Algorithm: Is Social Enterprise Sustainable?" *E:CO Issue* 10(3): 65-85.

Ussahawanitchakit, P. 2007. "The Influences of Management Capability on Export Performance of Leather Businesses in Thailand." *Review of Business Research* 7(5): 1-10.

Van Slyke, D. M., and H. K. Newman. 2006. "Venture Philanthropy and Social Entrepreneurship in Community Redevelopment." *Nonprofit Management and Leadership* 16(3): 345-368.

Waddock, S., and J. E. Post. 1991. "Social Entrepreneurs and Catalytic Change." *Public Administration Review* 51(5): 393-401.

Ward, T. B. 2004. "Cognition, Creativity, and Entrepreneurship." *Journal of Business Venturing* 19(2): 173–188.

Ward, K. 2006. *Is Religion Dangerous?* London: Lion Hudson Plc.

Warner, R. and Mandiberg, J. 2006. "An Update on Affirmative Businesses or Social Firms for People with Mental Illness." *Psychiatry Service* 57(10):1488-92. doi:10.1176/ps.2006.57.10.1488.

Weedon, C. 1987. *Feminist Practice and Poststructuralist Theory.* Oxford: Basil Blackwell.

Weerawardena, J., and Mort, G. S. 2006. "Investigating Social Entrepreneurship: A Multidimensional Model." *Journal of World Business* 41(1): 21–35.

Weisbrod, B. A. 1977. *The Voluntary Nonprofit Sector.* Lexington, MA: Lexington Books.

White, H. D., and K. W. McCain. 1989. "Bibliometrics" *Annual Review of Information Science and Technology* 24(1):119-186.

Whiting, B. G. 1988. "Creativity and Entrepreneurship: How Do They Relate?" *Journal of Creative Behaviour* 22(3): 178–183.

Wright, E. 2005. *Narrative, Perception, Language, and Faith.* 103–120. Basingstoke: Palgrave Macmillan.

Yujuico, E. 2008. "Connecting the Dots in Social Entrepreneurship through the Capabilities Approach." *Socio-Economic Review* 6(3):493–513.

Yunus, M. 2008. *Creating a World without Poverty: Social Business and the Future of Capitalism*. New York: Public Affairs Books.

Zahra, S. A., and J. G. Covin. 1995. "Contextual Influences on the Corporate Entrepreneurship– Performance Relationship: a Longitudinal Analysis." *Journal of Business Venturing*, 10(1): 43–58.

Zahra, S. A., E. Gedajlovic, D. O. Neubaum, and Shulman, J. M. 2009. "A Typology of Social Entrepreneurs: Motives, Search Processes and Ethical Challenges." *Journal of Business Venturing* 24(5): 519-532.

Zainon, S., S. A. Ahmad, R. Atan, Y. B. Wah, Z. A. Bakar and S. R. Sarman. 2014. "Legitimacy and Sustainability of Social Enterprise: Governance and Accountability." *Social and Behavioral Sciences* 145(1):152-157.

Zakić, N., A. Jovanović, and M. Stamatović. 2008. "External and Internal Factors Affecting the Product and Business Innovation." *Economics and Organization* 5(1): 17 – 29.

INDEX

A

academic entrepreneurship, viii, xii, 163, 164, 165, 167, 168, 169, 170, 171, 172, 190, 191, 193, 194, 196

acadepreneur, v, viii, xii, 163, 164, 165, 171, 173, 174, 175, 176, 177, 178, 179, 180, 181, 182, 183, 184, 185, 186, 187, 188

access, 49, 91, 99, 107, 156, 166, 241, 242, 270

accountability, 51

accounting, 128, 260

accreditation, x, 46

acdepreneurship, 164

adaptation, viii, 2, 3, 6, 10, 11, 14, 16, 17, 19, 20, 21, 22, 25, 26, 29, 30, 35, 36, 38

Africa, xi, 72, 121, 122, 125, 126, 129, 130, 132, 135, 152, 153, 160

agricultural sector, 137

agriculture, 123, 135

analyzer, vii, viii, 1, 3, 4, 7, 11, 15, 16, 17, 18, 19, 20, 21, 22, 23, 24, 25, 26, 27, 28, 29, 30, 33, 34, 35, 36, 37, 38

anthropology, 272

appropriate technology, 11

B

behaviors, 15, 27, 29, 255

benefits, 27, 32, 58, 73, 124, 156, 251, 254, 267, 288

business environment, 51, 60, 64, 100, 105, 123, 178, 222

business management, 50

business model, 3, 7, 13, 19, 57, 60, 61, 220

business strategy, 95, 179

businesses, ix, 45, 49, 53, 58, 80, 82, 91, 92, 94, 95, 98, 105, 123, 143, 166, 167, 180, 181, 182, 197, 220, 254, 260

C

capitalism, 164, 165

cities, 124, 125, 128, 152, 156, 161

citizens, 47, 259, 260, 274

cognition, 9, 40, 249

cognitive process, 244, 245

cognitive theory, 72

collaboration, x, 46, 67, 207, 222, 260

commercial, 49, 62, 63, 166, 167, 231, 258, 276

communication technologies, 62

competition, 5, 42, 78, 124, 182, 183, 203, 208, 221, 223

competitive advantage, 8, 13, 28, 41, 70, 99, 119, 123, 127, 141, 203, 220

competitive markets, 148, 203

competitiveness, 5, 10, 19, 20, 24, 25, 29, 33, 54, 55, 62, 78, 91, 115

competitors, 12, 13, 14, 15, 19, 22, 24, 32, 35

complexity, 49, 97, 100, 104, 106, 109, 114, 157, 270

conceptual model, viii, 2, 3, 38

conceptualization, 78, 179, 223, 228, 274

consulting, 62, 63, 166, 168, 170, 171, 183

consumers, 17, 22, 23, 29, 36

cooperation, x, 46, 57, 63, 67, 70, 175, 177, 208, 220, 221

corporate governance, 166

correlation coefficient, 140, 141

creativity, 9, 28, 49, 51, 78, 128, 146, 172, 178, 188

critical thinking, 56, 57, 66

cultural norms, 264, 276

culture, vii, x, 9, 20, 27, 29, 46, 48, 52, 57, 67, 107, 116, 166, 167, 168, 179, 180, 181, 245

culture of entrepreneurship, x, 46, 48, 51, 57

curriculum, 57, 66, 68, 69, 72, 173

customers, 6, 12, 13, 15, 16, 19, 20, 56, 92, 94, 179, 183, 208

D

data analysis, 11, 62, 63

data collection, 230

database, 131, 230, 238, 274

decoding, 203, 204, 205

decomposition, 6, 25, 35, 36

defender, 11, 12, 14, 15, 18, 19, 21, 29, 38

democracy, 159

demographic change, 118

demographic characteristics, 87

dependent variable, 144, 146, 147

developing countries, 84, 86, 105, 111, 178

developing economies, xi, 78, 86, 108

digital technologies, 38

direct cost, 124

direct investment, 150, 155

direct teaching-learning methods, 53

E

ecology, 159, 221, 271, 272

economic activity, 176

economic development, vii, ix, xi, 45, 47, 67, 81, 82, 86, 87, 95, 96, 106, 116, 118, 121, 122, 123, 124, 126, 128, 156, 157, 158, 159, 164, 190, 210, 211

economic empowerment, 141, 151, 154, 155

economic growth, 82, 84, 105, 109, 114, 117, 118, 119, 126, 150, 155, 157, 210, 211

economic systems, 130

economic values, 182, 267

economics, viii, xi, 114, 118, 121, 125, 133, 158, 164, 217, 255, 272

economies of scale, 128

ecosystem, 79, 84, 202, 207, 208, 212, 217, 220, 221, 222

education, vii, x, 5, 46, 47, 48, 50, 51, 52, 53, 57, 61, 67, 68, 69, 70, 71, 72, 74, 92, 96, 99, 166, 179, 195

educational background, 52

educational practices, 67

educational programs, 179

educational research, 240, 275

educational system, 177

empirical studies, 247, 253

empiricism, xiii, 226, 228, 247, 251, 253, 292

employability, 59, 74

Index

employees, x, 18, 19, 22, 23, 26, 30, 46, 54, 55, 56, 57, 59, 60, 64, 66, 75, 98, 115, 116, 118, 134, 166

employment, 20, 23, 24, 29, 123, 124, 130, 133, 134, 135, 138, 139, 142, 143, 148, 150, 151, 153, 154, 155, 158, 159

employment growth, 143, 158

employment opportunities, 133, 134

engineering, viii, 2, 5, 6, 7, 11, 17, 18, 19, 20, 21, 22, 23, 24, 25, 26, 28, 29, 30, 33, 34, 35, 36, 37, 38

enterprise orderliness, 122, 131

enterprise richness, xi, 122, 125, 136, 141, 142, 144, 145, 146, 147, 148, 149, 154, 159, 160

EntreComp framework, ix, 45, 48, 60

entrepreneur, ix, 8, 45, 46, 48, 49, 50, 51, 56, 70, 84, 94, 96, 139, 143, 174, 176, 178, 183, 184, 185, 186, 188, 192, 198, 206, 207, 219, 237, 253, 259, 266, 275, 293

entrepreneurial dynamics, xi, 121

entrepreneurial space, xi, 121, 122, 125, 130, 136, 137, 138, 139, 141, 143, 148

entrepreneurial university, 68, 164, 165, 166, 167, 190, 191, 192, 194, 195, 196

entrepreneurship education, vii, x, 46, 47, 48, 51, 52, 53, 57, 67, 68, 69, 70, 71, 72, 73, 74, 195

environment, ix, 2, 3, 10, 11, 14, 17, 20, 22, 23, 25, 30, 37, 38, 49, 56, 68, 86, 98, 112, 114, 166, 172, 178, 179, 185, 208, 260, 266, 271, 272

environmental change, 17

environmental conditions, 260

environmental impact, 259

epistemology, xiii, 193, 226, 227, 228, 230, 241, 243, 248, 254, 264, 269, 274, 275, 291, 292

epistemology of social entrepreneurship, 226

essentialism, xiii, 226, 228, 261, 276, 281

evidence, viii, xi, 6, 31, 35, 73, 121, 124, 125, 128, 129, 130, 135, 139, 144, 151, 223, 243, 244, 246, 247, 259, 267, 275

explicit knowledge, 215

exploitation, 7, 16, 20, 24, 31, 47, 172, 176, 203, 210, 213

external environment, 10, 11, 13, 14, 17, 20, 22, 23, 25, 34, 38, 205

externalism, xiii, 226, 228, 241, 242, 244

extrapreneurship, viii, xii, 164, 174, 175, 186

F

factual knowledge, 270

financial, ix, 22, 25, 27, 29, 30, 46, 47, 59, 62, 99, 106, 175, 182, 185, 233, 244, 259, 260, 267

financial capital, 27, 185

financial crisis, 106

financial resources, 22

formal education, 47

formation, 30, 142, 171, 220, 228, 234, 243, 246, 254, 255, 275

free state, 121, 125, 131, 132, 133, 134, 135, 136, 137, 138, 139, 140, 142, 143, 144, 145, 146, 147, 148, 149, 150, 153, 154, 156, 159, 161

funding, 16, 31, 32, 34, 74, 166, 192, 260

funds, 92, 116, 148, 150, 151, 154, 155, 166, 169, 259

G

GDP per capita, 84, 86, 87, 95, 100

geographical mobility, 187

global competition, 119

global entrepreneurship development index, v, vii, x, 77, 78, 79, 81, 83, 84, 85, 86, 87, 89, 90, 94, 95, 96, 97, 98, 99, 100,

101, 102, 103, 104, 105, 107, 108, 109, 110, 111, 118, 119
globalization, 6, 42
government budget, 116
government policy, 122
governments, 254, 267
growth, xii, 5, 12, 15, 24, 30, 41, 47, 54, 59, 62, 70, 71, 78, 82, 84, 90, 92, 95, 96, 114, 123, 129, 149, 150, 151, 155, 157, 160, 201, 202, 219, 229, 246, 259
growth rate, xii, 47, 150, 201, 202

H

heterogeneity, 29, 214
heterogeneous analyzer typology, v, 17
high school, 63
high school degree, 63
higher education, x, 40, 46, 69, 72, 74, 92, 96, 175, 196
high-expectation start-ups, viii, xii, 201, 202, 203, 205, 206, 207, 209, 210, 211, 212, 215, 216, 217, 221
history, 30, 91, 106, 108, 129, 248, 269
human, xii, 6, 9, 17, 20, 23, 24, 25, 27, 28, 29, 30, 31, 32, 33, 35, 36, 40, 51, 72, 95, 96, 112, 114, 116, 119, 122, 124, 125, 146, 152, 182, 203, 205, 227, 228, 233, 241, 242, 245, 248, 255, 265, 274, 276
human capital, 6, 9, 17, 20, 23, 24, 27, 28, 29, 32, 33, 35, 36, 40, 96, 114, 116
human perception, 248
human resource development, 72
human resources, 32, 95, 119
human settlements, xii, 122, 125, 146, 152
human values, 182

I

income, 84, 86, 87, 91, 95, 115, 116, 123, 130, 146, 167, 170, 233

increasing returns, 128
incubator, 166, 167, 169
independent variable, 135, 144, 146, 147
individual action, 206, 207
individual character, 216
individual characteristics, 216
industry, 7, 10, 40, 48, 67, 70, 159, 166, 167, 168, 169, 170, 171, 177, 178, 191, 192, 210, 211, 222
inequality, 122, 123, 126, 127
information processing, 66
information technology, 221
infrastructure, 123, 127, 128
integration, 8, 30, 38, 55, 96, 109, 113, 177, 183, 186, 214, 215
intellectual capital, 170, 172, 203, 221
intellectual property, 92, 170
interactive teaching-learning methods, 53
internalism, xiii, 226, 228, 241
international competitiveness, 68
internationalization, vii, xi, 78, 82, 112
intrapreneurship, viii, xii, 163, 164, 172, 174, 182, 183, 184, 185, 186, 189, 190, 258, 291
investment, 49, 92, 117, 123, 124, 148, 150, 151, 154, 160, 177, 259, 266

J

job creation, 122, 131, 150
job satisfaction, 117
joint ventures, 170

K

knowledge ecosystem, vi, viii, xii, 201, 202, 203, 206, 207, 208, 209, 210, 211, 212, 213, 214, 215, 216, 217
knowledge management, 43, 74, 202, 222

Index

301

L

labor market, 62
labour force, 78, 124, 159
labour force survey, 159
labour shortages, 118
leadership, 9, 20, 27, 29, 39, 50, 166, 169, 178, 179, 186, 194
leadership development, 178
leadership style, 178
learners, 23, 24, 51, 52, 53, 56, 58, 59, 60, 62, 63, 64, 66
learning, x, 23, 26, 30, 39, 40, 46, 47, 48, 51, 52, 53, 54, 55, 56, 57, 58, 59, 60, 61, 66, 67, 68, 69, 70, 71, 72, 73, 74, 146, 152, 153, 156, 164, 179, 181
learning environment, 52
learning process, 30, 58, 61, 69, 181
LED policies, xi, 121, 124, 125, 127, 129, 131, 138, 141, 144, 148, 153, 154, 155
life sciences, 31, 34, 191
lifelong learning, 47, 66
living conditions, 182
local authorities, 124, 126, 159
local economic development, v, vii, xi, 121, 122, 123, 124, 126, 156, 157, 158, 159
local government, 123, 124, 126, 127

M

market segment, 11, 12, 15, 17, 19, 21, 22, 25, 26, 31, 35, 38
marketing, 15, 40, 42, 166, 168, 260
mathematical methods, 249
mathematics, 63, 249, 253, 256, 275
media, 62, 63, 157, 235, 238, 257, 262, 263, 276
mental cognition, 275
mental image, 242, 275
mental state, 242, 250
meta-analysis, xiii, 226, 230

metropolitan areas, 123, 127, 128, 146
Microsoft, vii, ix, 2, 3, 16, 38, 41, 247, 248, 249, 250, 287
Miles-Snow strategic typology, 4
multidimensional, 78, 79, 80, 81, 249

O

opportunities, ix, x, 2, 4, 5, 6, 8, 9, 12, 13, 14, 15, 16, 18, 22, 25, 27, 30, 31, 34, 38, 45, 46, 47, 48, 50, 57, 58, 59, 60, 62, 63, 66, 78, 81, 87, 91, 99, 106, 107, 138, 141, 143, 150, 154, 155, 166, 167, 179, 180, 259
organizational culture, 12, 14, 19, 20, 21, 27, 37, 214
organizational development, 18, 22, 24, 25, 26, 35
organizational learning, 9, 22, 23, 24, 34, 55, 56, 152

P

paradigm paralysis, 122, 125, 153
paradigms, xii, 122, 126, 150, 151, 152, 155, 268, 281, 282
paralysis, 122, 125, 153
penalty for bottleneck methodology, 78
performance, v, vii, x, 8, 10, 13, 15, 20, 22, 24, 25, 40, 41, 42, 52, 59, 64, 70, 77, 78, 79, 80, 81, 83, 84, 85, 86, 87, 93, 96, 98, 100, 101, 102, 105, 107, 108, 109, 110, 111, 112, 114, 118, 119, 123, 127, 129, 164, 183, 193, 217, 258, 260, 278, 286, 287, 288, 293, 294, 295
performance indicator, 22, 24, 25
policy, vii, xi, 50, 78, 79, 80, 81, 83, 85, 101, 102, 103, 104, 105, 106, 108, 109, 110, 111, 112, 117, 118, 119, 122, 124, 125, 126, 127, 128, 130, 131, 133, 136, 139, 144, 153, 154, 157, 176, 181

population, 80, 82, 91, 92, 95, 98, 99, 116, 117, 118, 119, 128, 129, 133, 134, 135, 144, 145, 146, 147, 148, 149, 150, 153, 154, 155

population growth, 133, 148, 149, 150, 155

population size, 128, 129, 133, 134, 135, 144, 145, 154

poverty, xi, 122, 123, 125, 126, 127, 131, 133, 138, 144, 145, 147, 148, 149, 150, 151, 152, 153, 154, 155, 160, 289, 295

power laws, 122, 128, 144

practical knowledge, 245

practical-operational teaching-learning methods, 53

private sector, 72, 93, 123, 127, 170, 255

problem solving, 49, 172, 178, 180, 223

problem-based learning, 53

product market, 15, 22

productive knowledge, xi, 122, 125, 144, 145, 146, 148, 154

professional development, 52

professionalism, 66

professionals, 53, 151, 183, 221

profit, 8, 32, 49, 172, 176, 184, 185, 229, 242, 254, 259, 260, 267, 284, 285, 288

project, x, 46, 48, 51, 53, 57, 58, 59, 61, 63, 64, 65, 66, 67, 85, 89, 90, 94, 97, 104, 115, 116, 128, 148, 165, 169, 181, 182, 183, 186, 189, 193, 199

project reinnovate, x, 46

proportional relationships, vii, xi, 121

proportionality, 133, 153, 154

proposition, 124, 241, 250, 265

prospector, 11, 12, 13, 14, 15, 21

prosperity, 47, 114, 126, 128, 157

protection, 33, 62, 92, 99

public administration, 254

public goods, 266

public interest, 263

public sector, 255, 267

Q

quality improvement, 66, 67

quantification, xi, 121, 125, 144, 146

quantitative research, xi, 121, 125, 152, 153

R

rationalism, xiii, 226, 228, 247, 251, 280, 287

reality, 50, 116, 138, 150, 248, 249, 255, 261, 264, 267, 270

reasoning, 136, 185, 247, 248, 250, 269

recognition, 18, 56, 98, 99, 109, 172

recommendations, 53, 81, 101, 117, 151, 157

reform, 32, 33, 38, 112

regression, 136, 137, 145

regression equation, 136

reinnovate, x, 46, 48, 53, 57, 58, 59, 63, 66, 67

religion, 256, 262, 263

reputation, 5, 62, 181, 184, 185, 254

research institutions, 32, 34, 92

researchers, xii, 33, 34, 53, 79, 81, 111, 118, 129, 163, 165, 166, 172, 176, 193, 228, 239, 240, 255, 256, 257, 268, 274, 276

resource allocation, 79, 110

resource management, 9

resources, x, 8, 9, 15, 20, 25, 26, 27, 29, 35, 38, 46, 50, 51, 57, 59, 61, 62, 63, 64, 91, 99, 101, 102, 104, 105, 106, 107, 110, 165, 169, 172, 173, 182, 202, 205, 260, 266

response, 11, 14, 15, 17, 18, 260, 268

restructuring, 25, 26, 35, 122

revenue, 16, 31, 165, 259, 260

risk, vii, xi, 18, 19, 37, 50, 51, 54, 72, 78, 92, 94, 99, 100, 105, 109, 185, 187, 212

rural areas, 151

rural development, 155

S

scholarship, 116, 117

school, xiii, 31, 34, 181, 185, 226, 228, 236, 246, 247, 249, 256, 262, 268, 282

science, 40, 63, 69, 116, 151, 152, 169, 170, 182, 191, 192, 227, 261, 268, 269, 271, 272, 276

scientific knowledge, xiii, 226, 227, 228, 229, 241, 262

scientific method, 251

secondary data, 6, 37, 227, 229

secondary education, 92, 98

self-awareness, 51

self-employed, 84, 183

self-employment, 52, 80, 183

services, 3, 6, 12, 22, 56, 62, 92, 136, 137, 138, 142, 146, 156, 166, 182, 183, 213, 233, 258

settlements, xii, 122, 125, 132, 146, 152

shareholders, 13, 38, 39, 259

simulation, xi, 53, 78, 80, 104, 110, 111

skepticism, xiii, 226, 228, 248, 287

small business, 55, 71

small firms, 68

social benefits, 260

social capital, 9, 25, 29, 30, 112, 218, 266

social change, 258, 259, 260

social construct, 262, 263, 264, 276, 289

social constructivism, xiii, 226, 228, 262, 263, 264, 276, 287

social context, 228, 264, 276

social contract, 222

social development, 73

social entrepreneurship (SE), vi, viii, xii, 3, 4, 5, 6, 8, 9, 17, 25, 27, 28, 30, 33, 35, 36, 37, 38, 198, 225, 226, 227, 228, 229, 230, 231, 232, 233, 234, 235, 236, 237, 238, 239, 240, 241, 242, 243, 244, 245, 246, 247, 248, 249, 251, 252, 253, 254, 255, 256, 257, 258, 259, 260, 261, 262, 263, 264, 265, 266, 268, 269, 270, 272, 274, 277, 278, 279, 280, 281, 282, 283, 284, 285, 286, 287, 288, 289, 290, 291, 292, 293, 294, 295

social entrepreneurship and philosophy, 226

social entrepreneurship knowledge, viii, xiii, 226, 246, 275

social epistemology, xiii, 226, 228, 264, 276

social institutions, 233

social interaction, 262, 263, 264

social network, 113, 128, 186, 194, 217, 219

social phenomena, 235, 248, 249

social problems, 253, 256, 259, 275

social responsibility, 236, 254

social sciences, 70, 227, 244, 245, 248, 249, 256, 268, 269, 272, 276

society, 47, 49, 79, 82, 119, 144, 254, 260, 262, 264, 265, 270, 274, 276, 288

solution, ix, 2, 5, 6, 7, 11, 17, 18, 19, 20, 21, 22, 23, 24, 25, 26, 27, 28, 29, 30, 31, 33, 35, 36, 38, 48, 101, 152, 188, 253, 258, 266, 275

South Africa, v, viii, xi, 88, 121, 122, 123, 124, 125, 126, 127, 129, 130, 131, 132, 133, 134, 135, 136, 138, 139, 141, 142, 143, 144, 146, 147, 150, 151, 152, 153, 154, 155, 156, 157, 158, 159, 160, 161, 191, 286

Southeast Asia, xi, 78, 80, 86, 95, 108

specific knowledge, xii, 202, 211, 212, 214, 215, 216

spin, 167, 168, 170, 171, 174, 175, 176, 181, 182, 184, 193, 195

spin-off, 167, 168, 170, 171, 174, 175, 176, 181, 182, 184, 193, 195

stakeholders, 18, 23, 24, 48, 64, 177, 178, 180, 181, 208, 266

strategic entrepreneurship, v, viii, 1, 3, 4, 7, 8, 25, 26, 35, 39, 40, 41, 292

strategic innovation, viii, 1, 3, 7, 17, 18, 21, 25, 28, 30, 31, 33, 37, 39, 40, 41, 222, 282

strategic management, 43, 68, 70
structure, x, xiii, 5, 17, 20, 25, 26, 27, 29,
    35, 38, 40, 46, 54, 58, 65, 81, 128, 129,
    156, 158, 184, 186, 189, 204, 205, 207,
    217, 221, 223, 226, 228, 229, 256, 257,
    266, 275

T

technological change, 111
technology, vii, xi, 5, 13, 36, 62, 64, 72, 74,
    78, 91, 92, 94, 98, 100, 108, 112, 114,
    166, 167, 171, 182, 191, 192, 193, 204,
    205, 217, 220
technology transfer, 92, 166, 167, 191, 193
tenure, 19, 31, 32, 33, 34, 35
Thailand, xi, 78, 80, 86, 87, 88, 90, 94, 95,
    96, 106, 108, 109, 112, 115, 294
thoughts, xiii, 226, 258, 272
tourism, 123, 139, 143, 159
training, x, 46, 47, 49, 57, 62, 67, 68, 70, 71,
    171, 173, 183, 184, 185, 186, 274

U

unemployment, xi, 122, 124, 126, 135, 152,
    153, 155
unemployment rate, 135
universities, 5, 47, 57, 62, 68, 164, 165, 166,
    167, 168, 170, 171, 172, 173, 177, 178,
    179, 184, 191, 195

V

variables, xi, 78, 79, 80, 81, 82, 83, 87, 96,
    97, 98, 99, 100, 101, 104, 109, 117, 124,
    134, 262, 271
venture-sitter, vi, xii, 201, 202, 203, 204,
    206, 207, 209, 210, 211, 212, 215, 216,
    217, 221
Vietnam, v, vii, x, 77, 78, 79, 84, 85, 86, 87,
    88, 90, 91, 92, 93, 94, 95, 96, 97, 98, 99,
    100, 104, 105, 106, 107, 108, 109, 110,
    111, 112, 113, 114, 115, 116, 117, 118,
    119

W

wealth, 9, 27, 28, 29, 79, 122, 128, 145,
    147, 148, 154, 156, 192, 193, 196
work environment, 179
workers, 184, 260
working conditions, 182
workplace, x, 46, 48, 49, 54, 55, 56, 57, 58,
    59, 60, 66, 70, 74

Entrepreneurship Education: Opportunities, Challenges and Future Directions

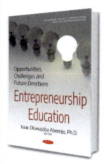

Editor: Isaac Oluwajoba Abereijo, Ph.D.

Series: Business Issues, Competition and Entrepreneurship

Book Description: This book is a collection of studies and experiences relating to entrepeneurship education, and the chapters are mixtures of conceptual, review, and empirical papers from different perspectives that provide learning tools for all stakeholders in entrepreneurship promotion and development.

Hardcover ISBN: 978-1-53613-246-5
Retail Price: $230

Entrepreneurship and Firm Performance

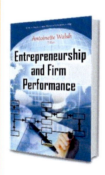

Editor: Antoinette Walsh

Series: Business Issues, Competition and Entrepreneurship

Book Description: Entrepreneurship has been the focus of considerable interest in the policy and business circles in the past two decades. This book provides current research on entrepreneurship and firm performance.

Hardcover ISBN: 978-1-63484-323-2
Retail Price: $160